ECONOMIC STEALERS

REPATHI KISHORE

INDIA · SINGAPORE · MALAYSIA

ISBN 979-8-89610-304-2

About the Book

This book discusses the old world's new systems, policies, and programmes that can help people to create a better place for themselves. It identifies the faults in ancient methods; it categorises the consequences ancient methods of political philosophies have on people.

Now, political philosophies are trying hard to be rational to everyone. I am accusing them of their mistakes, but the truth is that it is a never-ending cycle that tries to better itself from its flaws. All economic structures are like this, and no change in them. When something is identified as wrong or not working, it has to be repaired, but when it's not working after multiple repairs, our only choice is to replace it, but this does not happen in some cases. The system is trying hard to run along with it as much as possible. Damages occur because of it, but society considers it as collateral damage. This is ignored by leaders and people.

When we take any field, we can see 10% to 30% of extraordinary workers who strive to improve something in what they do, 50% to 70% good workers, and 20% poor workers, and 10% illegal workers. Managing this cycle, how to utilise them is the primary goal of any political philosophies that we are currently following. We can't avoid any segment of workers in current political philosophies. 'Reasons?' discussed in this book. 'What sort of world do we want and deserve? How to get that? What are all the struggles in it? Suggestions about overcoming it.' explained in this book.

We are facing problems based on differences. What are all those differences, why are they there? How are they constructed? What are they currently doing? How have they changed over the period? Everything is discussed in this book.

This book helps us to identify the economic stealers. It exposes how and why they are doing it.

This book is just a visiting card for the gate of opportunities. It can open the gate. We can explore an entirely new construction of the economic body, governance, and experience its wonders. Realise the values and importance of equality. This book aims to educate about equality and freedom to those who want it.

About Author

Passionate wordsmith with a knack for unravelling the complexities of politics. Unveiling the untold truths of politics and paving the way for a brighter future. I'm Repathi Kishore, a seasoned investment banker turned author. I'm crafting my debut book "Economic Stealers" - a thought-provoking exploration of new political philosophies and the shortcomings of the current system. After dedicating five years to this project, I'm ready to challenge conventional wisdom and ignite conversations that shape our future. Join me on this literary journey as I delve into the realms of poetry and novel writing too. Let's unravel the world together, one word at a time.

Contents

One

Work-based Economy

In the depreciating world, every living being needs to do something productive or should have someone doing something productive, which will give them food. Did everyone have food daily? The answer is a deliberate "NO". Is it their option not to have food? Or are they in a poor situation?

Did the world give equal opportunities to everyone? Did society update itself like technologies? No, no such continuous updates so far. We are still in the prototype stage.

We're yet to become one but not even trying to become one. We are divided by seven continents, four oceans, and more than 190 countries. The supreme issue here is that we're fighting with one another even after we realise that we have a 6th sense. We are trying to shift and test the economic policies by affecting the people's cost of living.

Few argue that 'capitalism will change the world,' few countries follow it; it helps the situation to favour wealthy people. Few say that 'socialism will change the world,' few countries follow it; it helps the situation to favour basic needs only, which get fulfilled. The rest is still a question mark. Few argue that 'communism will change the world,' few countries follow it. As long as money is a transaction tool in communism, it can't work to its full potential. In a country like India, there are arguments about a mixed economy, It does not have potential provide the change we require. Ordinary people in the world don't have proper knowledge of the different types of political philosophies. No doubt all the political philosophies help civilisation in one way or another in development, but they also struggle to help people move to the next stage due to their complicated structure and transaction tools.

Conquerors, Kings and Dictators played some important part in political philosophies. Evolution of society began from here. Different political philosophies arose during their time.

The world accepted Marx as a genius, so why is communism not followed by everyone? In fact, it is developed on the core principle of being common to everyone. "Common to everyone" exists in the world, but not everyone agrees to be common or equal. Those who have excess should share it willingly without hesitation, but many people with excess have the mindset that, "I worked hard, so I own everything excessively; why should I share it just for the sake of a philanthropist status." "I own it; I enjoy it" is the prevailing mindset among many here.

While existing political philosophies have positively impacted our lives, they fall short of addressing the needs of our rapidly growing global population, now exceeding 8.2 billion. comprehensive change is imperative to positively transform every life.

People must think about extremes of political philosophies, which should be measured. I'm suggesting all to think about extremes of capitalism, socialism, communism, mixed economy, dictatorship and kingdom. What will happen in the end? Will it bring absolute equality?

When you complete this book, you will realise what will happen at the end of all these political philosophies. Why are these philosophies not able to achieve equilibrium? When we introduced money into the economy at that time, we failed to regulate it. Educated people used it, became wealthy, then regulated it as if they were wise for their benefits. They curved the world around it. Later, it became too late when the good-hearted educated people identified it. They introduced new philosophies like socialism and communism. Those philosophies are structured to operate in the already existing evil transaction tool "MONEY". We don't have any other established option in the period when it was introduced. How can the world be organised and operate without money and stay equal? the current educational system around the world, except for those countries which follow communism and socialism, is aware of the dangers of introducing political philosophies to children because not much in-depth education is provided to kids. We aren't pushing them to understand the importance of equality. Countries are terrified of kids getting to know deeply about all political philosophies.

What kinds of problems may arise when kids start understanding deeply about all the political philosophies? The questions about absolute equality arise. The volume of protests will increase. It's why most countries don't want their kids to start learning deeply about political philosophies because when they become adults, they will start to act against it instead of operating along with it.

People who were enjoying unlimited privileges used their powers then stopped the well-structured philosophies spread across the countries. Rulers of communism and socialism failed to spread it to the world because at that time, more than 59% of people were uneducated. They were unaware of how to read and understand it. Another reason was the leaders; the early period of communism and socialism in Russia did not create a good impression. The USSR was spliced into bits and pieces but still Russia is big in landscape. It has more control over global politics. Capitalists utilised these negatives to stamp the impression that communism won't work. Currently, more than 60% of people are educated. Now they have to understand communism because education only gives them opportunities but understanding the concept of different political philosophies only brings growth. So, the real challenge comes after most people understand the concept.

What is the real challenge? It's overcoming the distraction. It's tough because, one way or another, people at some point in time educate themselves. They understand the concepts, but the phase of distraction has already started before we understand it and started doing its job better than ever. Even when we understand, it's hard to overcome the distractions caused by the opponents. It's hard because people are divided and entertained by trillions of contents every day. I carved the book to help understanding and overcome its distractions. It may take a while, but the work-based economy will get its way and make people equal forever.

Capitalism and mixed economy political philosophies only concentrate on particular sets of people at a time. Whatever it is, when concentrating on particular sets of people, the development, "Real Development," won't come. The real development is equality.

I don't know how to introduce the work-based economy and make us engage in it. Hey there! This is a work-based economy. Hang with it for a few pages. It will make us, and it will give us what we want. Here I introduced!

There is one unique matter with a work-based economy! All other philosophies like capitalism, socialism, communism, dictatorship, kingdom won't work out even if the world is united as one in the long run because all operate in the taste of money as a transaction tool. A work-based economy will perfectly work out because it will discard money as a transaction tool.

Who wants no border, who wants no starving, who wants their desired job?

Everything is possible in Work-based economy (WBE).

The work-based economy only works when the world is united as one.

The work-based economy is familiar; I plan to introduce the approach of how we can achieve it. What is that approach? We have been familiar with the approach for several years now. Yes! It's like a barter system. The future is with the barter economy and work-based economy.

The barter system is more than salt for rice things. We have to implement lots of norms in it. We should consider the whole bunch of opportunities. We didn't have Indirect Barter on the work-to-work method when we had a barter system. We just had direct barter on the asset-for-asset system. Direct barter on the asset-to-asset only benefits people who have assets. Those who don't have wealth or assets always depend on wealthy people; few used to provide reasonable remuneration to the dependent, but the majority won't provide it. It's not a mistake of them because no norms had forced them to provide good benefits to dependents. No laws in favour of underpaid and unpaid employees to punish financial crimes in the asset-to-asset barter economy. The communication gap and delay in timing and oppression are significant when communicating what we want. Wealthy people made use of it to control dependents.

Wealthy people used these situations and looted as much as possible with or without the knowledge of authorities. Most people viewed wealthy people negatively or avoided them as a result of these situations. This situation is where inequality started to spread its branches in the world. This situation is also the reason why 10 percent of the population holds 90 percent of the wealth. The asset-for-asset barter may be the first reason for inequity, then when it moved to the banking system, it got even worse. Bankers made all the people fools for the past 300 years. They collapsed the whole structure. We will discuss how it happened in the coming topics.

How will the barter system change the current situation?

The wrong method of the barter system was followed previously. ASSET for ASSET barter and the Fractional Reserve Banking System never bring equality. The proper method to follow is the Indirect Barter on the work-for-work system.

What is the difference between Direct Barter with the asset for asset and Indirect Barter with the work-to-work?

People will determine values of assets in direct barter with the asset-for-asset method most of the time. Although both food and gold are in high demand, gold is not as important as food, but still gold is overvalued by its owner. There are no norms and rules for the owners. Even if the norms came, we can't change the undervaluation of the employees by their owners.

But in the Indirect Barter with work-for-work, the government acts as a middleman. The government will measure our work; no owners' problem exists. No one will work for individuals. In this Indirect Barter with the work-to-work market, we no longer need to work for individuals to make profits. We can work for the needs and demands. No longer need to work when the need gets fulfilled.

When we don't have owner problems, we have absolute independence in our work and desire. I didn't mean only big owners; I meant all owners, like small, big, medium because owners need to run for profit. When they stop running, they stop dealing in business. That's the meaning of it. Pressure will always dump them when they are running for profit. This situation makes them money-minded people for life long. It won't make the owner think about their labour in the long run. It will result in a layoff. In the work-based economy, everyone will work for the government. It is not for the country's government. It is for the world government. It will be possible only when the world united as one. World people should decide and announce the regulations, policies and norms they have in mind. A single person, entity, or organisation can't structure a flourishing economy. We are going to discuss this concept in this chapter.

What is This System Implying to Us?

Indirect Barter with a work-for-work barter system denotes that people should exchange their work to get what they want. There is only one middleman, that's the world government. Like, if there is a doctor means their work is to handle medicine. The other one is the chef; their work is to handle the cooking. Suppose the chef required medicine and the doctor required food. What will happen? They can exchange their work. The government will act as a middleman to solve the hindrances in this transaction. Transaction tools will not be currency anymore.

Why is the Middleman Required in Transactions?

We require a middleman to avoid any crime, fraud, or misleading and to keep the standard stable and evolve from time to time. I am confident that the system never compresses or oppresses the public's feelings in any way. Everything will be researched thoroughly and then allocated adequately enough for everyone.

People will have a work card. Our work will take care of our basic needs. The government will provide specific points that we can use for our luxuries. The points will be the same for everyone, with no difference for anyone in the world.

The consistent points will be distributed all over the world by the government. These points will be adequate for a month. We can't save any points for the future. Monthly points will expire every month. It is only to store points for a short period. We can find the crimes with the help of this work card; if someone is not doing any work, the points owned by them will get blocked.

For example: If a person is going to a restaurant, it means that since we have a middleman as the government. While scanning the card, it will show whether that person did work yesterday or not, or was on leave for work yesterday. If it matches with the government database, that person can have food. If any system issue arises, they can still have food. But if an issue is found with that person, like not going to work properly or just roaming around the workstation without doing work, it means that person will be punished according to their crime level measurement.

Likewise, the government will act as a middleman, regulator, and protector. They will safeguard our enjoyment, environment, life, and society.

We have a "N" number of fields of work; how come equal segregation is possible in this work-based economy? Don't you think it's going to mess up and collapse?

Yeah, we have that much work in the world. But still, I see significant opportunity and versatility in each work. All works in the world will get bored at a certain point in time. People in the world don't like to stick around with only one work. A person should work on what he studied as a major and should work on any other work minor. Our educational system helps to implement this; In this minor work, he/she will be supervised by one who has taken it as a major work. Everyone will have two different jobs. We can choose our major independently. Minor fields will be allocated to us by the government based on economic requirements.

Educational System, we have to be engrossed in education no matter what political philosophies we follow. What students want to become should be decided by themselves. It should not be decided by others like parents, relatives, friends, or well-wishers. Few students always want to be with their friends, so they choose what their friends choose. Don't be led like this. Because what we study will decide what our future will be. We don't know if our friends will stay with us for the rest of our life, but education will be with us lifelong.

Every student should go to educational counselling to have one-to-one sessions with a counsellor for their SWOT analysis; afterwards, they should choose what to study. Most developed countries are following this. Once they graduate, they should not go to a job for a year. It is the time to explore and get exposure to the world. In the meantime, the students can do whatever they want. For example, if a student likes to go on a road trip to visit various places in the country and world and enjoy the journey, they can do that. If a student likes to do product research, they can do that too. Likewise, students will be free to do whatever they want in that one year.

Students get an opportunity to explore and experience the world. They can do whatever they want to do independently. While taking liberty, they should be aware of what not to do, like being addicted to sex and getting addicted to alcohol. Society gives the opportunity to students to explore. It's how society will grow a long way and get an update.

--------------cc-----------------------------------cc----------------------------

In the world, we have lots of illegal businesses as of now, like drug mafia, sand mafia, land mafia, sex trafficking, lots and lots. When converting to a work-based economy, everyone will be condoned by the government, but if it continues in the new economic structure, they will get punished. Why should a few do this mafia when given a chance to live happily?

Survival is not going to be tough anymore. The world will become an open forum to showcase our talent. No one will dumb down our voice in this work-based economy system. The important thing is, this is possible only if the world becomes one, as I said earlier.

"IF" is the best word because it always gives space to imagination. The work-based economy is the 'IF' factor here.

The world's most important disciplinary behaviours people can try to implement if work-based economy was possible:

- Everyone is Liable to Work until death or being deceased. Work will be reduced as age is considered. If people violate the rule, punishments will be given as a penalty.
- People in this world do not own anything but they have right to use everything.
- Everyone has the right to work in their favourite field.
- Artificial Intelligence strictly regulated in dangerous fields of work.
- Unethical work will lead to prison.

These are all the primary disciplinary behaviours to follow.

if you had considerable doubts about the above essential discipline. Raise your questions on the www.Economicstealers.com

For a few questions, I will answer here:

Why should everyone work?

Yes, everyone should work except students up till graduation. Currently, a certain percentage of people are not contributing to any work. Few are making money from money. I am not saying it's wrong, but they are unaware that their contribution to the world is missing. Few live in the shadow of other people, which explains that they are not using their education correctly. Few live on the assets their parents earned. People's utilisation is missing for these reasons.

People don't have the right to own anything, but the right to use everything. What does that mean? Don't we have the right to own our house?

Everyone wants to own a house, vehicle, and whatnot. Everyone wants to own everything as much as they can. It is creating a situation of massive excessive overproduction of particular goods. The rule is to avoid the overproduction of unnecessary goods. We will have a yearly meeting committee to announce the necessary goods and luxury goods. Everyone has the right to use necessary goods. Luxury goods will be owned with the help of work card points.

What if the majority of people choose to work in the same field?

We are all one; we always have a group mentality, whatever it is. In those cases, we make rational work diversity. People may do three ratios of what they wish to do and one compulsory ratio of what is necessary.

How are housewives or househusbands going to handle a work-based economy? Will they work?

They should work according to their studies and abilities. We may have too many questions on this segment. Adoption is the most important effort that needs to be taken. We can't just be housewives or househusbands anymore. It's hard to be a housewife or househusband. You may ask how people raise their babies in the early stages. Will it be easy to handle both? Yeah, it's hard, but they should have a long break of 2 years of maternity and paternity. But after that, they should make arrangements to take care of the child; there will be child care centres on every street where we can make them handle babies. Until they grow, there will be 100% assurance for their safety and education.

What if they don't like to work? A fundamental question arises if someone said that, as a child everyone studied something. Where are they going to use that study? If they don't want to work, do they really need the education? People always have some purpose in their life. They always work for that purpose. We have just crossed the stage of working for survival. What will they do if they do not work in that meantime?

Who will cook? Will housewives or househusbands not cook anymore?

In the current mentality, the world commonly views women as the ones who should cook for their family's daily routine. In some places, men are also cooking at home.

In the work-based economy, cooking is optional for women and men in the daily routine because, in the work-based economy, there is no housewife or househusband segment. They're not liable to cook compulsorily; they will be getting food that they want from restaurants on doorsteps. In the work-based economy, we can use A-to-Z services, which we will repay by doing our work. Since they are doing their work, we are getting A-to-Z services. So, we have to do our work so they will get their services. The world is interdependent. People are interdependent. One can't live without others' support.

Why should Artificial Intelligence be regulated strictly?

AI's growth has been tremendous in the last 30 years. We are witnessing software's growth in recent times with ChatGPT, deep fake, and AI voice generators. Many path-breaking and redefining inventions are under development. The accessibility is available to everyone. Therefore, mishandling incidents are registered in more places. We have to be aware of the potential dangers. We can't ignore the fact that AI can handle multitasking effortlessly. So, if we fail to regulate it now, then we will be in a critical situation in our future.

What if people share their work benefits with their children and relatives who never like to work and live in another's shelter?

There should be an e-evaluation for every person in the world. If anyone denies working and living under someone's shelter, they will be punished under the law. Everyone must contribute something to society in some way.

-----------------ccc------------------------ccc---

As per Newton's law, the moving object can't change its direction unless an outside force comes and reacts to it.

Be an outside force and make the directional change together. Scientists found the black hole with the Event Horizon Telescope. The Hubble Space Telescope found too many galaxies in space. Still, the basic system of society is like how we followed in the ancient period. No systematic updates so far. Few people may have changed, but it looks like a drop in the ocean.

When creating new political philosophies, we get a chance to implement rules to ensure that we have the discipline to take humanity to the next level.

In the work-based economy, politics will be in a different dimension. It will not be like how we are tolerating today. People want their leaders to be true leaders with leading qualities, but leaders mostly do not truly express their leadership qualities towards the people. Few countries have compulsory voting systems. Countries without compulsory voting struggle to achieve a 70% vote. We should follow how a country like Australia does compulsory voting. It makes people think voting is compulsory. Politicians fear the laws of the election.

Laws of election and quality of politicians - Our world forum should have one world leader. He/she should be elected by people who adhere to sign the documents of world peace, economic stability, public asset safety, natural resource welfare and safety, and policies should not be violated. If anyone finds it violated, crimes will be severely punished by the court.

World Leaders can't rule for more than four years. It's not consequent four years. That person should have a four-year break from when he or she last ruled. The world leader position will have a two-year time period. Their family members can't become the world leader for 15 years.

There is no single leader policy in the world. No single government policy in the world. There may be 200 governments according to their land, but leaders should commonly have this rule all over the world. They should report to one world leader for two years. They should obey the world leader or can leave the dream of politics. The motive is land without borders and governments without dirty politics.

The position of world leader will be rotational. No single country can limit the world leader to their own land.

---------------------------ccc------------------------ccc---------------------------

People use their names to confirm their identity, but it's not necessary to disclose our personal details to commoners. World citizens will have a common identity to introduce themselves. We can reveal our details only when we are wise to share them with people around us; else, we can introduce ourselves to others by using a world identity.

People have every right to follow their religion and ritual duties, but forcing that on another person is a punishable offence. Whoever is doing that will come under disciplinary proceedings. In the aspect of marriage, every religion follows different cultures and rituals. Many people in different countries find love on their own based on their likes and dislikes. They engage in matrimony, thus creating a family. Still, some people out there do matchmaking based on castes and religions. People may view it from multiple perspectives. Some may view it as an attempt to create an unwanted expansion of the circle, but there is another perspective to it. Adults who are not interested in finding love on their own or who haven't found love on their own have their parents, who are associated with these communities that have existed for thousands of years, looking for a match for their kids. They can move out of their community circle to search, but it's difficult to find a match outside of their circle. So, they choose the easiest way possible. According to the regulations of new policies, no one should express their caste on an open forum. People should not share their caste while searching for marriage. In the work-based economy, religions are accepted but not castes. The upcoming chapters will explain the reasons behind this.

We have to understand the importance of equality acceptance. People in a bad position on current political philosophies like to move to a work-based economy. People in a good and happy position on current political philosophies naturally may have the fear of acceptance of a work-based economy. They think and fear their positions will change for the worst, but it's not like that; no one will be going to be worse. The rich one has all the financial freedom on current political philosophies, so they won't like to get into a work-based economy.

We all like to bring about equality, but acceptance won't come that easily from settled people with current political philosophies. They have to believe that every person will be in a good position in a work-based economy. Rich and poor segments will not be available in a work-based economy. Monopoly and dictatorship will not be available in a work-based economy.

Private sectors will not exist in a work-based economy. That's the critical segment.

It is not like grabbing opportunities from rich people and then giving them to others. We must realise that governments can't operate a work-based economy through the private sector because of equality breaches.

I want to share something for people who hate closing private entities. In this changing world, private entities don't have the patience to see upcoming technologies. They always have a fear that someone is going to overcome them. It's true. New technologies are emerging every year, but still, we are sticking with some old technologies due to their profit motive. The important thing is that not everyone can start a business. Small people always get dumped by big players, so many new systems are destroyed in the drawing room itself. We might see numerous startups in new technologies sponsored by venture capitalists, but succeeding in the competition is brutal. Market competition creates a glut. It makes consumers and manufacturers suffer. The success rate of a startup surviving over five years is 51%. We are in a heavily competitive market. Big players will copy our concept and then execute it better than us. Risks of loss, pressure, and suicides are not widely publicised.

In a work-based economy, private sector owners and founders will not be ousted from their entities by governments. They have every right to participate in the industries, but control will be under the government's hand; they are all liable to play a secondary role in the economy.

What kind of roles will previous owners get in their entity?

They won't get roles in their entity, but owners will be transferred to a similar entity to avoid influencing their entity workers. Does it seem like damping the financially strong and rich people? Yes, we are forcing them to step down from their position, but at the same time, we are assuring them that they will not be ill-treated by society. The fact that they aren't going to be poor, but they are going to be equal. There are lots of differences between poor and equal. As I said earlier, there are no rich and poor. There is only one, and that's equality.

The government will take over everything. We will become government employees. We will have the right to question the government if it is doing something wrong.

How does law and order differ from the current economy?

Law and order matters a lot in any political philosophy. As of now, we are facing delays in judgements. It always makes people think about stopping going to court for small judgements. In a work-based economy, we should build a structure to provide judgements within 30 days. If the law gets delayed, then special divisions should take over the case. They complete it within the next 30 days with full force.

What is a Border Force-less Government?

For all countries, militaries are imperative to protect their borders. Here comes the work-based economy, with no border forces required since all countries will become one in the union.

What is the meaning of unity in the union? All the countries' leaders will have a world union meeting every year. They sign the agreement stating that all the respective countries respect each other's borders and will not assemble any border forces on their land under any circumstances. There will be invigilation at all borders before signing the agreement to make sure no invaders camp without permission. Once it's all cleared, all the agreements will be signed by leaders. No border forces exist. Rulers have no right to impose war on others. People have independence over their homeland. As citizens, everyone has ownership of their homeland. They can work wherever they want to work and live if there is demand and opportunity. Everyone has the right to go anywhere. We will have patrols to avoid violence. We will not remove any existing jobs, but we are creating opportunities to explore.

In the upcoming chapters, we will discuss how to avoid trespassers with hidden motives.

Why is a Structural Change in Education Important?

The purpose of education is learning, understanding concepts, experimenting, and discovering new things. A few top billionaires are not encouraging the school education system because they believe that it has not helped them in any way to achieve the heights they reached.

Theoretically and practically responding to those who said like above, the education system only provides an opportunity to create something but it will not act like a personal guide on how to create what we intended. We have to use what we learned from our education and think it through. We have to start with research, trial and error with the privileges that are available to us.

Currently, the education structure we are following is causing us trouble in understanding the struggle. It's because while some people see the same matter as a struggle, others see it as an opportunity.

- Is competition in the educational structure a struggle or an opportunity?

  People behave as they do now because of the competitions. Those who work hard can achieve success in competitions, enabling them to move up in the hierarchy. People support competition to gain this advancement and view it as an opportunity. Those who cannot afford to compete and those who fail in the competition see it as a struggle.

  The purpose of the competition is to select the most eligible one among other eligible ones. We need a society that takes people without competition. It means society is supposed to develop everyone as the most eligible one. It takes more effort and facility. It will be available in the WBE.

- Is Modified educational system based on political philosophies a struggle or an opportunity?

  People who benefit from a modified educational system view it as an opportunity. How are they benefiting? In their perspective, they are facing protests from common people within the range of what they think they can handle. Who are those people benefiting from it? Government authorities who manage the government. Why do they need to do it? It's the only way to make society move forward without more protests and calamities in their perspective with their political philosophies. So, they fear that if they impose an independent education system, then they will have to face twice or more problems than what they are facing in the country right now. How are they doing it? Through restrictions or a lack of information in certain fields of the democratic structure.

Children are influenced by the misguidance or false statements made by society surrounding them.

How can the whole society make false statements or misguide anyone without benefit?

We can understand why government authorities want it and do it, but why is the whole society supporting it? Different people from different countries have experienced different ideologies throughout their lives, which they have inherited from their ancestors. We all know that different countries have different political philosophies. We all know that people in different countries hate other political philosophies and ideologies for many unjustifiable reasons. Few people hate their own political philosophies in their country. We evidently don't know how the hate got spread or who spread these kinds of hate. It's like searching for a pin in the ocean. We can't ask the whole country's people to stop doing such senseless hate without proper evidence. Even if we do, one or two may change, but with a billion people out there, it's pretty hard to stop this kind of hate. So, it goes to the next stage. They collectively influence their children mentally with the same misguided information or false statements casually in daily conversations. If we try to research what they said, it means that the statement might be false or partly true, but the whole picture may be something different from what they understood. It's how the whole society, without their knowledge, influences children.

Who are the people who think that a modified education system based on political philosophies is a struggle?

People who are looking for absolute equality in all fields theoretically envision a whole host of opportunities. An independent education system can bring about even better political philosophies and create great new exchange tools. The creation of this opportunity allows for global collaboration on any subject related to the wellness of people worldwide without any ulterior motives.

- What does an unsatisfied worker mean?

  The person who works in a job without liking it or without being interested in it, 'Just for the sack of money' is known as an unsatisfied worker. How are they emerging in the economy? When a person is stuck in the trap of finance without having the independence to take risks. Why are they falling into that trap? It's due to the sole dependency upon them. If they stop doing the work that they don't like, then their family can't survive economically, or their standard of living may come down.

- Is it people's choice to be an unsatisfied worker or geeks?

  It's happening all around the world because of their family situation and relationship situation, mental strength. If a person is blessed with a good family situation, a supportive relationship and good mental strength, then that person finds a way to become a geek. If all these 3 are positive for them, then the chances of becoming a Greek at a young age are very high.

  If 1st two is not good but that person having great mental strength, then that kind of person has reliable chances to become a geek. They do unsatisfactory jobs, but they will keep pushing themselves towards their ultimate goals and improve their skills to achieve their goal of becoming a geek.

  If a person struggles with all three means, then he/she is most obviously stuck in the trap of unsatisfactory work throughout their life.

  Even if a person earns millions of pounds but does a job that he/she does not like, then that person is identified as an unsatisfied worker.

  It's not their fault because all these three situations depend on the country's political philosophies.

- Why can't everyone become geeks?

  All geeks have different motives. Not every geek worries about becoming a billionaire or millionaire. Therefore, it is unnecessary for geeks to always be rich.

Geeks will achieve what they intended.

Everyone comes from a different background in society. Societies within the same country have millions of differences. So, in addition to that, as I mentioned above, 3 factors play a major role.

The current educational system is creating competition among people. It rates people based on competition. The educational system has evolved over the years. It adapted to the political philosophies their country accommodated. The educational authorities lost their purpose. They started creating unsatisfied workers that required to run the political philosophy that the country required. It's inevitable, but so-called geeks educated themselves out of the systems, created something new. They hired both satisfied and unsatisfied workers they needed to run their business model from this educational system. Our education system is modified based on political philosophies. People's minds are structured based on that modified educational system. This is why most of us think competition is the only way to find talent. They believe that competition is the only thing that is moving us forward. People believe something is fundamentally wrong but they can't identify what it is. They believe victory is the only thing that gives us pleasure that no other can provide. When we create an education system that's not praising victory and a system that's not saying or imposing, being talented is a privilege that time we can attain immersive development.

Talented people get privilege, which is also a reason for global equality differences. I respect the hard work that they put into it, but why I don't want them to have that privilege. It's about the structural change I am talking about in this book. We are structured in the way we are doing things right now. Our ancestors developed our society to glorify talented people. We are not even realising that we are losing our well-deserved equality to them. We are happy about glorifying those talented people. WBE will build a society where everyone is treated equally, with no glorification or extra privileges for anyone who is talented. They are just one among us. These changes in the educational system will alter the complete structure of employment. People can learn and then do things they like with the help of what they have learned. They don't need to worry about comparison and competition.

The new education system will teach about the importance of equality and the uniqueness of individuals. Can you imagine what would happen if Cambridge liked educational services provided worldwide? Talented teachers will be available to everyone interested in getting them.

Education is the field that should be taken care of by the world government. The whole world should have the same scale of education everywhere. Students will study what they like. If more than a certain number of students like to study the same field, which is more than required, this will put us in the wrong position. When everyone corners the same field of study, we will have considerable gaps in other fields of study. The fields of study will segregate into the primary field and secondary fields. The primary field is the choice of students. The secondary field will be allocated based on the analysis and requirements of the world.

What Will Happen to Banks?

Bank – the word makes people rich and poor. Currently, banks are dealing with money. Our economy is solely dependent upon banks right now. There are multiple types of banks right here. One for investment, one for savings, one for lending, one for exchange, one for development, one for custody. Monetary policies make one segment of people well and good, which is educated and knowledgeable. However, there are several risk factors involved. Patience and passion are essential in travel. As I said, there is no money involved in the work-based economy. It directly means that banks will no longer exist, but no fear is required. We will not be firing the employees out of the banks. We have an extensive implementation called Point validation of work and luxuries. Luxury points can't be transferred or borrowed and used as derivatives. All new technologies will come to our doorstep. Point measures will be more likely to monitor people's work. A-to-Z category works get the same Point. Only luxuries like those out of our needs will cost this point. The share market will not exist in the work-based economy.

When there is no private entity, there is no fund creation. So, why should we need the share market? People in banks, share markets and directly in money-related fields like mutual funds, large-scale lenders, small-scale lenders, and insurance think that this work-based economy will suck our life, but the reality will be different. They will be going to participate in the Point validation system. To bring equality, we have to swipe out a few fields. Those fields are what I mentioned above.

When there is no money, then we don't need it immediately. For safeguarding any assets, there will be insurance in a work-based economy. In an emergency, whether health or disaster, the government will take care of us entirely. The government will provide all hospital services and nursing care without partiality for the work we contributed to the world.

Are you thinking that "we are replacing money with the alternative of another form of money (point measuring)?" That's NOT TRUE. We are creating an alternative resource to use instead of money. It won't be like money. It will not work like money. These points can't be lent to others and borrowed from others. The government is only a centralised exchange. Whatever we pay in the form of work will go to the government. Whatever we receive will come from the government.

While discussing exchange, we have a big stone in front of us, which is, 'how are countries going to handle this without money as an exchange tool to export and import?' We have to appoint the exchange council in all countries. The council will participate in all exchange meetings. Local government officials will bring their requirements to the council table. They will decide on import and export. These members only have the right to be involved in import matters of the country. They will be involved in only one country's exchange council. Another country will have another exchange council to decide.

Will these changes make people suffer for basic needs, and will these changes make people lose what they have earned up to date?

No one will suffer; everyone will live in happiness and love. These changes won't come overnight. All experts, common volunteers, and all field representatives will join together to test the methods and then execute them phase-wise. There will not be any immediate or miscalculated decisions.

The heart used to pump blood in and out consistently; if that stopped suddenly, what would happen? The person will die but if the heart is replaced by another one in time. The life of the person will be saved. During this transfer movement, there will be tremendous tension. For a few seconds, the soul seems dead but with expert handling, we can replace the heart. We assure that we won't make anyone stand on the road and suffer for food in this transformation.

Political management is crucial in a work-based economy.

We have to secure the same set of ministries worldwide. For example,

- Health Ministry - Agriculture Ministry
- Education Ministry
- Sports Ministry
- Space Research Ministry
- Entertainment Ministry
- Environment Ministry
- Home Affairs Ministry
- General Service Ministry
- External Affairs
- Ministry of Protection
- Ministry of Statistics
- Implementation Ministry
- Exchange Ministry - Animal Welfare Ministry
- Technology Ministry
- Consumer Affairs, Food and Public Distribution Ministry
- Transport Ministry
- Human Resource Ministry
- Ministry of Essentials and Luxuries

- Complaint and Justice Ministry
- Migration Ministry
- Ministry of Energy - Ministry of Emergency
- Ministry of Companies

The essential part of the work-based economy is politics and ministry. We have to concentrate on world politics. These ministries will be available in all countries. Ministries will work to shape the country and the welfare of the world. If anything is required, that will be added according to requests.

When speaking about the ministry of migration, we usually have lots of questions. What if everyone wants to move to one particular city to live? Then everyone will not be able to get what they wish. So, except for tourism, people will be allowed only on approval of the migration department's permission to work in other countries. When work requires, they can move accordingly. If they want to be with family, then they can migrate with the approval of the ministry of migration. If they want to live in another country, they can request the governments. The migration will be approved based on the available capacity.

In the world forum, all countries should participate yearly. They discuss their growth and problems, what to do, what to improve. The duration of this world forum is a few months. All country representatives must be available. All ministries should conduct yearly ministry meetings; all countries' respective ministers should compulsorily participate.

World leaders should not be involved in any country's politics. They should not be in dual-benefit politics like country and world.

Leaders of the world should not be leaders of the country. They should only concentrate on the world's peace, exchange, and environmental fields. They have every right to question any government in the world when they find something wrong in any field. Government ministries are answerable to them.

We should change some crucial rules in leadership. The officials will elect the leader of the party. The duration of the party leadership will be

4 years. Party leaders should not be the country's leaders. The party leader and country leader should not be close blood relatives. Party leaders should monitor country leaders' activity. If they find anything wrong or suspicious, they should report this to the world leaders. All elections will be relayed live on television to that area's people. There should be equal participation of women and men in the ruling.

World parties are subject to the same rules. Those who perform better in countries' politics will take place in world politics. All country's party leaders will elect the party leader. Party leaders only have the right to select candidates for the election. They have the right to decide and announce the country's leader and the world leader in the country and the world.

The leader will not be decided before the election. It will be decided after the results are announced. The party leader should examine who will be the best fit for the post and then announce them as the country and world leader in the country and worldwide. In this process, interviews and assessments will be conducted. Results will be announced. People who are not punished under disciplinary actions or criminal offences will be eligible for election for the post of world leader and country leader. Both party leaders should make sure that in particular.

Will these rules change politics? There are too many positives in these regulations. No permanent party leader or country leader will be there in any place. They can serve only twice in their lifetime. The dictatorship cannot be forced by it. No single-person politics will be implied. Since the leader will be announced after the results. No secrecy, adulteration can be made because of the supervision on leaders. It helps to avoid political games since no one will be only a politician; everyone should work on another segment of work apart from politics. No two or more country leaders meet or conference without the permission of a world leader. So, if anything like that happens, the post will be allocated to another one.

World leaders only have the right to produce weapons. The possibilities of achieving these policies are huge because I believe in technology. Humans are making, innovating, creating new technologies. All technologies should be under the control of humans. Technologies will push us to the next level of growth.

Every system has some problems, whatever we implement. We can rectify and reduce problems by making laws and controls. Here we go, see what problems people think will come while following the work-based economy. Please take a look at the solutions for it.

Problem 1: People may think that Independence on public opinion will be affected

Solution 1: laws which are adopted from existing laws will create space for independence in public opinions. It will increase. No restriction on public opinion in any field.

Problem 2: Wheel will be broken by changing to new political philosophy. It will collapse people's money and financial planning. The human effort of savings will be wasted.

Solution 2: People are going to be equal during the process of creating the new political philosophy. Everyone is going to gain more than what they saved throughout their lifetime from the new policies and procedures. It's the structural change that we are speaking about throughout this chapter.

Problem 3: Few people will start a mutiny to return to the old political philosophy. Most rich people may think that they will be affected by this new political philosophy. Few countries may dislike it. They prefer to avoid joining hands with new political philosophies.

Solution 3: Rich People lives everywhere. WBE will come to existence with everyone's approval including Rich people. If they are not agreed with it then it will not come until they accept it. everyone can do negotiations with them with reliable demands until they get convinced. Countries that do not accept new political philosophies can follow their existing political philosophies as normal. Newly converted countries will not face any hardships in any circumstances. When they need WBE, people in WBE welcome them to the new political philosophy. There will be no pressure placed on them by any country.

Problem 4: Even when people achieve a work-based economy, they have to assess people's consumption behaviour. How desperate people are behaving worldwide for products.

Solution 4: We have to implement the online test for the cool-down period.

What is the cool-down period? During this time, people can select anything that they want to buy. We will get to know how people behave based on this test. What sort of products do people reach for more during the cool-down period? This assessment should continue until the government understands the people's desperate needs other than their basics.

Let's view the struggles later, but how is it even possible to bring such a new philosophy into the world in the first place? Is it even possible? The audience may have this doubt.

How is it possible to implement a work-based economy in the world when a strong structure is present?

People need to understand the structural imbalance. They face problems because of current political philosophies. When people understand, the new wheel will automatically get started. It rotates itself stronger and faster.

How can people make it possible?

People can create understanding around the world. The most challenging job is marketing. When people start to make their voices reach out to everyone who is running fast in current political philosophies, make them take some breath, then feed them the truths. The chances of realising the benefits from real change are high afterwards, explaining the harmony behind the work-based economy.

This is about more than just the work-based economy. It is also world unity because all these are possible only when the world agrees with no borders. Borders that exist now will remain as they are but with zero border forces to protect them.

It may look like a larger-than-life thing, but all the above suggestions point out to make people aware that there are ways to be equal to all extents possible, but we need to have some discipline. Everything is stored in education. We are in place to create a new education system that bridges countries together. Everybody is aware of what is a possible way to make everyone equal. It will happen only when leaders realise the importance of it. Nothing has the velocity to spread all over the world without the leader's support. When people support, everyone can make it possible.

Those who do not like the work-based economy argue, "Why do we want this? We have everything in the world currently. Why should we bring this work-based economy to the world? Why do we need to follow new rules and regulations? We are doing great with money as an exchange. We can go wherever we want to go. If we want, we can work. If we want, we can live with the assets we saved. This is independence. In the work-based economy, do we have independence?"

Currently, rulers are not throwing stones at us. We are only selecting the rulers currently. Why should we want this world to be united? Now the world is separated into several countries, but we get whatever we want from the countries. We don't need any other country's borders to be joined with us. It will only create confusion and competition between us. We have absolute independence right now, so we don't need any changes. We will lead our future with this current world's policies and norms. Those who say the above things should read the upcoming topics to understand the essence of part 1.

Everyone won't agree with the work-based economy. Most people have even more questions about several hot topics. They have doubts about the work-based economy's success. People may ask, if everyone is equal, how can we find the best one? What is the validation that we are going to get for being extraordinary? If there is no validation for being extraordinary, then what if people do not want to give their 100%? What structure is there to encourage such misleading, empty, stupid hopes? Everyone in the world has a complete understanding that it won't work.

If everything is equal for everyone, how can governments plan to distribute daily consumer goods? We will have no choice for products then. How do we feel about that consumer independence? How do the governments expect kids to accept the forceful 2nd major role? What if the government forces us to do what we hate as a major portion? What if, for the sake of a name, they provide a small portion of time to do the work we love to do? What if world leaders try to abuse their power by over-controlling some countries, then try to destroy them for their vengeance?

These luxury points and work cards are entirely based on technologies. What if they're hacked and collapsed by hackers, then manipulated by them? What if they use it to their favour? What sort of security and assurance will be there to prove that we are falsely accused if those technologies are corrupted? How do governments expect everyone to be excellent and equal suddenly? These simple changes lead the world to equality, don't they? How does the author expect rich people to blindly accept and then sacrifice their position when they build the entire structure for their luxury purpose? Anyways, society also created ways to become rich like them when people had talent and knowledge, if they know how to market it. The rich people structured the world. Talented and patient people only could feel the richness. Talent is defined in many ways based on many fields in the current situation. When our talent creates some cash flow into the economy, if it establishes or improves, the monetary structures mean we will be highly valued by society. So, talented people always create opportunities for ordinary people to survive in different situations. In the absence of identifying talented people in the work-based economy, how can new ways be created for ordinary people to survive? Doesn't it damage the consistent growth of civilisation?

Millions of private companies exist worldwide. Talented, rich people lead almost everything. How do they permit WBE? Not all talented people are expected to be rich, but when they do and start to feel the luxury, it's nearly impossible to convince them to accept the world-based economy. How can this profound mindset change be achieved first of all? There is no clear picture of what sort of action plans, but instead of just some basics with unclear ethics provided. Isn't it unrealistic and stupid?

Why do politicians want to do what this book suggests? What sort of benefits are they going to get because of this? Politics is a highly complex field to judge. There are many possibilities that even a single misleading decision can turn a civilised society to act like animals. So, 'politically' is a word that can't be defined with one straightforward sentence. "N" number of nuances are hidden beneath. It helps to operate the world. So, they will stand against this work-based economy thesis. It's correct too. What if in WBE, the people working in the middleman segment started to manipulate the system to get benefits?

This book plainly tells us to erase all the things drawn on the board over these many years. It asks us to start writing fresh from the beginning. Not all segments of people can leave everything behind. They don't like to start fresh because everyone has their conflicts. People can't forget the struggles they faced to get a position in society. They won't easily say yes to start fresh because no one knows how different it will behave from the existing one; they don't know in what ways the evil can rise in the new structure. Not all people are interested in adventures; a few may be interested.

Ordinary people never accepted communism as a success story, so how can this work-based economy be accepted by people globally? Aren't both similar and have more or less have the same sort of features? What this book suggests is the end state of society. Making someone aware of it differs from making someone agitated about their situation. Why is this book a solution to all our problems when it blindly starts suggesting the end state of society as a solution to all our problems? Which is not possible shortly.

How come anyone other than government officials knows what will happen during the cool-down period? While discussing the cool-down period, how do people know that they're suppressed or over-liberated or in the middle ground? Isn't the cool-down period a lie? How come governments have that many resources when they're structurally controlling everything in the world if a work-based economy is implemented? Can't we leave the world as it is now and then wait for its time to change like it has changed so far? Didn't we evolve so far, why shouldn't we wait for other things to happen as well? This work-based economy model pushes the moving speed naturally faster than its normal movement.

All this 1st topic speaks about extremes and dangers, but it needs to open its eyes to see how far we have come even with the flawed monetary system. Humanity and harmony are not there in the world, which means we can't even come this far. Even if we try hard, we can't make the world all evil, but the first topic is making people believe that everything is wired in the evilest way possible.

For all these types of complaints, people have to move to chapter 2. Go forward! Complete this book to know what this book discussed. Why is it suggested?

Two

What We Really Want

Did humans want racism? Did humans want religion? Did humans want caste, power, money? Anyways, humans do have all these. All these components make it easy to stay divided and detached.

People should realise what the backbone of society is. Money, racism, caste, power, religion, will these fulfil that place?

If money is the backbone of society, that should have made us united. If religion is the backbone of society, meaning at least that should have made us united, or racism, caste, power, language, and land are the backbone of society, as of now those should have made us united by now. We are proud of all these identities. Diversely united in it but not in a good way, instead the worst way possible. Rulers of countries think these are the backbone of society. Each of us assumes that our pride is the backbone of society. We need to be more guided in the identification of the backbone of society. All that I mentioned are players of differentiation. People are fighting with each other in the contribution about who's giving more. People forget or do not identify that they are living in support of the backbone of society. People can't join together to stop the fights of players of differentiations because those will not allow people to join together. People are going to fall if they fight through these differentiations. People can stop fights but when? If they develop the understanding about what is the backbone of society, what are the issues in the players of differentiation. People have to develop their knowledge and humanity to understand.

What is the backbone of society?

What we want is indirectly connected with what is the backbone of society. We are alive on earth with the assistance of elements of the earth. It's giving resources to us. We are giving our contributions to the earth through work. It's like give and take. Our contribution is our work. It connects us with one another. People can't survive without our contribution. **Work** plays a backbone of society role.

Few leaders are leading us knowledgeably for better contributions. Till now, nearly all rulers have spent their time in players of differentiation. If all this is literally true, how have technologies and other technology-related staff improved to a great extent? Work connects us all. Leaders are unaware of it. They may have introduced schemes that only favour layers of differentiation but anyway, finally, those schemes find their beneficiaries who truly deserve it. Few people are real beneficiaries who deserve that scheme, that's why growth rates are very slow. Whatever improvements you saw in technologies and other stuff are not the real improvement. We are capable of achieving far better. The growth so far is not much improved but somewhat acceptable. Tremendous growth will come if rulers start supporting the backbone of society directly instead of prioritizing players of differentiation.

------------------cccc----------------------cccc-----------------------------------

We are living in this world for what? It is to be happy and to be loved. Our life is structured to feel all emotions irrespective. Suffering and joy are parts of our life. People feel nothing when they start living without doing anything. All our feelings are indirectly related to our work. If we want to be happy, we have to work. If we want to stop worrying, then we have to work. Work is given to us as a break from our feelings. It makes us feel refreshed. That's why people should do what they love to do as work.

Everyone should work on what they love. Instead of that, if they are forced to do what is available, the work becomes a frustration, and that will make everyone sick. So, people should be working at what they love. Humans always give importance to their emotions. No one will watch a joke with a sad mood. They don't like to hear the worst news when they are happy.

Emotions are plentiful in this world. They come based on people's actions. A person who realises that no outside actions decide their emotions will become happy forever inside. India produced plenty of people like that. For example, India had Buddha, Ramakrishna, Vivekananda, Ramana. Europe had Jesus. China had Confucius. Most philosophers have that quality. We also have a few examples, like Aristotle, Thales, Empedocles, Plato, Anaxagoras.

All these legends handled emotions very well. The most important thing is that no one becomes like that because of some sad thing in their life. They all loved to be like this. They were liked by others since they were like that. People in this world should realise the value of emotions. They should learn to handle emotions effectively.

It's easy to ask everyone to handle emotions effectively. Most people don't know how emotion plays a role in our life. It's complex. We have to add this to our schooling. It will improve our knowledge regarding emotions from childhood itself. Everyone has emotions in several forms. I like to mention a few, like relatives' emotions, work emotions, friends' emotions, acquaintances' emotions. If people take mental consultancy with doctors monthly, then that will allow people to handle it efficiently.

We have to handle betrayals and breakups effectively. It's hard to overcome. So many factors in this world trigger emotions, push us into the dark emotional zone and then shift our minds.

We came to the vital portion of life: to be loved. Everyone on earth wants to be loved. We are expecting love from others after our loved ones. While we expect love from someone, but when they ignore it, people get into a bad emotional mood. Everyone thinks it's a trap, but it is not a trap. We can't avoid those emotions, whether it be a work-based economy or current political philosophies. The problem of love is constant in any economy because it is not the problem of the outside world; it's a world inside us. So, no one has better solutions than our own, but we can get help. There are always trained medical people who are ready to instruct us towards peace, happiness and love.

-----------------------ccc--------------------ccc----------------------ccc---------

Humans want their families. WBE is likely to adopt the laws of current political philosophies. If any parents fail to follow them, their children will be given up for adoption. Parents will be allocated a counsellor. They will not carry babies until they are cured. For unique children, doctors will counsel parents on how to help a baby grow healthy mentally and physically. A happy family will make happy humans. We humans always want to be with family. We can't live without family. Families need support. The support I am referring to is from the government. They should not dump any families based on their colours, region, religion, caste, or language.

In a work-based economy, all countries and all families should follow only one set of rules and laws. Rulers may defer, but rules never defer unless there is a loophole. That's what is unique, that's what everyone need too.

-------------------cccc----------------------------cccc--------------------------

What do we really need?

What we all really need are food, clothing, shelter, and entertainment. These are humans' basic needs. All these are consumed based on money in current political philosophies. In the WBE, they will be consumed based on work. What is the average capacity that people are able to consume? In the WBE, this food and clothes will be available more than that for everyone. We can use a work card to consume it, but we should not waste it. As for shelter, it will be allocated based on our family size. When it comes to entertainment, whatever it may be, if it's a sport, they will have every chance to play, explore their talent, watch and enjoy. If it's a movie, everyone can watch whatever they wish to watch. Theme parks are open to everyone. No partiality, no money, no power. All entertainment is counted in the luxury points. We will discuss briefly about luxury points in the coming topics.

----------------cccc----------------------cccc-------------------------------------

All humans have their destinies. No one in the world lives without a destiny. People who say, 'I don't have any destiny' mean that is not true because even if they may not have one now, they will have it eventually. Most of us didn't have any destiny when we were in our comfort zone. We can't say that it's permanent. WBE never restricts any destiny that doesn't have a negative impact on the world. Finally, everyone wants to achieve the true destination of their life.

After we reach our destination, what will we do? Everyone has the same answer. They say, “I will fix my new destination.” For those, I share my opinion, “Please fix your destiny unimaginable by anybody. After that fix small destinies or milestones to achieve that unimaginable destiny. You make it a dream come true” because inner pleasure will happen when we achieve our destiny then it will become inner peace. When our soul’s destiny is tremendous, we won’t fix another one because it will satisfy us for a lifelong. When we achieved our destiny but haven’t felt that peace means it’s not our true destiny. We can achieve more than that. For that reason, Einstein tried new theories till death on his deathbed. The same thing made Che Guevara participate in the independence war till death. The change they brought to this world is extraordinary, but what they had in their mind to achieve is unimaginable. We also should have a destiny like that one. What if they achieved their destiny? The world might look different. I mentioned them because their dreams are achievable in a work-based economy. When that happens, the world will be in the hands of peace. Everyone will be equal.

-------------------cccc-----------------------------cccc----------------------------

What do we really want? The question has endless answers. The answers create endless opportunities. For that reason, I don’t know what to pick or leave. The question has 800+ billion answers. Here we come to know yours is not mine. Mine may not be your answer. As per ancient Hindu mythology, whatever is mine today will be yours tomorrow. The day after that, it belongs to another one. So, nothing will be permanent. We all must come to one point at the end. We have to be clear about that point, which should not be destructive. It should be diligently constructive.

People used to be allured by a few things. The alluring things are primarily addictive. These are needed, but they are not only needed or wanted for life. Addiction won’t consider listening. Deadly addiction leads us to death; here are a few deadly addictions as follows: No. 1 Power, do we want power? If yes, please think about it. All people in the world want power means how many of them will survive in the current population. Daily we have to dig a pit to throw the millions of bodies. Power can be consumed with the fight, whether it may be moral or physical. When something starts with a fight that can’t be ended without a fight. The population automatically becomes zero in a few days when everyone starts to fight physically. The peace of mind will collapse if everyone fights morally. It's not possible for everyone to hold power. So, we have to understand a few things about power. When people decide to remove a person from power means, nothing can control them. Power relies on obedience. Power relies on diligence. A person with interpersonal intelligence, obedience as a skill with experience and peace of mind can only hold power in any field. So, one can't simply take the power of another unless they have these skills. So being addicted to getting power on hand is foolishness without developing these qualities. Sometimes even if we have all qualities, people won't accept us because of various reasons. Our ideology is not relatable to them or inspired them, which may be worst from their point of view. Power should not be centred on a single entity or person because humans are more vulnerable when they feel weak.

"Being an alcoholic, drug-addicted... Is that really what I want?" If "yes!"

"What an idiot?"

We all want to get high and unconscious for a few hours, but how long and how frequent matters. If it's really often, it means we're wasting our time and energy. It's not advice for alcoholics and drug addicts. What if? All are becoming alcoholic, nothing but alcohol and drugs that we drink, eat and taste. No productive work will happen. It's just a short pleasure. People may get drunk and use drugs occasionally but should not get addicted to them. It is what we want from us. For those who say, 'I really want alcohol and drugs all the time,' this will lead to a lifetime of misery and assault on their surroundings.

Few people work actively when they are under alcohol and drugs. Their creativity works when they are under drugs and alcohol. They can't work without it. Few people smoke 12 to 100 times a day. They can't move through the day without smoking. Their work won't happen properly if they stop smoking. How do they have such capacity to handle such bad habits and be a creative person? Sometimes the body changes to adopt that behaviour. Few may function like that, but it's not possible for everyone. People should not be influenced by them.

---------------------------ccc-----------------------ccc-------------------------

What do we really want? Sex. A person shouldn't have non-consensual sex. Sex is something that can produce endless pleasure every single time it happens. Educating people about sex is very important from childhood itself.

Currently, we have many genders. People consider the gender of males as the dominant one. Males often violently take steps ahead and may sexually harass other genders. They sometimes harass their own gender. In a work-based economy, forcing sex, child abuse, and harassment will have deadly punishments. It is essential to have sex education from pre-KG until death. Yearly, we should have exams on this as well.

----------------------------------cccc-------------------------cccc-------------

Few people are extravagant and spendthrift. It is bad because that is a deadly addictive one. There is no use in spending more on something because it's entertaining and stress-relieving unless we gain something out of it in the physical world. We can gain happiness; it's a short pleasure but that can destroy us in the long run.

----------------------------------cccc--

The world is filled with diverse individuals, and everyone approaches every aspect differently. Few may think some incidents are wrong. The rest think that's right. Few don't have an idea. They don't bother about it. Every possibility is there. All kinds of thoughts may arise within us like everything is perfectly imperfect and imperfectly perfect. We are in a world that has given us endless possibilities. It will give us the same until humans become extinct. Sometimes we can change. Sometimes we have to accept. Like how money came into the picture. WBE will come into the picture. Sometimes we can change. Change is in our voice.

"I want to have a big house, super-fast brand-new cars, huge assets in the bank." Almost everyone used to ask for these luxuries when we asked them, "What do you really want?". In WBE, we are all going to get these materials, but the important thing is we are not going to show off with them. There is nothing to show off when everyone has them.

-----------------cccccc-------------------------cccc------------------------------

What we really want from ourselves and from others? It's honesty, fairness, courage, caring, straightforwardness, dependability, cooperativeness, determination, ambition, loyalty, self-control, and imagination. People should have these aspects inside them. Our above-mentioned qualities are often sacrificed due to the fear of survival. The battle for survival of the fittest won't be here anymore in the WBE. The WBE will make everyone the fittest and wisest. Think that if we have bad aspects like lying, laziness, not being punctual, and lethargy, how essential things will work around us. Behaviour will decide the path that we are going to travel.

---------------------------cccc-------------cccc--------------------------------------

Sovereignty – A supreme power or authority. Most people have God as sovereignty for them. For those, I would like to clarify a few things. Even when we look deep into this, we can't find the true meaning of sovereignty. We almost forgot it. Our ancestors made us think worshipping God is absolute sovereignty. Those people are atheists. So, God will save us all. That's what our ancestors spread all over the world. We started following it blindly. It made billions and billions of gods. We added billions and billions of beliefs with that afterwards. We joined trillions and trillions of procedures to worship it. In the whole world, we don't have any country without God's belief. The world is occupied with significant religions like Islam, Christianity, Hinduism, Buddhism, Shinto, Sikhism. We can't even imagine how many sub-branches were in each religion. In ancient days, there were wars that happened to spread religion. The priests had control over so many things. They are even treated as God's messengers, few of them supported improving our society. Few were spoiled. Both pros and cons are there. We can't deny it.

Non-religious people existed in ancient times as well. Those who don't have a belief in God are called atheists. Over time, the number of atheists constantly increased. It's about expressing the freedom of choice and independence. In ancient days, if anyone expressed anything contrary to God, the punishment would be a death sentence in a brutal manner. We can't even imagine how painful that was, but today both groups live equally without significant trouble.

A significant gap in the concept of God has existed for thousands and thousands of years, which means from the existence of God or the concept of God's arrival. When I look into this gap deeply, I discover something inquisitive. It made me speechless. Do we know what God is doing?

Most philosophers also agreed with the point I discovered. We have many perspectives on God. We can take this perspective into consideration as well. Few perspectives argue that God is true and not true. We can't be conclusive about anything because, like most people agree, God works in mysterious ways. People use it to unite and at the same time they use it to diversify.

I have many perspectives, and one of them is that God is separating one another from joining together. The concept of God belief separates one individual from another, after which it unites them all with the concept of God.

The atheist's mind used to think that opposing God is enough to be an atheist. Few atheists have the realisation of how to overcome it. Almost everyone got it the wrong way; people don't know how to overcome it. Few have not realised that there is still a gap.

How did God make us separate? Before knowing that, we need to understand the butterfly effect. It's a sensitive dependence on initial conditions in which a slight change in one state of a deterministic nonlinear system can result in a significant difference in a later state. This is the so-called book definition of the butterfly effect. At the beginning of history, we used to have sovereignty as the sun, moon, land, water, fire, sky, and air. Through continuous development, it evolved from these to worshipping the best among humans. We named them as gods. They were named based on their locality.

The Stone Age people are those who still have their sovereignty as above. On a few islands, there were still ancient human civilisations following the same. Currently, evolved civilisations follow both cultures.

Based on our religion, if we are Christian, we used to go to church; if we are Hindu, we used to go to the temple. If we are Muslim, we used to go to the mosque. All religions have their worshipping place. When we pray, we take apart the pressure from us then submit it to God. It is how more people enjoy relief, but the problem still used to exist. It will not go anywhere from us. It is why we have relief for only a few hours. If the solution came, we wouldn't think of it. Are those solutions coming that easy? No, we have astrologers in many religions. They have a greater earning capacity. Our problem is their money. If we don't have any issues in life, then we stay normal. People like astrologers won't exist. Few are worthy but 1 in 100 possibilities. Rest all doing it to earn money. Countries like India are mad about astrologers. Few people were doing everything based on astrology, even brushing their teeth; that habit may disappear from the current or coming generation.

Most religious-oriented rituals become a money-making business. We have to pay to see God in the temple. This kind of thing became a money-making business. The rich got priority but the poor did not. In the temple itself, partiality started in a few places. People do business based on belief in God.

How are our problems finally getting solutions? If we have a problem, we leave it to God and then come home. We used to tell people around us what our problem is until that problem gets solved. We share the pain of that problem with our family, relatives, friends, and neighbours; if people solve that problem, we will also thank those people in the name of gods. Spread the incident that happened because of God's grace.

Here the problem is not solved by God, but we are praising God. We have to understand who God is. People understand it like that God has been created that opportunity. If we ask this question to people, they used to say supreme power, the creator of opportunities. The one is having access to whole knowledge. Do we have an understanding of how supreme powers were created? The person who knows who he/she is, used to become the supreme power. We should understand that knowing ourselves is not only knowing our interests. It's the purpose of knowing why we are here and knowing what our prime duty is.

Most of us don't have any idea about our prime duty. It is why there have been no drastic changes in the world so far. The core motive of sovereignty is 'compromise, sharing, unity, and forgivingness of mistakes.' We should develop our humanitarianism to have these. It's the basic need in any economy structure and society. We can't survive without it. It is not the thing to achieve; it's the aspect to develop. Without it, we can't even understand what we really want.

Who is that sovereignty or God? The person who exceeds the expectation of others in these things. We will not become saints, sages if we start following these things. It's a long process of realisation of all the aspects of the world. If people want, they can work on it to that extent, but it's not that easy. That's why we have a "N" number of ashrams, churches, mosques, temples. Humanitarianism is the first level to achieve that great extent.

-------------------------ccc-------------------------ccc-------------------------

What is Humanitarianism?

Caring for everyone. Loving everything unconditionally without considering or thinking of its nature, its kind, its position, its race, its character, without manoeuvring and being envious, considering our benefits. Suppose we started developing humanitarianism. We can grow stronger than anyone in the past centuries. We have to develop humanitarianism within ourselves.

What do we really want? Desires to fulfil, enjoy again and again. Everyone has desires. All our desires are influenced by external forces like things we see, things we read, things others do, things we listen to. Mostly, the things that make us excited will become our desires. We will be happy if we get what we desired. This happiness will be reflected on the outside as well. We can't reach our desires all alone; that needs some help. It's essential to have positive, good desires that won't destroy others.

The track has reached the field HELP. Help is not like work. We are not supposed to do it daily. In some areas of fields, we are doing it subconsciously daily. It may occur at any time when one who needs it. It may be small or big. We will remain in the person's mind forever after we do that help. This help can make a tremendous change in that person's life.

Big Bang Theory is a help that space did for us. Just a vast blast became AI now in our world. People may say it has evolved. We are still trying to discover how many planets are over there in space like us. A small help can change N number of things we don't believe in. So, helping tenancy is what we really want in the world to live and love together. Everyone will benefit only from it. It may come in good qualities of humans, but I am saying this alone because all good qualities will improve us but helping quality is the only thing that will improve others without benefits.

What we really want is to help when it is necessary. People will help others who want help, which will increase humanity. It always makes us feel high and happy. No one is going to ask for anything that we are not able to give. So, assess the level. If we can offer that help, then do it. Nothing is wrong with it. The loving and helping tendency will make people's lives happy.

--------------------------cccc---------------------cccc---------------------------

What we really want is humanity and self-respect. If someone says, human blood is not red, no one will believe. People will instantly scratch their body then show the drop of red blood. They shut down the speaker who is proposing it. They symbolise him/her as stupid. It's because we know it's unchangeable or unarguable truth. We are not able to get into the same kind of argument when we talk about humanity. It's because few people take a side with the world has humanity all over and few people take a side with the world has no humanity. It means we have not achieved the unchangeable or unarguable truth in humanity. The same applies to self-respect as well.

We have both good and bad sides. We should only have a good side. Why is it not possible? Why does the bad side exist? What is triggering the bad side? It's nothing but selfishness. When we have selfishness, then we can't achieve humanity and self-respect. What is causing the selfishness? It's the structure of society. It doesn't have enough supply for demand. So, people are forced to compete for supply. People became selfish due to competition. We can't blame people for it. The time has not yet come to build a structured society that has enough supply for demand. So, people are not educated towards it.

Self-respect is different from self-pride, but people often confuse both. What is self-respect? It's respecting our body and respecting ourselves. We are tolerating whatever unforgettable tortures, shames, or harms that we are facing in hard times which hurt our self. Why are we tolerating? We are tolerating it in fear of survival. It's happening to both educated and uneducated people. It's true that survival is important. We feel the pain when we remember it. It will mentally affect us. Every second of life after that is hell. So, don't ever lose your self-respect at any cost.

WBE will make sure that the system encourages and respects people's humanity and self-respect. WBE will stay on the paths that lead people with humanity equally to everyone. The system will make sure that it won't hurt anyone's self-respect.

Happiness won't come that easily to everyone's life. Few have earned it, few have bought it, few have sold it, few have loaned it, few have lent it, few have struggled for it. Happiness will come when we get what we want. We never get what we want, meaning how happiness will come to us.

Whatever political philosophies, the primary matter is to realise what stops us from being happy. We have to examine it society-wise; we have to examine our personal life. We have to find a resolution to solve the issue. If it's not solved softly, we must start acting against it. We should have the capacity to stand against the matter.

I will say only one thing to the protestors all over the world. The protest may be for land, food, cloth, work, nature, water, culture, survival. Please keep only one thing in mind. The protest will never come to an end until the political philosophies have the same rules, regulations, powers, and controls. Even when we won in the place we protested, that is still happening in some other places; who will win for them? It's a never-ending process. It's better to guide world politicians to create a new political philosophy. The WBE will have the space to accept all the requests with a permanent resolution because it will not operate based on money. It won't encourage differences that current political philosophies have in their system. We will see differences in upcoming topics.

----------------------cccc----------------------------cccc------------------------

Politics – we have to know the meaning of it first. Did people in the world know the exact meaning of politics? I will share that last. Here, we see what Google says,

The activities associated with the governance of a country or area, especially the debate about power.

The activities of governments concerning the political relations between states.

A particular set of political beliefs or principles.

The principles relating to or inherent in a sphere or activity, mainly when concerned with power and status.

Activities aimed at improving someone's status or increasing power within an organisation.

These are the explanations that Google delivered.

It's what I am sharing here below: - The real meaning is so simple, "politics is the word which has an inseparable relation with people and tricks; people will come to power with tricks that impress people. They want to play a game to stay in power with some tricks. Sometimes that favours citizens. Sometimes that favours rulers.

We have politics at every level of work. We have to stay aware of it. We want to learn clean politics, which favours people. So, we can improve people's lives.

---------------cccccccc------------------------cccccccc-------------------------

Most managers in private organisations don't identify who is doing well. Person 2 has the quality to escape from responsibility. Person 1 has the quality to take responsibility. They didn't identify based on it. They identify based on errors. There is no rating and ranking anywhere on the WBE since everyone will be identified equally. People's faults will be rectified by providing constructive feedback. We do not want any rating and ranking, which is possible only on the WBE.

Without rating and ranking, what if people get lazy to do work? There will not be competition among them. How can they improve without competition? It's a dilemma. People are going to work in what they love to do. When they work on what they love, the chances of being lazy are too low. The real competition for a person is with herself/himself. They don't have to compare themselves with others. People with these current political philosophies think they want to be better than everyone. It gives them fear. It makes them run without awareness of what they want and their goal. There will be zero motivation for competition when there is no rating and ranking. So, dirty politics will be avoided. We have the open choice to do what we love without any competition. They don't like to escape from responsibility. The competition is to better yourself than you. It's a self-competition. You're your competitor. We don't have to point to others and then say he is doing less; I am doing more. It is not going to happen in the WBE.

So, how does the adequate work segment operate? Don't they behave lazily without rating and ranking? We have independent working hours. Our labour policies will be structured to make people cooperate with those who consider it their main work profile. Will the government force workers to cooperate terribly? No, the adequate work will be allocated based on their education, to which they have already agreed to cooperate.

-------------------cccc-----------------------------cccc-----------------------------

Globally, everyone has something in common. One who doesn't have this should be in a mentally weak stage. Everyone hates to have this. No more thinking; it's the so-called fear. Fear and fearless, there were two terms. People can't be fearless in all matters. At the same time, they should not be feared for all matters. Why do we have it? Any guess?

Fear will raise its wings when something we don't know or aren't aware of, or haven't heard, or are ignorant of. The fear of what others think when we say something or ask something. The fear of losing something. Fear of trying out. This fear may appear at any time. The truth is that we can only be focused if we fear what we care about. When we really want something, at that time the fear will rise.

When we have a fear of anything, it means we have to try that thing. We have to clear our fear that way, but before that, we have to know how it works. We need to be trained on it.

Why should people really need to be feared in a few situations? They should fear doing lousy work or bad things that harm society. They should fear influencing others in a wrong way. They should fear spoiling others' lives. Actually, what we don't want others to do to us—that stuff we should not do to others. It will be helpful if we have fear about it.

We don't need to fear: speaking with others, asking for something from others, gaining knowledge from others, accepting others' points if we feel they are correct, even if everyone is against it for support. But before accepting any points, we must do our research on it from all perspectives possible.

Everyone is a victim of fear. There are 'n' number of fears, but people should not fear doing something right. There are ways to overcome all kinds of unwanted fears. The complete cure will come once we start fighting with it. Practice is the better one that we can do. I know it's stereotypical, but overcoming fear is something that needs to be appropriately guided, which can be done by therapists well and good.

-------------------------cccc-------------------------cccc-------------------------

In our life, a whole bunch of people, waggling in the world to win over something. Animals have to win for their food. They have to win for their life. They have to win for having a partner. Humans also think that way; it starts from birth for every person. We were born when our parents successfully communicated. We have to win to complete our studies. We have to win our job. We have to win our business. We have to win our partner same as animals. We may say couples will join together when they love each other, but most of us treat it as a competition. For a few of them, even survival is also a competition to win situation.

What we really want is to win. It's a default setup in our minds, which I call wrong.

Not only in the games that the win mattered, but currently, it matters in every aspect. All because surviving itself became the competition. What is the reason? The reason is current political philosophies. Money is needed for everything. We have to win for the money.

The laughter point here is every win varies based on time, location, field, situation. In football, if a person plays, we may take game days as work days. The player works full seven years, most probably scoring a maximum of 1000 goals. For the rest of the day, they will practice to be better at performing, which means every workday, but they get paid in millions of dollars with an average performance of 50 percent. When an employee in a corporate works for 20 years, he/she practices for a maximum of 5 years to be better at performing each day, and they earn thousands of dollars with an average SLA achievement of 96.74 percent. The pressure is the same, but the field, time, location, and situation differ. An actor portrays a field character for two years and earns a million-dollar salary. In contrast, individuals working in that field must toil until the end of their lives to accumulate the same amount of money

Two percent of people will win a little, but with that, they hold 70 percent of the world's wealth. Eighty-seven people have to win daily to manage their day-to-day. The pressure of the work was the same. The benefit of wealth only differs.

The people have to realise how our wins make others enjoy enormously.

Winning is necessary when it improves us along with the world's improvement. Winning will improve confidence and happiness. A win in current political philosophies always has a material benefit, which is incorrect. The win should bring about a material change, notably in the world's improvement and inner peace. In sports, competition is fine, but a win should not be a pressurised part. Games are all for self-confidence in WBE. No one can only be a player. As we said earlier, they should have a second profession. We will see in the players of differentiation part why we have these differences.

-----------------------------------ccc-----------------------ccc-----------------

What do we really hate in this world? There might be different answers for everyone, but commonly, the loss and defeat is something that we hate for all our life. People always have wrong ideas about loss and defeat. People think that loss makes people scold us, forget us, bully us, hit us, sadden us, making us poor. These ideas need to be cleared from all our minds. Loss and defeat make people gain some perspective. Loss and defeat can't happen when people are not trying or learning anything new. Losing is the first step to self-learning. The reasons for loss and defeat

- inexperience, carelessness, laziness, negligence, unawareness of field knowledge. When we try something new at that time, we have no one to guide, which means losing is the best guide. No other master is better than one experience of loss. We may earn tremendous gain by repeating the event while rectifying the error.

The pressure of loss and defeat has a number of deaths in its hand. If we lose, there will be another chance over anywhere. A life not meant to close out. People should take that failure of loss then grow with it. We should not make any decisions immediately when we fail. We should take people's reasonable advice, don't listen to scolds and laughs. The new invention will come with 100 to 1000s of failed ideas and attempts. Few losses only show who's our real supporters and motivators. The most hateful time in the world is to be losing, but without learning any lessons from losing is the worst loss. The reason for losing should not repeat. The focus on the goal motivates us. The result of happiness that's what we have to think.

When we lose something for our loved ones, our love will increase. That kind of loss will strengthen the bonds and relationships, but we should not lose what we love willingly to someone because that loss might hurt us and them both in terms of happiness.

-------------------------ccc---------------ccc---------------ccc---------------

There were several emotions and feelings that are common for humans and animals. Those emotions and feelings will come out according to the situation. Anger is the emotion that comes when we are disappointed with the behaviour of some uncertain events. The pressure will build up if we do not express our anger correctly. We will feel bad. We become cowardly when we think about that situation. Anger should not necessarily be expressed in a loud manner. Anger always has the loud face of portrayal. It should be expressed politely. It should be pointed out with a suggestion of the corrective step.

People shout out due to anger; sometimes that will be portrayed as funny if that anger is meaningless and frequent. They will be mocked by their surroundings. Anger that comes to us should be politely expressed so that the person won't be hurt. It differs when it comes to some illegal activities. If bad things are happening in front of our eyes, there is no need to be polite at that time. In the work-based economy, people have the right to ask if anything goes wrong in front of them, I mean any illegal activities. Even the WBE will have a policy that gives people the right to take action on illegal activities. The public will have the right to capture the person if that crime seems to affect others in a threat to life. There is no need to wait for the police to come once we have reported. There will be a camera for surveillance in every public place. I am saying this because in the current political philosophies, people report to the police. Some people only do that because they don't have the right to take action, and witness responsibility is an extra burden on their daily routine.

If any big scam or malpractice is operating near us, we feel angry about it. We can oppose it in any economy. We have to express our thoughts in public first. We must collect all evidence about that illegality and spread it to the public in a way that they can connect with it emotionally. People who feel the same can join hands with us, then we become us. Some day in the future, people will change the system. If we see anybody who has already started it, please do start supporting them. It will make an enormous change. So, there is no use in fear of something we feel is wrong. Raise your voice against it. It's the best action we can take.

We really want to be angry about the wrong system, illegalities, and crimes happening against us.

-----------------ccccccccc-------------------------------ccccccc-------------------

There are limits in every aspect. If we cross that limit, destruction is the only result. There is no other option. Take our body for an example - naturally everything is aligned at the perfect level for our body to survive as per medical elements. If that crosses its limit, it indicates we are sick. Like that, from A-to-Z, there is a limit. We have to realise what the limit is. Suppose we've crossed the limit, then we need to face unnecessary consequences. There are a lot of differences between being within a limit and making decisions without being within the limit. We should not argue that "we are within the limit" when decisions have to be taken. We should not argue when our limit is over. If we cross it, destruction will be the result. Knowing the limit is the best knowledge in learning.

The limit is the word that should be used only in certain places. When we realise something wrong is happening, we have the right to raise our voices against it. Few do not realise what is wrong. They don't know what natural consequences are happening because of doing it. If we have explicit knowledge about the consequences and dangers of that matter, we have to raise our voice against it. We should not be silent at that time. We should not say that we are at our limit without taking any action. How will it look? It looks like we're also supporting unlawful, stupid, or destructive policies.

What we really want is to realise the meaning of the limit. People need clarification about it. People must realise when they should be within the limit. When to raise their voices. Since then, we have been facing 'n' number of outbreaks of unnecessary losses.

------------------------------cccc--------------------------cccc-----------------

Business requires this. Success requires this. In every plan, it is the most following phenomenon. Politics require this. The competition's results are based on this. Every bad person who wants to rule the world will have this. This heavy introduction is for none other than "Strategy." People in the world have it naturally. Strategy is the most important thing to take revenge. It's essential to get success. It's required to beat the competition. Movies mostly have a strategic villain and an innocent hero, but the villain gets defeated by the end. That only happens in the movie.

Everyone has their strategy. Few don't know that they are playing with a strategy. Everyone operates based on a strategy with or without realisation. You know that successful theft will never be found; even still, it's running on its way because the theft strategy is so strong. It's not only used for wrong matters. We have one saying in the world, "the person who does illegal activities in the wrong way may get caught, but the person doing the same in the right way will never be caught." I am not influencing people in the wrong way. I am giving awareness to people to find out the strategy of the other. The best strategic game is chess. Even only with a single king, we may draw the match. We may quickly lose with all guards. In the world, we have infinite strategies happening around us. We have to realise what the motive of the strategy is. How others are playing strategies with us. Even people we love have some strategies to fool us around. They make us lame because the core motive of them is to make others spend for their causes. Few may be an exception. So, we have to communicate with everyone to know about others. So, we may get 'n' number of visions about the people around us and their strategy against us.

All wars are won with strategies. There are two kinds of innocents: those who are truly innocent and those who only pretend to be. People who are truly innocent can react to a few miseries, but people who pretend to be innocent never do that or overreact. If we have people who care for us, that's cool. We can feel the difference by our instinct or through some behaviour.

I just diverted you to the people behaviour strategy. There are a number of strategy types. If you are interested, then learn on your own.

If we have a plan, we should have a strategy to make it. If we don't have any plan, others will use us to make their plan work by using their strategy. It is Dhirubhai Ambani's quote.

If an ant has a plan that works well with strategy, it can defeat an elephant. The book "Good Strategy and Bad Strategy" has all the details about it.

The strategy should contain a diagnosis, a guiding policy, and coherent action. These are the three main things.

We can't ask people about their strategy because it's always a secret. We have to discover it on our own. We have to make a counter-strategy and protect ourselves from it. People want to identify the strategy. Suppose a strategy works for a good cause. It's OK to be in it and support it. Avoid the bad ones. We should come out of them quickly.

----------------------------cccc--------------------cccc----------------------------

We have to understand what we want instead of lusting after the material desires that we need for luxury. What we really want will be available in the work-based economy.

How can we identify what we really want? It can be identified with necessity. If we can't lead a life without that, it necessarily means it's what we really want.

WBE never forces people to play in a small circle. It will erase the circle. It educates the people about the availability. It asks them to draw their circle considering the availability. It makes them comfortable in it. WBE encourages them to widen the circle by their work.

2K kids will have a better understanding of everything than the other generations. It is because the internet has made the world small. Technologies are better than ever. We have to move forward without crossing the limit.

What we really want is knowledge. What is restricting us from being a knowledgeable person? Is it society? Or is it our personality? Knowledge is nothing but knowing what we like deeply. People always want to gain knowledge in a vast majority of different fields which are not correlated to one another. It's not humanly possible for a person to know everything in every field. It's only possible up to a certain level. We are not robots to store everything in our memory without a point of difference. All the restrictions related to society that are stopping us from gathering knowledge will vanish in a work-based economy. We can independently learn and gain knowledge in whatever field we want.

What we really want is to be beautiful. Why is this addiction towards being beautiful? People from ancient times themselves educated wrongly. They defined white with some facial shapes and body shapes as beautiful. They defined clear skin as beautiful. It's fundamentally wrong. It's stereotypical and a closed mindset. The definition of beauty will change from one person to another person. The media world, starting from the beginning, showcased similar or the same types of structures and shapes and colours as beautiful in advertisements. Viewers got influenced by it. The truth is that there is no defined shape or structure for being beautiful. Few people like a fat body. Few people like a slim body. The majority of people defined as being fat is ugly. It's not a fact. It's one of the body types. It's an individual's right to represent themselves how they would like to be represented. We should understand that while beauty is subjective, it also means recognizing that not everyone will find the same people beautiful. Even a Miss World isn't attractive or beautiful to some people. At the same time, not everyone can look ugly in everyone's eyes. People with misguided knowledge are trying to fit into the mould that society created as beauty.

What we really want is to be an entertaining person? Most people are attracted to people who have a jovial personality. These people keep entertaining their surroundings. There is a saying in Tamil Nadu: "A garrulous fellow survives easily." You can change your personality if you practice how you want to live your life without thinking too much about it. We need to know why we change our personality. If it's harming others, then we can change our personality. The process of changing personality is a hard one. We can't start today and achieve tomorrow. It's a long process, and mentally we have to prepare for it. We have to accept the consequences that are going to happen, good or bad, because of that change. Most of the time, people like to look for magic in these kinds of things. Some people get jealous of these entertaining persons. They try to act like one. We can act like an entertaining person for a short time, but we can't do it for long because it's not our original nature. We eventually come back to our real nature within some time, within an hour as far as I know. Some people naturally get this personality based on the kind of situation they grew up in, the kind of people they are surrounded by, the people they saw, and the things they read and listen to. I took this topic to make people realise what they really need, but some people are misguided by society. They are falling for wrong ideas like beauty and personality. People have to realise that loving ourselves as we are is true happiness.

What we really want is to be talented. Everyone in the world likes to be talented. They are hardworking too. The opportunity is the problem in the world. Every talented person is not getting the right opportunity. They are struggling to find the opportunity to prove themselves. The players of differentiation are also playing their role in it. Why is it hard to provide an opportunity for the deserved one? It's because of the tiny demand. The waiting period is huge. Middle-class people with dependencies can't survive the waiting period. We can't definitely say whoever is the best because an even better performer than them might not have got the opportunity that others got. The work-based economy is the place where all talents are recognised, and opportunities are given to prove them. The system will mentor them without any difference. We can't achieve it with current political philosophies.

We will see what all the hindrances are in current political philosophies in the upcoming topics that restrict what we really want.

THREE

MASKS OF COUNTRIES

What is a country? How is it made? Why is it made? The same kind of people who follow the same culture, God, correspondence live together in a place was called a country in the initial periods. Now it's changed a lot from all perspectives. When humans stopped hunting and started to cultivate food, they decided to live in a stable place for a lifelong. So, with their belief, they developed their culture, language, protection. It is made to express their identity and avoid dangerous thieves from another group. In ancient days, most tribes never allowed trespassers into their tribes due to security issues; they either killed or warned them.

Do you know what countries are doing now? They have formed a government. There are 28 types of governments. All governments follow four types of economy.

Traditional Economy

Command Economy

Free Market Economy

Mixed Economy

The traditional economy is a barter system. It is now followed only by ancient tribes. All other economies are operating based on monetary policy. All countries were fighting over the power of trade; countries were fighting to become a superpower. All countries have a desire to dominate other countries. Everyone is playing with their strategies. The countries are using several masks to fool people. Do you want to know about these masks? Do you want to know how to tear masks?

People of their own country are brainwashed by their government. People believe they are the best or worst country in the world, but they are not because all governments are fooling people from some perspective. No country is an open book for its people. It has to be like that in the current situation. Masks are created to rule us separately without hesitation. All the situations and circumstances are created by the country itself. It acts like it's not the reason for that. Once we know all the masks, we won't hesitate to join together to love other countries' people.

Trade Mask

In any circumstance, unless we explain the concept from the beginning, people won't understand. The buying and selling of goods or ownership, or IOU, is called trade. Where are the biggest trades happening daily? The place called a market. It's rotating oceans of money; from fish to whales, one who swims smartly can get anything they want; even fishes get power to eat whales but only sometimes. Whales are ruling the market. The fishes rarely survive. Few only do more than survive. Decoding the market is not that hard, but encrypting it well without identifying fraud is hard because we have regulations and programming. The regulators are the fish traps. Do you know why the share market was created? It was created to fund companies. It plays with paper money. Why am I stating it as playing? Once the primary market investments are made based on the company's future, forecast, management strength, growth, returns, then the secondary market will take place. It's where psychological, global, domestic, industrial situations and companies' performances take place as factors that decide the price of the shares and growth of the shares. People who do not understand will lose. The investors and traders are fooled by too many frauds and advertisements. Grounds are covered with a number of tricks and codes. Survival needs a complete understanding of the market behaviour. FII and DII people have been playing with a joystick. They bet on the market index or securities or bonds or currency to grow faster and quicker. Sometimes they force the downside. Sometimes they force the upside for any market instruments in the above. Which may not necessarily need to mean perfect or correct. They try to confuse the directions of the market whenever they need to make money.

All goods are sold for money and bought for money. There are four significant trading components: commodities, shares, bonds, and communication. Whatever country rules these will have a massive impact on the world forum. Most trades are happening around these parts. If a country wants to start a trade war, it will start based on any of these components. If we want to tear masks off, we can try to stop depending on them entirely. We have to know how countries play with these first. Oil is the most critical tradable commodity. When we plan a trip, when we like to buy eatables, when we like to transport something, all the places need oil for the manufacturing industry. We depend on oil for food, manufacturing industries for A-to-Z operation and transport purposes.

There are many countries producing oil. The top countries are like the USA, Saudi Arabia, Russia, China, and Canada. The United States is just making alliances with most of the Middle East countries like Saudi Arabia. The United States influenced other countries to sell oil in dollars. A few countries other than the Middle East like to sell their oil in their currency, but they got threatened indirectly by the United States. In Iraq's case, false accusations were made against them. War was imposed on them. It destroyed them in the name of peace. So, to reduce the dependency on oil, we can start using alternative sources for transport or form a new union with small countries who are willing to sell oil. We can create a common currency that may be fiat or gold-backed with the help of venture capitalists around the world. We can avoid supremacy. All countries that like to trade may offer protection for the suppliers.

The share market was created by Europeans. It was adopted by every country worldwide. It was created around the 17th century. Shares were bought based on credibility. They were sold based on credibility. Money circulated because of it. We can't make money out of nothing in other fields except gambling and casinos, but we can do that in shares with strategies in the secondary market. Companies make money through IPOs; then, in the secondary market, shares will rise and fall based on news, performance, deals, and agreements. These are accurate most of the time, but sometimes false. Why should we try to reduce dependency on this? Because it's one of the main reasons for inflation. No country's market in the world has collapsed entirely. It continues to rise due to inflation. Sometimes individuals' growth is hindered if they don't participate in the market. The country's inflation rate leads to poverty due to a lack of knowledge about a particular sector.

Bonds are IOUs. There are several types of bonds; the most important are corporate and government bonds. Bonds and shares are interrelated. They depend on each other. Governments and corporate companies can issue bonds to attract investors of various kinds. Trading is a complex geopolitical game sometimes. In uncertain situations, ordinary people panic and then do something wrong. Intelligent investors grasp the situation, using it to their advantage. They earn more during this time. People later realise the situation and start to get involved again. At that time, up to specific points, it will rise, cross certain points, then grow more than its capacity and potential. After that, again, people realise that it's overgrowth, then common people bring that down. So, it's never been at its correct valuation for an extended period. It's always either over or under. It might be at the correct valuation for some short period. It's what the art of trading is. Those who understand the concept can sustain. Others lose in this game.

Money is not like technology. It may be in the form of technologies like debit and credit cards, UPI, but the nature of the money in these technologies remains unchanged. It uses technologies to come in different forms with the same characteristics. It's just a transaction tool that needs to help people to transact. It is always reachable by everyone in need. Technology's growth will move society to the next level. Inflation will never move society to the next level. It just alarms people to stop consuming fast. We can't stop inflation when using money. We will discuss it in detail in upcoming topics.

Communication's latest form is the internet. The mixed result of the internet is unavoidable. Everyone knows the good side of the internet. It's helping people to learn, grow, earn, and entertain. When speaking about the wrong side, it does inflate fake news and incorrect information. It is used as a tool to steal people's data. The threat of viruses and blackmailing for money. Most of the time, these crimes end up for the motive of money.

The intention is always money for most of the crimes on the internet.

We can't say it isn't perfect. We are enjoying the good side of the internet more. Few people are affected by it. We can follow the protocols strictly to avoid the wrong sides—sometimes, internet hackers leak more truths about governments and countries. Society needs the internet to voice out independently. Society needs the internet's help to change. The only way is to understand the power of communication.

People may have doubts about where the country's mask is hidden in it. Countries are financially secured by these components. Countries will do anything to gain a leap of advantage in it. We have a classic example called the "British Empire". How they looted innocent countries via trades. We have another classic example of corporate companies' loot, that's "Shell". They spoiled Nigerian lands for oil. They play smart, which can be identified after all the damages done.

Every country tries something daily to become one step ahead of others in trading. For that, they are building strategies, alliances, creating structures. It's what we are reading in the daily newspapers. People may say it is healthy competition. We can't have healthy competition where the general public is affected.

War Mask

Wars have served the world continuously from the beginning until now. Wars happen for multiple reasons, but people only suffer from this. The main motive of war is desire. Someone's desire is someone's fear. Someone not getting that desired item means he/she makes war to occupy it. Countries have a desire for other countries' resources, leading them to initiate war. Weapon-powered countries frame false accusations against emerging countries and oppress them. People should be aware of why countries are fighting now because there was a need for war until 1700 AD. After that, the modern evolution of industrialisation happened. Countries sought independence from occupants. Occupants never liked to leave, but due to the certain compulsion of evolution, that became inevitable.

We are encountering wars against countries in most places. Some are on the edge. Most of it is against terrorism and invaders. Soldiers do not even know the cause of war or what happened that caused the war. They are always the order observers and executers. The primary task here is decision-making. The soldiers decide the results of the wars. Whatever it may be, the soldier has every right to decide whether he/she wants to go to war or not. They must know the reasons behind the war. Rulers always decide whether the war happens or not. Rulers have decided most of the wars that have happened to date. So, in N number of wars, soldiers were guided to do war for rulers' selfishness. The disgusting part of war is the soldiers' behaviour after the victory in battle. Humiliation, destruction of the opponent's civilisation, demolition of property happened because of them. It didn't only happen in the ancient days. Even now, we see soldiers misbehaving. The violence during the war is less than the violence after the war. Why hasn't this changed a bit? Because of the hatred planted within every soldier by rulers, here I would like to point out the mask that is the influence of fear, the odd one out. Most wars happened in ancient days because of competition among brothers, siblings, sisters. Why should soldiers die for the problems and competitions between relations? Vigorous nepotism went through royal blood in those days. Some countries are still affected by nepotism. There are bright chances for war due to nepotism even now. Before that, we must be aware of it and avoid it. Wars always make people hate opponents. Somebody unknown creates most war threats to make people hate their neighbouring country, because of that most people always curse each other. They feel good about being separated from them. This somebody can't be identified and they are doing it because they have benefits in it, due to that people are separated. Unity is the way to tear the mask. How to unite? We may stand against any wars universally. How to stand against any wars? There are many ways. We can choose our own way.

We can identify civil wars in all countries over the years in these times, all of them against their government's illegal activities. If a country needs to be destroyed, enemies won't attack directly from the outside; instead, they create problems inside and then cut off trade chains. So, the destruction will be fierce and quick.

War is dangerous among all masks because the power of destruction is vast. War always consists of four stages: orders, prewar preparation, war performance, and post-war activities. In each stage, a number of wicked and unkind things happen, but countries publish newsletters to people only about cooked-up stories that make them feel proud, strong, and challenged. It's called the mask of a makeover. How people feel is a vital essence of war.

A and B are allies. They do war against D than in the meantime, A secretly allies with C. 'C' leaks secrets of B to A. It causes damage to B and D. E makes a secret ally with B to damage A. Outsiders and insiders think that A and B are warring against D. Still, the reality is A, B, C, D, E are at war with each other but truth never reveals. Economically strong countries finance the war for both countries. They use situations favourable to them. They let the loser breathe for some time. They are making them a borrower for the rest of their life. Later these financiers occupy their resources. There will always be a third party who makes use of it when two are fighting. So, before involving in the fight, always think about the consequences and terribleness of its results—the mask of mediators.

Invaders initiate war on borders to occupy the neighbouring country and their land. Why can't we open the border to neighbours then ask them to come and go? People say, 'what if they start to stay in those border places?'. We may also stay on border places like them, right? Let them come in. We also go out. Governments can't let it happen because occupants make cooked-up stories to their people. They destroy neighbours without humanity—a mask of cruelty.

For example, a country thinks that it allows some innocent people into their land out of humanity, but those people stay in that land and buy more places in that land for a high price from that country's landowners. They later try to occupy the whole country and name themselves as a new country. It is such a shame for humanity. It's the mask of innocence. They suppress the native people's voice through war.

War makes people separate. War makes people suffer. War affects innocent lives.

Economic Mask

The economy is a combination of production, supply, demand, distribution, and consumer behaviour. When we have balance in the curve of economics, then we have balance in the country and the world; for the profits curve, corporate and government made 'n' no. of sacrifices in principles of economics. It results in poverty and deficiency in countries, which earned different names like 3rd world countries, 2nd world countries, 1st world countries based on the crimes of corporate world wealth exploitation. The incredible thing is that people of 1st world countries discriminate 3rd and 2nd world countries, but there are poor people in all countries. 1st world countries also hold the poor people; those people feel the pain same as 2nd and 3rd-world countries. 1st world country people feel that they are the best around the world. When the truth opens up that time, specific statistics will make 1st world people understand the heat they are all in. When a corporation completes its exploitation in 3rd and 2nd world countries; it will turn towards 1st world country people. What is an economic collapse? As of now, we have several countries as an example of that, like Greece, Venezuela, Sri Lanka. The fall expresses the failure of economic expertise. Most of the time, the fall is purposely planned and implemented by rich countries to occupy vulnerable countries. When we follow monetary policy, we must understand its structures and controls. If we take a step away from structures and controls, we have to pay for its side effects; sometimes, it costs whole countries' lives. In 2008, Zimbabwe got hit by hyperinflation; its currency notes cost less than the value printed on it. These countries ignore economic experts' education, growth, importance. All foolishness is happening because of people without consciousness and knowledge. No countries are ready to express their true selves from the perspective of economic wisdom to their people. They take us till the end to express the defeat. For example, one day before, we may think our country is so strong, but the next day, we will realise that it's not true. The economy is very simple to collapse; no big math is required. The economy contains many loopholes; Powerful and intelligent people can quickly demolish countries with it and that's what countries are trying to do. People have a right to vote to select authorities. Authorities have a right to make decisions, but people don't have a right to accept or reject their decisions. It is called a mask of superiority.

Courts were there to bring justice. People can file a case against the authorities' decision about economic decisions taken by the government. Almost whenever we stop it, it comes closer via other rushes and pushes, the so-called mask of rationale. There were 'N' numbers of economic summits around us like World Economic Forum (WEF), G7, G20, APAC, G15, SAARC, BRICS but does any summit discuss global unity? Yes, they do discuss, but why in the first place only a few countries participate in summits that become the talk of the town worldwide? Have any tremendous decisions been taken via (WEF)? Maybe some that are based on write-offs, reconstruction supports but not much; these summits mostly discuss and get away; there was yet to be a compelling take in. We are following monetary policies. Does anyone speak about the single currency use all over the world? It's all about the import and export ratios of the country. If countries are willing to sacrifice their wealth for equality worldwide, then we can dream of a single currency worldwide, but no one is ready to bring up a speech about it at the summits. For every country, its wealth is vital to them. So, whether in any economy, monetary policies never bring world equality. Even if the currency becomes the same in all countries, people's incomes always vary. Equality is in the hands of people's support of changing the political philosophies.

Big companies' founders and CEOs know how to create wealth without tax. They pay taxes, but these are comparatively lower than those of the common man or woman. Taxes are one of the primary sources of income for the government to keep the economy healthy. Wealthy people have managed to handle their finances tax-free. They, in some ways, efficiently exploit countries with loopholes and corners of the laws. It is also a part of the economic setbacks for countries. A commoner doesn't have many options; they can't prevent governments from taking money from their pockets as tax. The savings rate and risks of inflation make all the matters complicated—a mask of economic differentiation.

A threat to the economy is illegal activities. Few are hiding goods. They are creating demand manually. It's making people suffer from high pricing; in the same way, overproduction leads to undervaluation based on this entrepreneur earning part of their illegal money. They do smuggle the goods to skip the taxes to the governments. Here comes a legal way to do illegal activities; the country offers entrepreneurs some concessions for the growth of the people in their country, but by using loopholes in it, they started skipping colossal amounts of taxes. They are enjoying a mammoth number of turnovers. These effects always go to the people's heads as tax, job cuts, underpaid. Governments allow these illegal activities to go freely due to the absence of strictness and close monitoring. If ten got benefits, 1000 got affected by it.

The 1st world countries never allowed their country's natural resources to get spoiled by any business. So, what do entrepreneurs do? They search for countries that allow doing that in their country. Anyhow resources will get spoiled. As a result, that country's people will get suffer. Entrepreneurs get a lot but they share a little that's even due to the country's compulsion. We must understand that they are looting that country's natural economic resources in the business's name.

Corporates are damaging the world, but not only them. All countries have an equal participation in it. Countries create the projects. It involves people working on those projects. It's circulating money through that project. Some projects do not succeed in earning back the money that was invested. Countries that are fully dependent on that project try until the last deep-hit stage instead of stopping after some limit. This is spoiling the funding that was invested by other countries. It's creating an economic recession.

What kind of mask are countries wearing in this segment? Countries know how much entrepreneurs are benefiting from them. They can increase the taxes to balance the Gini coefficient. It's the mask of ignorance.

The imbalance results in unemployed, underpaid, and undesired working-class people and abnormal work-life balance. These people are the economic stealers.

Food Mask

Family should care for its members even when few cannot succeed. A good family always cares for its members. Every country is like a family; If a family fails to care for its members, it fails in its duty. So far, countries have yet to pass on their duty. Why were countries created? For protection and care, when it's small in size like a tribe, it never fails in part of caring, but when it becomes big, it's unable to achieve it.

No masks are separate. They are all interlinked. One leads to another. One can't survive without another, like a parasite. Over 90 million people die yearly due to food insufficiency and food-related issues, but whose responsibility is it to save them? Who made them starve for food? Countries are dumping on each other for wealth. Whose responsibility is it to bring equality in the first place? It's the country's responsibility. Why is the country not assessing the right food requirements of their place? If it does, no starving will happen anywhere.

Natural resources like water are an essential item in food. Countries should inspect factories continuously, but they have failed in their duty. As a result, many people have been affected by factory waste. Most of the time, it's a failure of authority's responsibility. They do it for money. The mask of wealth plays a role in the fate of the country. Only some countries are checking seeds and fertilisers. Because of that, we have had land immunity failure and high-level chemical-related issues in the human body. Scientists work on agricultural research and development to create new innovations and inventions that save humanity. They initiated the green revolution, blue revolution, silver revolution, gold revolution, yellow revolution, and white revolution to resolve people's starvation. The first agricultural revolution was called the Neolithic revolution. In 10000 BC, humans started farming. Everyone works in the world to resolve the starvation of people by finding new solutions. People took the initiative to find a solution. When a country does not support revolutionary ideas due to some corporate wellness, it gets spoiled. Mask up to pull back the fast growth.

21st century is well-known for the COVID-19 pandemic. The leading cause of the pandemic is people's starvation. In previous centuries, all countries were starved at some point in time. It made millions of people lose their soul. When that happened in China, people started eating all kinds of flies and wild animals for survival. Everyone complains it's due to the population, but when speaking of that topic, who in the first place encourages it? Due to protection and production, health issues, lack of knowledge, all countries encouraged to have more kids. They let people have lots of children but failed to feed them—a mask of selfishness in the name of the country's welfare.

Governments should conduct food inspections daily. Failure in that leads to big manufacturers adding harmful chemicals to food items, making artificial sweeteners, extra-long durability, making the food a slow poison. All these illegalities are for money. Money should act only as a transaction tool; instead of that, it's started being an extra comfortable status item. A mask for money looting.

People who eat food once a day always live in hell, but death won't kill and take them that fast. What makes this situation exist? It's because of the political philosophies of countries. All political philosophies have a hierarchy. Benefits are distributed based on hierarchy. Money as a transaction tool is deciding the hierarchy. It's the only item common in all philosophies. Those who can't earn it more are cornered and ignored. Governments provide support to them, but it never equals people who earn more money. If countries treat them equally to those who earn more, people who earn more get demotivated and stop working hard. People should know and feel the difference. That's why governments cannot treat or provide for them equally.

Poor people in inefficient countries without money always starve because countries can't do anything; political leaders of countries can't do anything because corporations sponsor politics. Corporations want capitalism, but not all countries are cooperating with that. There were some exceptions as well, but in all countries, certain people starve to death for all the above reasons.

Now, the World Bank, the United Nations, its members are focusing on automation and robotics and slowing down manual intervention. They are encouraging technologies. There is nothing wrong with it. Their report on poverty and investing in opportunities establishes only their significant members' growth rather than global growth. How to fire the mask? Some people think that what if we stop using big corporate food products, which will automatically lead them to the fall? The truth is that we can't stop using it because 90% of food items that we are using currently are produced by corporates. We have to understand that something is fundamentally wrong in the name of keeping the balance in the world to set the fire on the mask. People need to gain an understanding of it in the first place. When everyone understands it's a ground reality, that is enough. The next step will automatically happen without pushing. All the politics are like a mask of favours to corporates to make the country survive.

Terror Mask

Gaming is the best entertainment. Children play video games. Sometimes, they don't know what reality is and what a game is. We are like those children fearing terrorism. All games have an antagonist and protagonist because without that, the game won't be that interesting. What if the antagonist is evil? Terrorism is that evil. How countries use terrorism? How it influences people to do and be something they don't even want. Countries make terrorists in two ways: with consciousness and without consciousness. A common fear of life occurs wherever we hear the word terrorism. We have to accept that we are responsible for their terribleness. We choose our country's leaders; it's not possible to be liked by everyone as a leader. Leaders are responsible for countries' decisions. They favour people close to them using leadership, which sometimes creates people as terrorists who are against that favour. So, we somehow become a reason for their behaviour. We should raise our voices against anything that is happening wrong. So, if we are not doing so, we're also helping countries be masked. WBE may be a chance to make our system flawless.

Terrorists are sometimes used by one country to threaten another country. It makes sure each country's people hate each other. Yes, unless both are friends by their trade agreements and conditions. Countries always create negative impressions on neighbouring countries' people by nature to avoid them binding up. Countries subconsciously use terrorism as a weapon to avoid binding up. Have you ever thought about how terrorists get weapons, missiles, bombs? First, they make it with supplies they stole and smuggled. Second, they will get it from an illegal market. The market exists because of the government's incapacity to provide equal opportunity. It is how people are suffered for their own mistakes. Here, Countries always wear a mask of protection but behave the opposite to it.

It exposes the evil world around us. What are all the masks of the country making a person a terrorist? We should feel happy and blessed that those masks have not played a role in our life as of now, but reading it and leaving it just like that will increase one count. Process it, feel the guilt, rectifying will make 'n' number of counts down. The reason for involving in terrorism has been mostly unemployment and refusal of rights. Suppose it's a minority in animals means humans protest to make it live. Still, when the case changes to human cultures and beliefs, people in power always want them to fit into a mould. Countries try to make them fit in the majority. When refusal arises, they will be labelled as a terrorist. History has proved it many times. Moulders always wear masks of good people and kind ones. The hardest part is we can't realise it's a mask.

Few countries make terrorists on their own. I don't know how to call them. Is it terrorists or assassins or secret agents? If they get caught, then they are terrorists. If they escape, they are assassins or secret agents. It's because no one can create terrorists. If they're created, it's not called terrorism. People's lives are collateral damage for them. Countries use them to steal other countries' secrets. They make use of them to blackmail. They get more significant gains from other countries. These countries act like saving people from terrorists then leave both in the middle of nothing and seize resources of their place without a trace. It is a pure mask of hypocrites. A few of those agents were killed by their own countries, but a few escaped and got revenge for the consequences they faced by hurting innocents and superiors of the country. Countries are captured by their agents with the help of other countries. They suffer without being able to tell outside.

There is one terror mask above all that society is wearing, but to remove it, we have to work too hard. It's the Mask of Blindness. We face mass murders at school buildings, malls, parks, and grounds. What hurts more than anything? Harsh words, behaviours, bullying. When these things start happening around a person more often; at that time, violence within the affected person begins to hurt those who made them. It hurts the society who saw but haven't raised their voice against them. It's not only hurts or kill them but it kills others who haven't related to the incident but happen to be in that place when that violence happened. It hurts everyone in society. People within countries also are making terrorists with or without their knowledge but they blindly cross that without acknowledging it. We have to support each other in a public place. When someone happens to be involved in a fighting or bullying, harsh situation, at that time we have to be the first to stop them. They should not necessarily be our relatives or friends. Even for a third person, we have to stand on the ground. All of us should stand against it to stop it. It will give society confidence and courage to raise voices against wrong things. We can escape the terror in the future.

We're the only ones who lock our inner selves with doors and locks. We can venture outside our imaginary limits if we want to, but we will always be in our cell until we do not want to. We might feel comfortable in our cell, but it won't bring us anything new.

Protection Mask

Secret services, patrols, intelligence, military, air forces, navy, missiles protect the country. These government bodies always act on commands of superiors in governments. What countries possibly do for our protection? They build walls, draw a borderline, get the forces to guard us. What should get protected in the first place? A possession. A soul, is it? What is important there to protect in all the countries? It's memories; all our memories are priceless. The rest of the items that get protected will be gone eventually. We don't even have the capacity to save a single person's memories with the help of servers and databases. It's that much huge in volume.

What countries do in the name of protection? At the border and inside the border, secret agents or spies of other countries, loyal to their own countries, try to spoil other countries. Some protectors have a mindset of corruption. It leads to the enormous black hole of power abuse. Since, a number of people's lives are affected. While power gets abused in other masked fields, people suffer from money, but life threat is there for everyone in the field of protection and terrorism.

Corrupted governments and ruling parties never allow people to protest against them. They always use their forces to control people's rights and suppress the crowd's emotions. Sometimes, countries kill the protestors to threaten the people, indirectly controlling their behaviour. This proves that government ruling parties can do anything they want to keep the calm. It's terrible behaviour, but countries present themselves as protectors of civilisation. A mask of a good protector.

Government authorities should not control patrols because while controlling like that, Ministers and higher ruling authorities misuse patrols. They are making the surroundings uneasy; patrols sometimes commit illegalities in favour of political party members. It's called the mask of independence. Patrol members know those hard feelings.

Why do border forces not have a proper work-life balance? All humans are born to spend time with their loved ones, but why aren't border forces getting that in some countries? Is it that hard to protect borders? Yes, it's hard because countries must be in a mutual relationship to remove guards from the borders, but they are not. So, countries want soldiers to be stubborn. Countries are competing about who gets in first, who gets a lot of land. They like to be separated by borders, as I said earlier, a mask of separation.

In WBE, no border forces are going to exist all over the world.

All land-capturing stuff is happening in the name of protection. In ancient times, Britain captured all land in the business's name. Well-equipped military-based countries offer training camps to developing or underdeveloped countries. They send their forces in the name of training. After that, it makes the forces stay there to protect as well for some time. It makes the silent move. It captures the excellent hide place or creates the hidden place. They move back to their own country for a name sack then fall back to attack the country for the purpose of capture. Force them to be under big countries. Countries do the cruellest betrayal to their people to avoid a clash with neighbours; sometimes, the country sacrifices its people, but they are not even soldiers. They consider it as collateral damage. They are innocent civilians who live on the border, a mask of protection.

What should be protected in the first place? Memories are essential to protect. In WBE, no individuals will have possessions. No life threats to the soul. So, the only item that is precious is our memories; our memories will be transferred to our generations. They have our memories as a base to build further improvements. As I said, we don't have that much space to store everyone's memories, but all our milestones will be captured. We make them a lesson for the future. So, I am sure all our visions will come true even if we are not able to achieve them; our generations will make them live.

Health Mask

We have an infinite number of viruses, but how many harm us? Have you ever thought about how many human-made diseases kill humans and other species? Everyone knows that if the 3rd world war comes, bio viruses will play a crucial role. Countries are working on creating viruses and antidotes for future war manoeuvres. We don't need to worry about the 3rd World War anymore. It's already started. It's ended silently in the name of the Covid pandemic masks of prevention.

Humans made viruses like HIV and a few other viruses; there are no cures unless the body cures itself automatically; a slow and painful death is the only way. We feel bad for them, but the cure is not in our hands. As Einstein said, "no rats build a rat trap for them," but we are bombing people. All scientists must say no to creating deadly things. It harms our humanity. If someone blackmails to do something harmful against humanity to rule the world, it's better to stand against it, if not possibly die—mask of innovation.

For 8 billion people, how many doctors are there in the world? Even in developed countries, for every 1000 people, we have one doctor, but in other countries, we have three doctors for every 10,000 people. It's a weird ratio. In disasters, we require a large number of doctors, but since we have only a few doctors, we can't save more crowds. Why is there such a terrible ratio of doctors in the world? Because the field of education has become highly knowledgeable and money-oriented. The system is sorting people based on money instead of sorting them based on their knowledge. Since there is a mammoth drop in the ratio. People with interest and knowledge sometimes can't enter the field due to a tiny margin of marks or rank shortages. They can't afford to be doctors. The medical field only has a small number of seats available; not everyone who is qualified can get in. Countries can open a large number of seats, but considering the tight supply and demand, and the money involved in the field, they don't increase seats for education. They know that if there is more supply, demand will be reduced, and they can't make money. It makes a living itself a critical one. Few jobs are always treated as larger than life; medicine is one among them. If something goes wrong, it's difficult to find what went wrong in the medical field within that deadline; even doctors make mistakes, and few doctors don't reveal them. Every year, 138 million people are harmed due to doctors' mistakes. What makes the count increase every year? Why is it not going down? It may be because of hard shifts and long hours of practice, impatience. What actions have been effectively taken by countries for all these issues? The Mask of Education.

Given the commercialisation of education, the treatments also cost a lot. So, medicine became a top-selling business. Insurance also plays its part. Since then, it has become hard for middle-income people. They spend a day's income on normal fever and checkup. There was a time when hospitals were not accepting critical cases due to showcasing the high mortality rate for business purposes. It's still happening in some places. Most essential medicines are sold for high rates to make a lot of profits from patients. The manufacturing cost will not be coming under a penny but will get sold for great rates; manufacturers formed communities among them. Even if one likes to sell for a low rate, others will not allow them to do so. It's a brutal mask of business.

Some private firms produce low-quality products to make profits. Some hospitals recommend low-quality, whole hazardous medicine to people. It makes people struggle for their life. Big and economically self-satisfied countries test their products on developing countries' people. It is killing people without their knowledge. It's a wild mask of testing. Why aren't they testing on their people? Due to legal problems and in their country, volunteers should be monetised for this testing legally but no humanity and patriotism for sure.

Organ transplantation is a big issue in the world of medicine. All over the world, there is a high volume of wealthy people involved, driven by the power of money. The illegal organ market revolves around $600 million to $1.2 billion a year. Wealthy individuals often bypass the proper channels, seeking shortcuts to expedite the process. What can we expect from doctors who spend all their money to obtain a degree? Some are resorting to these illegal practices to quickly gain money for their needs and luxuries. It's a facade of vigilance.

In the industry of medicine, health insurance is the most extensive money-making business for countries. The global health insurance market was valued at $1.98 trillion in 2020. It is projected to reach $4.15 trillion by 2028, growing at a CAGR of 9.7% from 2021 to 2028. Common people are bankrupted many times when they go for reimbursements of their medical expenses because the insurance company delays or denies repayment. Hospital charges are very high, but insurance covers very little, which people end up paying from their own pocket. No money, then no honey concept, but they advertise everywhere and influence everyone that insurance is the lifesaver. Mask of a saviour.

We have a close-ended behaviour all over the field of medicine. In WBE, we educate people in medicine based on interest, qualification, and talent. We have to video record all kinds of activities on operations like most of the hospitals are following now. Six eyes cross-check must be done on all the prescribed medicines and medical reports. For every 100 people, there will be one doctor. So, it will be easy to get treatment in any situation. Medical education will start from the 4th grade itself. Everyone should be educated in adequate medicine and first aid.

Community Mask

Religion is the primary practice for connecting with people. In all countries, at least one religion plays a dominant role. Most rules are implied based on that religion. All religions have communities like Christianity - Catholicism, Protestants, etc. In Islam, we have Sunni, Shia, and so on. These communities are split due to ideology. There are communities in the world split based on work and other stuff. All the communities follow a unique set of rules for themselves. We will see what countries are doing with those rules' loopholes.

For an election, they are influencing people in the way of community, using them to win elections. So, for them, it always needs to be separated. Even though there are no significant problems, they used to showcase minor issues as big ones. They make different communities hate each other. So, they can pedal easily in political games without a clash. It's called a mask of influence.

All religions say that people should be united. Trust each other with love, humanity. Political parties are creating a clash for political purposes like Sunni Vs. Shia, Muslim Vs. Hindu. All problems always start from a dirty political perspective of who is big, great, powerful. So, they start to clash with each other. In the end, leaders of political groups will come and enjoy the confusion and benefit from interruptions. We have to realise why they are doing this. They want to occupy the land. They want to rule in the name of God and ideology. For that, they will do anything. It's a mask of a religious rebel.

The black community in America is still suffering from racism. If a country truly desired not to have slaves, there would have been no enslaved people from the 1800s. What was essential for them at that time? It's money. It will always be money. They used the black community, made them work worse than animals, slaughtered them. Why have governments not taken any action? Because rulers had hundreds of enslaved people at their service, how can they ask for support? The whole society grew on that mentality. There may be few exceptions. It's a damn mask of utilisation.

How did a dictator like Hitler change the world? As everyone knows, enigma is the code that helped him to transfer information secretly every time. The first-ever basic computers built by scientist Mr. Turing to break the code. This changed the war, freed the Jews, boosted innovations and evolutions of technologies. How many Jews were killed in that war and before the war? What a cruel mentality for a person!

It's a great example of what happens if power gets into the wrong hands. What consequences will happen for a community. It's called the mask of the ruler's mentality. No one knows what is inside a person's mind. So, while choosing someone to rule, we must also be aware of precautions. Mainly what happened to Mr. Turing who was the ultimate reason for winning the war. He was gay. Britain had laws against LGBTQ+ communities. It forced him onto conversion medicine. He suffered because of his identity even after being the reason for the world's tremendous change. The mask of support.

The labour community gets affected in all countries. There is no assurance for work-life balance for daily wagers, except in communist countries. Factory workers cannot get specific insurance policies due to assured risk factors. Why should one get employed without insurance or security when there are assured risks? What are employers doing about that, why are countries not looking at it? It's not an astronaut job patrol job to risk a life voluntarily. Even for that as well they will be providing insurance since it's a government-oriented job, but most factory labourers are not getting it. It is what governments should look into, but they never do. It's impossible to do particular massive work in any country without a daily wager. The volume of workers is large. If the government started providing insurance for this, money would get wasted. It's what they think. So, it's a mask of equality.

Few communities have feared showing their true selves due to countries' ancient, outdated laws. The LGBTQ+ community is the best example of that. There is nothing wrong with that community. A few countries say it will spoil our culture. No evolution happens if we cling to culture. It's their life; forcing them to do something they don't want to is a kind of crime. Why are few countries doing this? Because they don't want to change the pattern of society. Many communities suffer from the truth like this. They don't want to show themselves to the real world.

All countries have people who don't like LGBTQ+ even after it's legally recognised in some of the countries. These people humiliate LGBTQ+ in public. They speak nonsense about LGBTQ+. It's the mask of culture.

Political Mask

It's extraordinary that every country follows the same tactics in political masks. It's a universal pattern of ruling people against their will. Two different parties with contrasting tenets ally and rule people.

Two conflicting tenets make people think in two different ways; that time, people will go on to the 1st tenet or 2nd tenet. Few people will get attracted to both. Few people who selected the 1st don't want the 2nd and vice versa. If these two tenets joined means, those first two types of people would not choose this party. Most of the time, people do not vote because of the above reason. How can parties with conflicting tenets rule without sacrifices? So, they sacrifice their tenet. Since that, politicians need to sacrifice tenets in taking decisions for the government. So even for the small, good decision, no two big parties with different tenets join together, but the small parties with different tenets will join with these two big political parties based on money and power at the time, who holds most. Parties are identified as small and big based on their followers. It's a mask of alliances.

Politicians are using their powers to approve unwanted projects for commission or donation to parties and their pockets. Governments and political parties are getting donations from entrepreneurs in favour of those parties providing some favours which will harm the small business or medium, developing people. It's the Mask of favours.

There were leaders in every place working on their ground to improve society. If national leaders worked hard for society with a pure service mentality, this book is not required to change the model. When changes started happening in society from remarkable leaders that time to stop it or change track of it, good, obedient leaders got assassinated by unknown people for the political gains of opposite parties or business people. Sometimes to take over a throne also political murders happened, for example – Martin Luther King Jr, Malcolm X, JFK, Lincoln, Subhash Chandra Bose, Francis Ferdinand, Gandhi. These are all only a few famous worldwide, but it's happening in all countries from small to significant levels. It is to stop changes in society. The changes that they initiated may be good or bad but we can't know because it's not implemented. We never know it may have gone bad as well but by killing them it got stopped. So, it's always a mystery to common people. It is called the mask of development.

The election is the best drama in the world. They will make 'n' number of promises while asking for votes. While watching the drama, we feel fantastic and energised by its content, but after the drama is over, we won't have anything to take away. Our money and time are only gone. Most countries still need to fulfil half of their promises. All kinds of fraudulent activities would happen at that time, like bribing votes, illegal voting, exchanging vote boxes, and hacking into vote machines. It's the Mask of Promises.

In the digital world, almost everything is digitalised. Social media is the primary medium of politics, so the most effective campaigning happening on social media platforms. Corporate companies started to brainwash people for elections psychologically like Cambridge Analytica. Fake news becomes a threat to the world. All politicians have started consulting corporates for elections. Technologies are improving; currently, tech wizards are playing in politics instead of politicians. They cover up all the foolishness of politicians. They are showcased as true leaders in front of people. Truth and tenets are just the last part of the election. The power of attracting people via social media plays a vital part. How do people with criminal backgrounds participate in the election? Most of the records are modified by hackers and insiders on the internet. It is a mask of technology.

Politicians always allure power more than anything. When power comes, all situations will automatically fall into place. They use all information whenever and wherever it's needed; there are both good and bad sides. They are misusing information and hiding the truth from people. Politicians help criminals to wander around independently against the law for their personal benefits. It's a mask of information.

Mistakes can be corrected next time, but when it comes to crime, which has happened with the knowledge of others, there won't be a correction anywhere; the only solution here is punishment. When superiors commit crimes and then escape from the law with their power, they become the worst example for subordinates. Subordinates start following their path. Other departments will also start doing the same since another department is doing that crime. So, the whole system will get corrupted by ignorance of crime, which will lead to mass disobedience of the crowd, so the harmony of the country will get destroyed by their own hands. Early identification will save the country from collapse. It's a slow process that takes at least three to four decades to corrupt the whole system. Currently, some countries have already fallen for politicians' crimes. They are trying to regrow again. It's a mask of power.

The most important thing is making decisions in politics. All decisions must be well reviewed by multiple sets of people, experts, professionals of various departments because even a single wrong political decision can create a war and destructive situation. So, when it comes to the responsibility of decision-making, every leader must be careful. In history, we saw how a single decision made a soldier into the dictator Hitler, from a soldier to the terrorist Bin Laden. It's the mask of decisions.

Disclosure Mask

What needs to be shared with the people of the country? All things that governments do need to be shared with people. There should not be any secrets because when the country is doing good things and making good alliances, why should they keep that a secret? The secrets are kept to hide something for future purposes. This truth harms others, so all countries have their secrets to keep. It's called the mask of secrets.

Countries know when and what to open up to the public. Without revealing their true identity, we never know how many undercover people died for their country. From A-to-Z sectors of government, there must be something to hide; sometimes revealing it might have a chance of showing their weakness as well. It might lead another big country to occupy or take advantage.

In the WBE, there will not be any secrets between countries, since everyone is equal and there is no motive for power and money.

Media Mask

Countries can effortlessly manipulate public focus through entertainment, steering attention away from critical issues. How are they doing it? Take all entertainments which get the most media attention, like drama, sports, fashion, and concerts. Countries are not diverting protestors' attention because that's impossible.

They are turning down the viewers' attention by changing the media topics. All people in the country are joined in only one place: the media. Media is an intermediary between people from different places. The issue becomes more prominent when the viewers increase. When attention reaches a larger audience, governments have no option other than to make it up to the people's side unless the consequences would be terrible. So, to stop that, governments always turn the media's attention to different topics. When topics change, viewers avoid getting stuck with the same issue. They forget and move on to their regular routine. It's because they have their preferences. It's essential for them. It's the Mask of Attentions.

Most Media are owned by political parties or their proxies in most countries. It makes people view the news that they allow. So, it makes people not even know the severity of problems and rest happily in their place. Media is under the direct control of the government in a few countries. There is no media independence in many countries because most of them are owned by corporates. These corporates are donors for political parties, so when anything comes in the media against the government ruling parties or them, the telecast licence will be revoked. A few private media outlets that post the truth are threatened and bribed by the government ruling parties to cover up. It's a Boogey mask of media independence.

The brave and bold reporters are still continuously writing the truth on other platforms like social media and blogs. Most terrific truths come out to the public just like that in the millennial, but the consequences are tragic for some people who show it to the limelight. They are getting life threats. A few reporters were murdered to make them shut. The risk for life has been there in the media. They do not even have job security because few people are forced to field out. Why the continuous torture for these people? Media has the power to bring down the government. It's a mask of Reputation.

During election time, most political parties are partnering with media companies. They promote their tenets and influence people with mesmerising fake news. The media uses worthless news to cover politicians daily. They are making those faces familiar to people. It's a mesmerising mask.

Countries use entertainment figures to divert people from significant issues. The media is one reason people learn from history to science, but in some countries, history is wrongly taught to them for their gain and control. In a few countries, people have grown up away from the truth. Due to partialities, not all countries' people gain access to all information and technological knowledge. We have a knowledge gap. Most underdeveloped countries are unable to cope with more powerful nations. It is in all fields and media as well. It makes one segment of people feel left behind. They desire to come out from these knowledge gaps, but funds are not readily available. Media and the internet are influencers, but still, in some places, electricity itself is not available, how can people come out to learn and gain expertise? So, leaving people in ignorance is the biggest crime that is happening in some countries.

Knowledge should never be partial from one place to another place. Media is the primary medium for that thing. It's a mask of knowledge.

These are the masks governments are wearing. They are making everyone a fool to date. It's possible to remove the masks of countries, but only when all the people try to see beyond selfishness. Once we see reality, it's easier to march towards goals faster and quicker.

Money is the primary and secondary reason for all the masks. It directly and indirectly fuels all the differences and inequalities we face. I want to showcase how money has become a failed element in the world.

Four

Money – A Failed Element

When did we start using money as a transaction tool? It's been so long; it's approximately 4000 years old. No one thought that it would last this long. What is defined as money? Money is a tool that helps humans to get anything without a fight. We can't evolve further without a proper tool. We all go back to fight again if we don't find a new one. We had cattle transactions before 9000 years. Various precious metals, including gold and silver, were accepted as a payment method in the name of money several centuries ago. Farmers exchanged gold and other metals as a primitive method of payment. So, the transaction tool evolves from time to time as technology evolves. It's time to say goodbye to money. It's never been rational at any time. Why is it a failed element? Long ago, people looked for a transaction tool that was handy and easily movable, less weight. Since then, they made coins to transport and safeguard easily. It has worked so well, but this transaction tool slowly becomes destructive.

A transaction tool is essential for society. Money - without it, a human can't survive in society. There are ways to survive outside society. Transaction tools must be common, easily accessible, transportable, and equal for everyone. From the beginning, we haven't understood the principles of money. This is why we all suffer from some kind of money-related trouble at some stage in our lifespan. A few people's lives come to an end due to this.

When did transactions become a part of human life? While we were roaming around places like animals and cave people, we used to share food with our group. Food was the first income for humans, the only income in those ancient days. Humans never looked for a place to stay during those periods, so there was no need for anything other than food and water. As they started to evolve, everything changed, such as staying in a place, cultivating food grains, petting animals, and bartering food. This structure evolved through kingdoms and landlords.

What aspects make money awful? the banking system is ruling the world, money is ruling the world, or the rich are ruling the world. Banking operates based on a fractional reserve system. So, what is happening here means our money's worth becomes less and less and less and less every time they lend out based on our money.

New digital money is created by banks when people take out loans. Yes, banks play a crucial role in creating money in the modern financial system through a process known as "fractional reserve banking." Here's a simplified explanation of how it works:

Deposits: When you deposit money into a bank, let's say £1000, the bank is required to keep only a fraction of that amount in reserve, typically as mandated by government regulations. The rest can be loaned out or used for other investments.

Lending: The bank lends out a portion of your deposit to borrowers who need loans, such as individuals, businesses, or governments. Let's say they lend $900 to a borrower.

New Deposits: The borrower takes the $900 loan and deposits it into his/her own bank account. This creates a new deposit in the banking system.

Repeat: The process can continue as the new $900 deposit is also subject to fractional reserve requirements. A portion of it is kept as a reserve, and the rest can be lent out again.

This process can repeat multiple times, effectively creating new money in the economy. It's important to note that the total amount of money in circulation can be much larger than the initial deposit. The money supply expansion is constrained by reserve requirements and regulations set by central banks.

Central banks, like the Federal Reserve in the United States, also play a role in money creation by influencing the reserve requirements and conducting open market operations that can inject or withdraw money from the banking system.

So, in summary, banks do create money through the lending process, but this money creation is subject to regulatory oversight and is influenced by central bank policies.

How do banks account for that new money in their balance sheet?

When banks create new money through the process of fractional reserve banking, they need to account for it on their balance sheets. Here's a simplified overview of how this accounting typically works:

Initial Deposit: Let's start with an initial deposit of $1,000 by a customer.

Assets: The bank records the $1,000 deposit as an asset. This is because they now have $1,000 that they owe to the customer.

Liabilities: At the same time, the bank also creates a liability. They owe the customer $1,000, and this is recorded as a liability because the bank is obligated to repay this amount when the customer requests it.

Lending: When the bank lends out a portion of the deposit, say $900, it doesn't actually reduce the customer's account balance. Instead, it creates a new liability.

Assets: The bank records the $900 loan as an asset because it expects to earn interest on it.

Liabilities: The $900 lent to the borrower is recorded as a new liability. This is because the bank still owes the customer $1,000 and has now created a new liability for $900.

New Deposits: When the borrower takes the $900 loan and deposits it into their own account at another bank, a new deposit is created in that bank.

Assets: The bank records the $900 deposit from the borrower as an asset because they now have $900 which they owed to the borrower.

Liabilities: the same liability entry that we saw above will come here too. For $900 this process repeats itself until it reaches '0'.

The key point here is that the bank's liabilities increased with each step of the process while its assets also increased. The net effect on the bank's balance sheet is an increase in both assets and liabilities.

It's important to note that banks are required to maintain certain levels of reserves based on regulatory requirements. The reserves act as a buffer to ensure that the bank can meet withdrawal demands from depositors. These reserves are what are accounted for as assets on the bank's balance sheet.

The specifics of how banks record these transactions on their balance sheets can vary depending on accounting standards and regulations in different jurisdictions, but the general principles outlined here apply to most banks engaging in fractional reserve banking.

When a loan holder does not pay back the loan, then that bank cannot reduce their reserves. So, the reserves of the bank will increase. Central banks will be used to provide repo interest. When reserves pile up because of the above similar scenario, due to loan holders not paying principal and interest to the bank, at that time repo interest will go down automatically because the central bank can't provide more interest due to this huge volume of reserves.

These reserves can lead to a recession. If it's the fault of the country's economy and monetary policy, then this burden falls on the public as taxes and pay cuts increase the price of goods and services. If it's the fault of a bank, then that bank will end up bankrupt. This kind of reserve always needs to be within the central bank's guided limit; that's an indication of good banking and a viable economy.

Governments are printing money that they don't have in their hands in the name of treasury bills and bonds. Governments transfer that money through banks to various industries. This process of mediating makes banks get richer and richer and richer with the help of the Fractional Reserve System's multiplier effect. Governments print money with the guidance of the central bank and monetary requirements.

Banks lend out 80% or more money that they have as a deposit using the fractional reserve system. Modern monetary policy killed the sound money already. So, in the name of the multiplier effect and fractional reserve method, they're creating credit money without any resources to back it. While gold standards were in place, they created more money than the value of the gold. Either they had to increase the value of gold or increase the gold reserve to avoid complications; They announced fiat currency to avoid the complications. They stopped following gold standards, which is why money became fiat everywhere. So now they don't need to back it with anything. It is how money devalued itself over a while and became fiat. The new money is a debt. So based on debt, money is created now. If corporates, governments, people decide to stop dealing with debt, if all debt is repaid means, then there is no more money created as per current policies, but they can rotate money that is available in hand, which will lead to an increase in the value of 100 dollars. It's not healthy for the monetary system because as per the mentality of people, it should grow. We can't increase the value of 100 dollars more than we can imagine. For a joke, can we imagine buying a house for 1 dollar? We roll on the floor and laugh. If no one is ready to take debt, there is no way for growth in the monetary system. It leads institutions to rotate money within what they have. It is just one of the outcomes, there is no way that everyone decided to close debt simultaneously.

Banks are operating based on faith. Governments can create money they don't have in hand. Banks can lend it to people on a requirement basis. People who need to pledge their tangible assets worthy of that money while getting a loan, if they fail to pay, banks will undertake that asset. Debts between countries due to war and countries' inefficiency renegotiated million times. Debts between corporates renegotiated when they have hard times but debt renegotiation is unthinkable or unimaginable when it comes to poor or middle-class people. Why is renegotiation not possible or very rare for these people? The volume of people in these segments is huge. If anyone is approved or renegotiated then a whole bunch of people will take that as an example and request renegotiation or write-off. The banking sector will collapse due to this. The bank is creating money for our loan through the multiplier effect. It's not giving money from its hand but it's providing it from its customers' pocket or account from that 1/9 of the portion. If that money becomes worthless means we can't ask banks why? But if we fail to pay the money back, banks will undertake the assets we pledge. The truth is obvious banks will not trust us but we need to trust banks, but still, educators, socialists, experts didn't like to find other ways to resolve this issue. So, the issue is unsolved. These people used to ignore it. They practiced to suffer in the unrealistic and irrational world.

The solution for this is within the political philosophy. People have to understand the monetary system that is operating them. How are they struggling to operate with us? How are we struggling to follow them? The struggle is rising from both sides. Why is there a struggle on the operator's side? When years pass in the world, demands rise for everything, but operators do not know how to balance everything and lead the world equally. The number of people in the economically lower class with excellent education is consistently increasing. They started raising knowledgeable questions about the system's inefficiency over decades. They are creating attention on social media. So, currently, operators have a limited amount of luxury they had several decades before because of the open-source internet and networking of common people. We need to know how it all started.

How was it all started? The biggest scam in the world is still happening all around the world. Think of it like a fictional story, how it all may have started. People started to store their wealth with someone trustworthy to safeguard it while they were out of town. Those trustworthy people wanted to gain something out of it in their absence. They monitored what was happening outside and realised that people used the receipts of wealth deposited with trustworthy individuals to buy goods. Sellers also accepted them. So, the trustworthy people started lending receipts to those who needed money for interest, then gained profit without any investment in others' wealth. Later, they shared that gain with the people who stored wealth with them, so the interest rate for loans went high due to profit sharing and maintenance. The credit demand increased as Europeans spread this method worldwide. Here come evil thoughts and the idea of trustworthy people; by that time, they had become institutionalised. Now, they ran out of money to lend to people due to the minimum storage of wealth. So, the institution started creating receipts for wealth that they didn't have in hand. They issued them to the world because they analysed that all depositors were never going to come together and ask for the whole sum of money, so they didn't want to pay out all that was deposited in a single payment. Only the institution knows how much holdings they have in hand.

The dollar was pegged to gold once upon a time. What happened after the 2nd World War? Most of the world's currencies were pegged to the dollar. It happened because the Americans were the official financiers of the 1st and 2nd World War. They financed the side that won the war. So, the rest of the countries in the union accepted the dollar as the world's reserve currency. This occurred because no other countries had that huge amount of gold. Other countries owed America for the war expenses.

The United States should have been in the position to supervise these gold and currency transactions between countries, but they failed at a point when the Vietnam War and oil shocks happened. These incidents made the United States lose its credibility.

The system is always ready to collapse at any time. It's not rational in any circumstances. Structures like this are tough to save. Running a collapsed system to be on track is abnormal. It's consistently collapsing, but we still follow the same monetary system. The collapsed system went out of hand already. Regulators can't say yes to stopping it now or zeroing out everyone's money. So, regulators made a scam out of this scam then made that scam legal with the name of modernising the fractional reserve system. It was the solution provided by John Maynard Keynes.

Let's dive in a little deep. During the 1920s, the USA, England, and France were heavily affected. The exchange between them became complicated. England took a step forward and came out of the gold standard, as advised by John Maynard Keynes. After that, all three countries came to an understanding. They created a tripartite monetary agreement to avoid a currency war. Then during the recession period 1929-33, John Maynard Keynes wrote a book regarding the multiplier effect. Banking systems are structured on and operating based on the multiplier effect successfully. After the book's completion, he sent it to both the USA and England banking. Government officials implemented it after making considerable amendments to it.

The IMF and World Bank were created in the year 1944, July. The Bretton Woods meeting aimed to bring balance to monetary systems, which have 190+ member countries all around the world. When it started, only 44 countries were there. The system is funded by member countries. During a recession period or a pandemic, countries borrow from the IMF to avoid the economy's collapse.

All collapsed structures were affected after the United States came out of the gold standard in 1974 entirely by declaring they would never convert the dollars to gold anymore. Regulators might have stopped it using their power if they carefully considered its effects, but they let it happen. That's why we are all suffering with this transaction tool.

Currently, all banks are interlinked and used to operate together with cooperation and understanding. Their first motive is to create debts then circulate money through them. We are all living based on that scam currently.

Banks mostly convince wealthy people and private institutions, companies to push to take loans. Unless they take loans, banks can't circulate money. Why not use taxes that they received from the public and corporates to circulate money? How does the public receive money? People get a salary from their employers. When employers run out of profit to run the business what they do they can either lay off or take a loan. If they lay off, they can't manage to get more work from their clients if the situation changes. So, they need to keep the employees with or without salary, but the employers can only hold the employees without salary for a short time because they will move to another employer. It is one of the reasons they are taking loans. Why are countries continuously building infrastructure and real estate? Because they are creating wealth through the government's treasury. Countries all are circulating their money based on this.

WHY IS THIS MONETARY SYSTEM A FAILURE?

All developments will come after lots of testing and failures. No new things get successful in the 1st attempt itself, but a few things are there as exceptions. So, only some attempts will make a systemic return. Failures are significant reasons for failed repayments. So, from here, we can understand only one thing: Failures are never accepted in the system, society of banks. Banks only aim for return, never consider efforts as a material thing, they dislike failures. All collective failures make the system collapse again and again. It will continue to happen until the system exists.

What kind of structure operates in the world? The structure of debt creation operates in the world. Are there any exceptions for any countries in the structure? No.

In society, all basic needs were deferred based on the class of the people. The most prestigious class, that's what they call themselves. Rich, like 'riche rich' rich. All their basic needs are just some ten cars minimum, a few billion in the account, a handful of servants, 20 to 30 bungalows. The next class is the upper class; all their basic needs are three cars minimum, a few million in the account, 3 to 7 bungalows. After that, the upper-middle-class minimum of one car, a few 100K in accounts, two bungalows maximum; followed by the middle class, a maximum of one car, a few 10K in the account, 2 to 3 flats maximum, then the lower-middle class, two bikes maximum, one flat maximum. Here comes the poor, one bike maximum, without these basic needs they can't survive in their class. They have to step down from their position. What is defining classes here? 'Money'. Most inequalities come from earnings of income. Transaction tools cause problems.

If we say all troubles are because of money. Others will say, try to adjust and tolerate structure; you don't know how to play. It's because of your mistakes, lack of concentration. If we make a mistake in corporate, they will put their hands on our salary. If we're making mistakes in society, that will cause us problems. We have to handle then clear our mess. There is no tolerance in any corporate, society, or science. No mistakes are acceptable in science; it never sacrifices its standards, but people must tolerate and accept the mistakes of society, corporate, and science. Why has no tolerance helped corporate, society, or science? Because they developed the structure through every mistake, but those who caused those mistakes are removed or ignored from time to time. Nothing is going to change when we tolerate it, but transaction tools will transfer its shape and control us.

Transaction tools should not act like independent bodies. The purpose of the transaction tool is to support transactions, but instead of that, it has started to act independently. When a transaction tool acts like an independent body, what will happen? Examples: Landlords started lending money to get interest; everything went well for some time because few made big strokes. After that, when it started to spread all over the world, lending became a big business. Landlords lent money to people if they pledged something worth of money. Few people started struggling to pay back due to failures; lack of self-control led them to a lack of money. This made business people get others' property in the name of pending bills. It is why people who lend become more and more potent with money. Later with various financial bodies like the share market, hedge funds, private equity, bond markets, Treasury, 80 percent of the money went into the hands of 20 percent of people. So, when people started using money to get money, money became an independent medium to stand alone and survive. Now it's both a tool and an independent body. We can't achieve equilibrium with money on our side.

I am curious to know what percentage of people are involved in finance worldwide. I am sure everyone knows how badly it operates around the world. They know all faults in the system, what needs to be improved to make it right, but most people have a mindset of "A bird in the hand is worth two in the bush." Why should we leave the position that we earned hard? Sacrifice is the first step to success. No pain, no gain. But there is no pain at all. We can expose items that made money as a monster. The first item is finance.

Finance is all in all in direct and indirect contact with money and money only. The transaction tool independently plays all its master strokes here. For a few, it's gambling; for a few, it's a strategic match like chess, where either money earns money in the end or money gets lost. Finance has helped society in many ways. It has productively contributed to the world's next level of scientific and educational growth, but it has always shrunk its availability space. Sometimes the most deserving items get ignored. Sometimes foolish items are motivated by finance. Finance is a tool that has served people in its ways possible, but we want something better than finance. Why am I claiming that? Today's money acts as an independent transaction tool. People make money from money because of it. They spend it for the standard of living. Few are only in such a field compared to the world population, but the rest of the people also get inspired by others who earn money from money. So, if everyone invests and trades on the financial market to earn money in that sense without doing any other jobs, who will actually do works that potentially trigger the other industries to move forward? The world is confident that 100% of people are not going to involve only in the market fully without doing any other job. The world is confident that most of us will take it as only side hustles. It might happen for now, but in the near future, everyone will move towards the market. This hazard may be controlled by regulators by forcing people to provide their money to asset managers to earn money and make us do the works that help other industries to move forward. So, it will affect people who led their life as individual investors or traders without doing any job. There is a chance that regulators conduct eligibility exams to become a trader and set the qualification criteria very high. So, the importance of the asset managers will increase. Therefore, qualifications to become asset managers will get tighter. If the world doesn't care about it, then the fall will not be like what people imagine. All people with and without knowledge try to earn money in the financial market without doing any other jobs. All other industries will get affected because of people shortage. If the market collapses, people will be pushed to step down from their respective classes where they are at that time. There won't be any classes after that sort of collapse. Everyone will act like monsters. When that collapse happens, everyone will get to know their own position.

We have 247 countries currently. 162 currencies, which means money type. Why do we have different types of currencies in most countries?

Every country has a different value for its currency based on its country's value. It's decided based on exports, imports, reserves, consumer behaviours, inflation rate, Purchasing Power Parity, GDP. In different countries, inflation is identified through different currencies.

If countries want to exchange between themselves, they use an exchange rate. What is an exchange rate? How is it determined? An exchange rate is a tool that makes a transaction between two countries possible. This calculation is made in types that are floating and fixed. Floating rates are calculated based on the interest rate, demand, supply of the prime good of the country, currency trading in foreign exchange, and foreign markets. Underdeveloped and developing, emerging economic countries in most places have more volatile currencies. This will affect their position in trading and transactions. Those countries like to peg their currency to strong currencies like the Euro and USD to avoid volatility, which will give them a fixed exchange rate in trade. It makes the trade easy and steady. There are multiple types of foreign exchange agreements based on countries' relationships with world nations.

How foreign reserves are acquired by one country from another country? When money is withdrawn internationally from one currency against another, that time reserve currency shifts from the national bank of one country to the reserve account of the foreign banks. These foreign banks have relationships with local banks that allow the local bank to hold foreign reserve currencies while not being a part of the central bank scheme at local central banks. (e.g.) When 1000 pounds are transferred into Rupees in India, a United Kingdom bank will agree an exchange rate with the rupee area bank, perhaps 104.10 Rupees to the pound. The UK banks will then transfer 1000 pounds of the central reserve currency to the UK partner bank of the rupee bank, while the rupee bank will transfer 104,100 Rupees of reserve currency to the rupee partner bank of the UK bank. These reserve currencies need to be spent in the country of origin or exchanged into other currencies. Most foreign banks do not have deposit-taking accounts outside of their national borders, and as such, the foreign reserves they hold do not come back to them in the form of deposits.

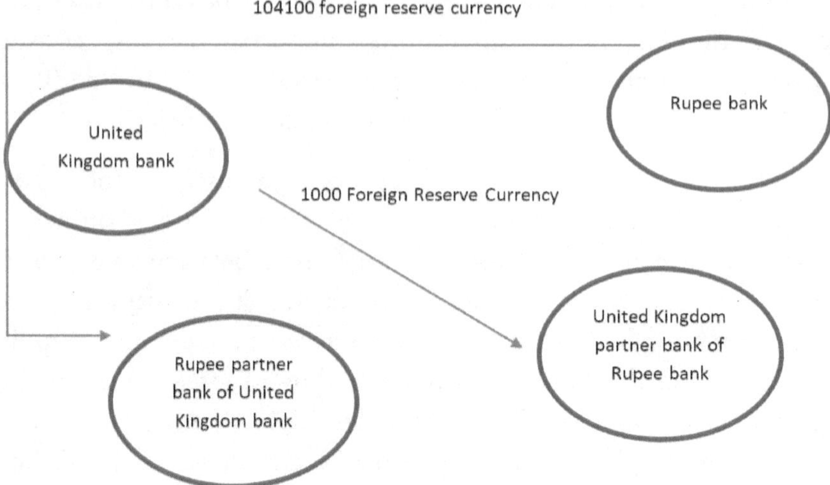

What happens when a trade imbalance occurs between countries?

There are two types of imbalances: surplus and deficit.

Surplus: Countries accumulate foreign reserve currencies

Deficit or negative: Countries spend their own reserves.

Trade Imbalance vs India		
USA	Negative (Spend)	Own USD reserve currency
	Surplus (Accumulate)	INR, the reserve currency

Trade Imbalance vs the United States		
India	Negative (Spend)	Own INR reserve currency
	Surplus (Accumulate)	USD reserve currency

Countries with a large deficit of trade imbalance rely on their creditors to spend the imbalance accrued in their own market. The IMF and World Bank are created to deal with these imbalances. These institutions prioritise the trade side. So, all countries settle their imbalances through an international clearing account.

Purchasing power parity (PPP) of a dollar is continuously decreasing. Fiat currency note value is declining prosperously. Governments can control up to certain limits. The limit was crossed long back. They can inject money into the economy indirectly. It makes businesses and industrialists happy but not ordinary working-class people. Why? Behaviours and attitudes of most people are almost similar when they get money. What do they do? They save it. The purpose of injecting money is to circulate, but if it goes to ordinary people, they won't like to circulate. Actually, there is no way that it goes straight to people because the government can't give money to people for free to spend; then it will suffer like how Zimbabwe suffered through hyperinflation. It will reach people in indirect ways like price drop, discount, offer, subsidy. The injection of money will always act as a painkiller but not a cure. An economy needs 70 to 80 percent of working-class people with medium and low income. The world always keeps rotating the wheel to balance it anyhow. We must realise that we are being used for others' wealth creation. We can't feel safe or happy in being middle because of the nature of the transactional tool. It's imbalance.

------------------------cc---

We have various large types of debts. One of them is public debt. All countries are obliged to lenders outside of themselves. Public debt is nothing but national debt. A few countries add state, municipality, province as well. Why does debt take place in the country? We all know we can't spend outside of what we earn.

You may ask, "The governments are printing money that it requires, so why should they need to borrow from others?" But governments are not creating wealth. They're just creating money to equal their debt. So, if their economy collapses, it means they have limited power to do quantitative easing of money. They can't do what they are wise to do without limit. If they do so, it means that is taken as a crime. It will make other countries crabby. So, all countries will come to a trade war with them. Governments know quantitative easing only helps countries up to some limit. There are a few countries exceptions to it. It's called developed countries, superpower nations like the USA.

So, to spend outside of our budget, we have to take loans called debts. Public debt is the accumulation of budget deficits. Public debts can be helpful for a country's structural development. Politicians think that it's better to raise debts instead of taxes. When countries exceed the maximum debt limit threshold, growth slows down.

Public debt is good when it's taken for a short lifespan. It makes situations easier to increase economic growth. When used correctly, it's an excellent way to increase people's standard of living. It encourages people to spend more instead of saving for the future after 60. This makes more circulation of money possible, which helps the market to grow faster.

Public debt is terrible when the government's ruling party tends to take on more debt to make their party and themselves famous in front of voters. It's terrible that politicians are only increasing debt. Investors check risk factors in a country. They compare countries' debt with economic output, debt to GDP ratio to analyse how countries pay off their debts.

When debt reaches its dangerous level, investors generally begin demanding a higher interest rate. They want more return for greater risk. When a country does not keep up to the mark, the rating of its government bond will get affected, and the value gets reduced. The country moves to default. As interest rates rise, it becomes more expensive for a country to refinance its existing debts, while most income goes to repay its debts and less towards government services.

All countries have public debt. Countries are connected as a web of debts. So, there is no way all countries fight each other because they're invested in each other. If anyone gets affected, it will also affect others. Then why do we see in the newspaper daily that war clashes are happening? It's because of gang formation. Countries form a gang. They support each other. Different gangs' members want to take over the opposition's position, which means there will be a fight. It is what is happening in the world. First, countries should not gang up because that only results in a fight.

These components will likely impact the country's structural development. It makes loan interest more expensive and difficult to pay. Where are all public debts wasted? Debts should be used for structural developments, but they are spent frivolously on elections; politicians act as if all the burden of this money is due to economic and global conditions.

IMF analysed and identified more than 50 countries as underdeveloped countries in the year 2018. Only some countries, like Mozambique, announced a default on some of their loans. They need to be on track with the repayment schedule that they agreed to. A few countries, like Afghanistan, were under the protection of the United States military but are now in the hands of the Taliban and local protestors because the United States does not find it noteworthy anymore. Day-to-day operations and circulation of money get difficult in these countries.

When countries default on their payments, it makes their daily activities challenging to operate—the operating cost of countries is affected. No countries like to invest in the defaulted countries due to their inefficiency. It makes it hard to take new loans.

What reasons are there behind this sort of default? There are several reasons, like the need for more expertise in all fields. Natural calamities, corruption, misuse of available funds, loss, wrong and useless investments. Few countries depend on their natural resources, which will not work long-term. They have to find alternatives like Arab countries. Defaulted countries' earnings will go towards the maintenance of employees, but they won't be able to improve infrastructures.

The situation gets even worse when we cancel the debts based on kindness. Rulers made the situation worse. They will start all over again and make it worse again and again, just like an endless loop. We have to realise the situation, consequences, and reasons behind them. We must try to eliminate the reasons. The main reason is that rulers thrive on money, poor management, and immediate economic crisis. Most of them can't avoid it. So, we must realise that this situation will happen when we follow money without knowledge.

-----------------------------------cc---

What is a currency war?

It is known as competitive devaluation, a condition in international affairs where countries seek to gain a trade advantage over other countries by causing the exchange rate of their currency to fall compared to other currencies.

All countries are competing with each other in trade, import, export to gain domination over one another. For that, they devalue their currencies against other currencies, accumulating other countries' currencies through trade. All centralised influencers, organisations control their member countries to avoid engaging in a currency war. A war would have an economic impact, leading to a recession affecting people's PPP and consumer freedom. No country is wise to devalue its currency extensively as it would impact themselves, but a small margin will have a practical effect on other currencies. G5, G8 and G20 summits used to be organised to enhance financial understanding among countries to prevent unnecessary clashes.

The average non-performing loan of 183 countries from 2015 to 2020 is 8.105906983%, bad debts restrict countries' growth. It should not cross 5%, but in the current situation of 5 years average itself is greater than 8%. Why is it happening? Lenders are not proactively reviewing the nature, capacity of businesses, their marketing ways, risk limits when it comes to big firms. They are just giving loans on stupid plans, business, marketing. Risk reviews are not happening diligently. So, business people get more leverage of money without a proper model. The final results are getting worse. It is becoming bad debt for lenders. On what basis interest percentages for loans are increased and decreased? It's based on public debts, bad debts, inflation. Ordinary people are finally suffering because of foolish decisions by bank authorities and government officials.

If people think about what made them push forward and pull backward means, we only get two solutions: Technology pushed us forward. Money pulled us backward. What's so wrong with moving fast and correcting all backlogs?

The reasons behind the historic recessions of the past 200 years are mostly a weakness of money and its associated factors. In each recession, millions of people died, became homeless, but significant players with billions of dollars in wealth, increased their working capital and evolved from each recession. An ordinary person has to suffer for learning it. Money modifies its loopholes every time. We haven't got complete technological advancement for all human races. We are using the technologies that billionaires think we want to use.

World Bank data states, "Bank non-performing loans to total gross loans (%)".

Working-class people are not the deciding authority of our technologies. It's because entrepreneurs and industrialists invested in some technologies and industries that they need to earn back. They wanted to taste some profit in it. They hired employees for developing, maintaining, constructing, designing, and promoting purposes. They can't just leave all that behind and jump into the new technologies or alternatives within a short span of time. All their investments and the future of employees who depend on it get ruined. So, we can't just blame them for it. The monetary structure is designed in that way. Sometimes it seems like pushing us forward, and sometimes it seems like pulling us backward. Is it pulling and pushing at the right time? Sometimes it is, and sometimes it is not that.

We will wonder why currencies were backed by gold and silver once. What standards is it operating on now? We should know the gold standard.

WHAT IS THE GOLD STANDARD?

Currency was valued based on a volume of gold for some time. Money was backed by a hard asset like gold to preserve its value. Governments issued currency tied to its value to the amount of gold they possessed.

Under a gold standard, anyone holding paper money can turn it in for a fixed amount of gold from the country's gold reserve, which means those paper banknotes can be exchanged at will for metal; we could bring paper money to a bank and then exchange it to get actual gold in return.

Initially, actual metal coins were issued, governments started using them in trade. Since gold was the most durable of all metals, it had the most staying power. Lydia, in modern-day Turkey, is noted as one of the first cultures to document their use of gold as currency.

While various countries have adapted their currencies backed by gold over centuries, the British Gold Standard was one of the most notable examples of backing currency with hard assets. Gold spurred exploration in the 16th century. It helped to standardise world trade when it boomed in the 19th century.

Along the way, governments introduced paper money to make life more convenient. Carrying metal became a frustrating behaviour. The easy solution was issuing little slips of paper. For example, a person went to McDonald's with a $1 bill. When the paper itself is worth nothing, a $1 coupon paper bill is only worth $1 if McDonald's is willing to honour it. Therefore, governments backed their paper money with gold, merely allowing paper for convenience but with the full backing of a hard asset. McDonald's accepts it because it's backed up by a hard asset.

Gold Standard History

Silver reserves were depleted due to wars and trade deficits within Europe. Until then, silver and gold standards had both been in place, but by 1821, a gold-only standard was adopted.

Silver was still used in coinage (along with gold), but by this time, the use of banknotes was increasing. By 1816, Bank of England notes were backed by a specific amount of gold.

As for the U.S., it began using a bi-metallic silver-gold standard upon passing the Coinage Act of 1792. Copper was also used in coinage but was not convertible at specific rates like gold or silver. The goal was to use big denominations, silver for small denominations, but this required a gold-to-silver ratio, which kept fluctuating based on market forces. The rate was fixed at 15 ounces of silver to one ounce of gold, with the market rate typically ranging between 15.5 and 16 to 1. Significant gold discoveries starting in 1848 decreased the value of gold compared to silver, thus making silver worth more on the open market as a currency. The U.S. continued efforts to maintain a bi-metallic standard, but by 1873, it had adopted an unofficial gold standard.

The 1900 Gold Standard Act required the U.S. to maintain a fixed exchange rate with other countries on the gold standard. It was suspended from 1914 to 1919 due to World War I. In the early 1930s, the United States, France, England had different opinions due to the exchange rate issue. They were in and out of gold standards for some time. They came to a solution with a tripartite repo agreement. In 1944 the Bretton Woods Agreement established the International Monetary Fund (IMF). The World Bank set par values for currencies in terms of gold. Countries were to maintain their exchange rate within one percent of that par value.

From 1968, other countries started demanding gold from the United States since the United States was printing more money. It resulted in a U.S. Congressional repeal of the requirement that Federal Reserve Notes be backed by gold. The age of standard gold prominence has passed, although many countries still keep significant gold reserves, including the U.S., Russia, France, the U.K., Germany, Italy, China, Switzerland, and Japan.

In 1971, the United States closed the "Gold Redemption Window". It ended the practice of issuing sound money. It decided to join the ranks of most other nations that shifted to purely "fiat currency" with no value other than what is implied except its exchange values based on international trading activities. Whichever country exports more has more value for its currency.

HOW IS MONEY VALUED TODAY?

Does gold back currency? The simple answer is "no."

Many countries are failing in financial knowledge, which proves the destructive power of fiat currency. It's just 50-60 years old.

While some foreign currencies – like the dirham – are pegged or essentially pegged to the U.S. dollar, the U.S. dollar is not pegged to anything. Countries around the world have tied the fate of their currency and their population's welfare to a USD currency because they have the mindset that the United States will never fail.

When our money is in the financial system, it's subject to the whims of central banks and politicians. President Roosevelt's famous gold confiscation forced all banks to hand over their gold to the government's Fort Knox. He forced private companies and citizens to hand over their metals at a steep discount in exchange for dollars.

The government devalued the wealth of its citizens overnight. Not only was wealth devalued, but private ownership of most forms of gold was banned unless people held a licence. The government had confiscated wealth and prohibited an exit for its citizens.

For some reason, zero central bankers believed it was a bad idea. It's because it's their idea in the first place. Bankers and politicians prefer to manipulate the value of their fiat currencies simultaneously to achieve their political objectives and beat inflation. The idea is that a hard asset with intrinsic, long-held value can't be manipulated the same way paper money can to achieve the whims of the moment.

Some people tried to change that, but it did not happen.

There is no global currency, but reserve currencies are used in transactions by central banks, corporations, and governments.

The U.S. dollar is the world's most widely used reserve currency since the U.S. economy and its financial system are stable.

More than 60% of central bank currency reserves are held in dollars. Many commodities are priced in dollars.

Dollar as the De Facto World Currency

Many commodities are priced in dollars since the dollar provides a stable medium of exchange between international companies. Dollar-denominated commodities include crude oil, Natural gas, Gold, Silver, Copper, Aluminium, Platinum, Wheat, Corn, Soybeans.

More than 85% of foreign exchange transactions are done in dollars. Forex transactions involve currencies converted or exchanged into other currencies due to investing in global trade, such as exports, imports, and financial transactions from corporations.

Other countries developed over the years; Their currency's value increased globally. Today, two other major reserve currencies are the euro and the Japanese yen (JPY).

While the U.S. dollar remains the world's reserve currency, the world can be divided into three main currency blocks, with America mainly dealing in dollars, Europe dealing in euros, and Asian countries becoming more connected to the yuan, rupee, yen, Singapore dollar, and ruble. China has implemented capital controls, for example, which prevent Chinese investors from transferring their yuan out of the country. Conversely, the yen, euro, and dollar are freely traded without restrictions.

Less dominant countries, such as Australia, had a situation some years ago in which Australian dollars (AUD) were first converted into U.S. dollars and then from U.S. dollars into Japanese yen. Today, there are many cross currencies, for instance, even when a currency pair is not associated with the U.S. dollar, it's possible for Australia to transact directly with Japan using AUD/JPY.

---------------------------------------cc---------------------------------------

Cryptocurrency, a new evolution that started evolving in 1983. It evolved into a decentralised form in 2009 by Satoshi Nakamoto. He developed blockchain technology. Bitcoin and similar other cryptocurrencies emerged as opponents to the world of currencies and gold. Cryptocurrency had no value when it started. Slowly, the market value picked up because of people's demand. It was less than a dollar in 2010. Why is it a hindrance? As all know, it's a cyber network. It's easy to hide the transaction and its purpose. If anyone wants to hide their payment for an illegal purpose, then it's a great tool. So, we can escape from all the official databases and security: no struggle and risk. There are no regulations for it in many countries. Most countries are trying to regulate it. NYSE added cryptocurrencies to the index of portfolios and started investing in it. Other exchanges in several countries are doing the same. It's challenging to track a person unless someone shares, "it is my crypto id." Few countries have approved it already. Most countries are willing to approve it in their territory in the future. More people will try to adopt cryptocurrency when technology develops. So, people will freely transact without an intermediary, but when countries approve it, that time, it will ask for their crypto id to track the database. People are trying to utilise crypto with digital inventions like Nonfungible tokens and a few other things. They started trading with it. If we watch closely enough, we can understand one thing: people all around the world who found themselves in technologies created something to change some principles in finance that exist currently.

Conspiracy theory states that a group of people created cryptocurrencies to hide their transactions. They influenced the general audience that it's the new kind of money that helps us evolve to the next level. They inspired tech people to mine and transfer the cryptocurrencies between themselves as much as possible when they're created. They made a future contract between them using bitcoin as their underlying asset. Now, these cryptocurrencies have a noteworthy market which helps them well in hiding their transactions. It's significantly used to hide transactions across borders. It's one of many features in cryptocurrencies. There are rumours that it can collapse if that group of people wishes it to collapse. They start influencing the general audience towards its collapse if they want it to collapse. We can't conclude what is true and what is not true, but one thing is true: we can take a few technologies like blockchain which are great to build an ideal transaction tool.

---cc---

People started circulating crypto-decentralised finance among the same kind of people who also attired in the same way. Market forces and financial systems of the existing world didn't force them to stop because the people who created the crypto environment are fundamental to developing entire software systems and technologies of the existing world. So, acting against them will entirely create unbearable side effects on the financial system. So, the existing system started to adopt it and coexist with it. Even though the existing system doesn't like this sort of shift, it's not in a position to wipe it. The existing system is trying to absorb it, modify its ancient methods by using its popularity, fame, advantages. Undisclosed flaming fights articulated between two different systems that are running the world.

Changes like that are what we want. We can slowly shift to another level as time passes. It may even be a starting point for something like a work-based economy or something new that is better than a work-based economy.

Ordinary people aren't even aware of the existing monetary system entirely. These crypto concepts are all alien topics to them. So, most people won't understand the concept, which is sad. Why it is essential to understand the concept without blaming our knowledge gap. So, how to spread awareness worldwide? So far, readers have learned how it started. Several intelligent people structured the monetary system. Later, wealthy and cutting-edge advantage people used their knowledge to modify or collapse the structure to their advantage.

I'm not an advertiser for crypto, but it's a movement taken by a knowledgeable crowd. It needs enormous attention. The globe should see why it is essential.

Why should we try to hide transactions as ordinary people from the government? Because equality in earnings is a massive problem in common ground, the person who owns and earns more thinks about how to hide transactions. Why? We have to understand that even a person with knowledge and skillset that high and earning huge has problems with transactions tool. They are trying to hide their privacy of finance. Middle-class people don't have a purpose because earning itself is a hindrance for more people. Why is the highly earning crowd hiding transactions? It's to earn more, hiding it for privacy, saving tax.

We can see many layers if we take centuries of data on how crimes evolved over the years based on finance and the monetary system. The system itself is bogus, but it's operating in the world. The system is upgrading itself from all its visible and affectable crime. The 17th century held illiterate people high. Crimes oriented to finance were committed by illiterate people. If any financial crimes happened in the 17th century, police would start to investigate only illiterate people. The 18th and 19th century as well had the same sort of situation, but the situation of shift started happening in the 20th century, educated people as well started facing the same sort of financial troubles that last century illiterate people faced. So, crimes had mixed participation. Police had to investigate both sides in these times. When it comes to the 21st century, it became complicated because educated people increased, the situation of struggles in finance existed like in the 17th century. Crimes in finance increased to different levels. Society is still the same, even with education. The purpose of education has not served well. Should we put our education quality as a question mark? Why? Because it's not giving the changes that people expected; instead, it's giving struggles that existed in the 17th century. Now comes to the 21st-century quarter century almost crossed. The material worth of educated financial frauds increased more than illiterate financial frauds. Now, we have to raise a significant question about education. Does education teach people how to commit fraud systematically?

So, education is not something that helps in the practical financial world. We must create a new system that understands the value of work and its importance unless we can survive healthily in society.

Problems with the Former Gold Standards

There were various problems with the gold standard.

One of the main problems was that the systems ultimately relied on central banks to "play by the rules." The rules required central banks to adjust the discount rate to allow for proper inflow and outflow of gold to bring the exchange rate back to par with trading partners. While many countries followed the rules, several did not, like France and Belgium. Any system requires the cooperation of the parties involved. The gold standard was no exception.

A second problem with the gold standard was that while it did maintain average price stability over the long run, short-term price shocks needed to be absorbed by economies. The California gold discovery of 1848 is a prime example of a price shock. The gold findings increased the money supply, which raised expenditures, price levels, and created a short run of instability.

Deflation may arise when there is a lack of gold supply.

As I said, we may analyse every way to stabilise the economy with the tool of money and gold, but the truth may remain the same. Instability and loopholes will always make people suffer. One segment of people will always perform beyond the bar.

Failure of Free Market Economy

If the world agreed on the United States dollar as a common currency, the United States may need to redefine its monetary standards. They should not make mistakes by printing money whenever they want without other countries' approval and opinion. They should not play other countries. They should not dampen other countries' growth for their country people's wellbeing. They should not exploit other countries' wealth and make other country people enslaved. Even now, some 1st world country people think of 3rd world country people as lab rats. They should provide the assurance that the 17th and 18th-century slave economy does not arise again. These are all uncompromising tenets not only for the United States but if any other country's currency becomes a common currency, they need to stick to these rules which are very hard.

In this situation, the free market economy has already affected many people but is still destroying people's lives. All fields are already filled with skilled labourers, yet there are still excessively skilled people waiting to enter the same field. People who were forced into that field of study are also too high for the available jobs due to corporate misguidance. All the country's corporations are trying to achieve a 100 percent free market economy, but most corporates do not care about the people who are waiting for the opportunity.

When will corporations stop running for profit? When they start analysing fields, requirements? When they guide people towards balanced growth?

Corporations function in the world with a profit motive. They hide their dim-witted decisions and losses with the help of creating new wealth with the support of banks in their hands. Corporate to corporate, they back each other. A free market economy may be good when they work together well-organised with a social cause without inner and outer competition, but with money as a transaction tool, that's not possible. Regulating themselves matters a lot while saying it. No one can regulate others' businesses in a free market economy. Self-control beyond greed is more important. We don't want to push people to WBE when that happens.

Those who support the free market economy have to think: "Only talented people should live happily, and others should always work on their skills to get better and talented until death. Why should we argue about rational systems everywhere and every time?"

All talented people have relatives with no talent or less talent. Even people who are recognised as talented will not stand or speak of this complex problem of society."

Equality is supreme change. Didn't we expect someone would come to safeguard us from this evil world? How is that someone going to change? Will someone magically bless us? It makes us overnight talented or a billionaire. It's not possible. Political philosophy is not structured to accept that; it can only happen in dreams.

The one we expect is absolute equality. The person will not come from anywhere because that person is within us. We want to express that to one another first.

So whatever growth we see is not real growth, but it's a suppressed growth of this failed monetary system. Growth of three percent is constant year on year means it's not a straight line because the resources available will get reduced, manual efforts always increase yearly. This year's five percent is less than next year's five percent. We have to beat inflation with our growth if not we will not stand on the market profitably. So continuously, our work and resource exploit more than required over time. The monetary system perpetually operates based on debts subsequently, so it's time to start taking care of it and change.

Money is just communication; in that sense, we can say it is a transaction language. So, we should not shut down others' language unless it's violent and harmful to others. As I said, we have technologies to create an equal transaction language.

Finally, what have we concluded in this chapter? Why is money a failed element? Money is created by countries based on demand and supply in the economy. These notes are transferred through the central banks of their respective countries to other banks. These other banks use the fractional reserve system to lend money to people and industries. The fractional reserve system uses these currencies for credit creation through the multiplier effect. This causes an increase in digital currency at the banks' reserves, but physical currency usage is comparatively below the desired level. These digital currencies can't be transferred to the public, and at the same time, they can't be used legally by these banks and governments. The public can't know what happens to these currencies because of their centralised structure and lack of a public ledger. This is why blockchain technologies are supported by people, as they have a decentralised structure and a public ledger. This closed-ended behaviour creates speculation that something wrong is happening around the world as a dark secret.

Five

Players of Differentiation

Differentiation is fundamentally wrong but we differentiate from our friends; our parents differentiate from our relatives. Their parents do the same. What has this differentiation given to us? Our position!!! With the help of differentiation, we assess our position in society that we are low or high compared with another. How are we travelling? Fast or slow. It gives a typical kind of happiness, aspiration, inspiration to move forward in the race for most people. Some use it in other ways.

Some influencers use this differentiation. They keep on separating us from mingling with others. Why are they doing it? What benefits do they get through it today? How are they doing it?

Most people use differentiation as a ladder to achieving big things in one way. Few people are falling into the trap of differentiation and then spoiling their happiness. It is another way. Few people are spoiling others' lives due to differentiation. Some people are using differentiations of society and ruling the country.

So, what is a common factor that encourages differentiation? It is pride! All people will get pride above their happiness of achieving something over others. This pride will never allow them to resolve their differentiation but encourage dipping others.

There are some common differentiations in society. We can't do anything with a few differentiations. We must accept it. We can avoid fighting through unchangeable differentiations. All we need is to integrate our mind to acceptance of unchangeable differentiation. It will prevent influencers from getting into our minds. A few differentiations we can change and eliminate. How has that been playing us?

Poor VS Rich

What makes people put on a smiley face? The survey says money makes most people happy. When money is in hand, people feel independent and pleasure. So, money is a tool for happiness. It makes people smile too. Happiness has started to be rated. So, we can get happiness for the amount of 100, 200, 300, 1000, 100,000 and million dollars. So as per the survey shall we take it like this; rich people are happy and poor people are not that happy at all. As I said in previous topics, we can see how many endless loops are created around these current political philosophies and monetary system. After reading this; ordinary people as well think that when a transaction tool is involved in the happiness of people, then the economy never achieves absolute equality. It's because all want more happiness. More happiness involves more money. Certain people only earn a large portion of it. Ordinary people get affected due to it. Keeping it perfectly imbalanced is the only way to make many people work highly for happiness.

The feeling of happiness is the same for everyone, but the cost is very different. Few luxury materials in the current situation can't be distributed equally to everyone, even in WBE, because there are no resources in the world. A few examples are palaces, luxury cars, rare diamonds. The reason why luxury is called luxury is that it can't be occupied by everyone equally. It's limited, rare, can't be distributed to everyone. If everybody can have it, it means it's not a luxury anymore. Whatever the rich can enjoy and experience, that same thing can be enjoyed by poor people, but the cost, the luxuries for that are different. What? How come happiness costs more when people become wealthy? Where do they go for food? Where do they go for entertainment? Where do they go for vacation? How do they enjoy travel? Where are they going to gather? What clubs are they members of? For all staff, they spend unimaginable amounts.

The structure is separated based on facilities. Where there is more money, there are more facilities. People who enjoy more facilities are called rich. What do the rich think of the poor and what do the poor think of the rich? Generally, the rich always keep in mind that they should not become poor in any situation one way or another, but the poor people mostly always keep in mind that they should become rich one way or another.

Globally, there is a subconscious thinking that poor means dirty and rich means pure. So generally, they criticise people based on that mindset.

This mindset makes a global impact on every item we use. Costly means sustainable. Cheap means poor and only lasts for a short time. There are always two price categories for the same product, High-end and low-end. The fact everyone knows that low-end products are sold highly in society. Who is producing it? Rich. Who is doing that segregation? Rich. Who's getting huge gains of wealth from this? Rich. Why are they doing it? Because luxury can't be affordable by everyone, there aren't many resources to produce luxury for everyone. It is why luxury is limited to a few people. Rich has the status of enjoying those limited resources with the power of wealth as per the current philosophy in society. Those who are buying cheap are symbolised as poor.

How do both sides perceive it? How are these things registering in the minds of poor people from different perspectives? These were being registered in several ways, but the most common perceptions that the poor have are: the rich are the ones who help us live our lives, and we are indebted to them; the rich are superior to us. We should also strive to reach that position. Another perception is that the rich are the reason we are unable to get what we want. We have to avenge them.

How are these things getting registered in rich people's minds with different perspectives? These are getting registered in several ways, but the most common perception that the rich have is: - the rich can use the poor for their luxuries. Anyone will do what elites order them to do for money that elites are going to give. A few rich people may think in other ways as well, that poor people are the reason for our position, so we have to help them come up in society.

The problem in the structure is that all these perspectives create pain, happiness, gain, and loss. These perspectives are manipulated by society and encouraged by everyone. Perspectives will only change if the system changes.

There are several ways to become rich and stop becoming poor. At some point, in a few places, the rich moved towards crimes to avoid becoming poor. The poor moved towards crimes to become rich. So, these crimes create an imbalance in society. In a few places, the failure of lawful ways, cross roots, crimes make agitation to common people push towards becoming rich and stop becoming poor in unethical ways. In this race against money, a few may become rich in evil ways as well. A few may become poor in reasonable ways, but the structural imbalance exists without any change or improvement. The so-called wrong and good ways are defined based on political and philosophical construction. An identical thing is called evil, excellent, grey in different political philosophies—only a few things are defined as wrong in all political philosophies.

Money is something similar to drugs. It gives some addictions to those who fall for it. In some cases, it makes people arrogant if they have more money. Arrogance becomes their behaviour. It leads them to make others suffer and insult others. Those who are affected by these addicted people like to get revenge. It may be in a good way by working innovatively and growing higher than what they were named in that insult. A few may take revenge in the wrong way by spoiling the person who insulted them, making them suffer. Positive reinforcement is good, but the pain that people endure until they overcome the insult is high. It may turn negative sometimes, stopping us from moving forward and ahead in life. Negative reinforcement is wrong. The pain in it is comparatively even higher. It may provide fast relief, but people's real motives in life will be ruined by it. The situations, our surroundings, and many other factors like education, knowledge, peace, and family are reasons for one's growth and decline. We can't just argue with others that we are richer than you and you're lazy and poor without knowing others in detail.

The global inequality ratio between the poor and rich is very high. 1% of people hold more than 50% of the wealth in the world. According to the survey, 775 million people are in severe poverty.

All political parties come to power in a democracy with one promise regularly without fail. What is it? Poverty reduction. Is it happening? The progression is evident. The world has developed into a better place compared to 1990 to date. Globally, the focus is on poor people and helping them move towards becoming middle-income earners. However, the issue arises when educated middle-income individuals start doubting that something is wrong. This doubt can have a severe impact on the social structure if the system collapses without an alternative; then it's catastrophic. Nobody wants it.

All analyses about democracy, non-democracy, redistribution, inequality fail to find a definitive solution for achieving equality systematically concerning current monetary policy. The reason is demand and supply chain management of worldly things are not connected in any other ways but monetary policy. The financial system favoured the side of the rich. It made many devastating policies to dampen the failures of the rich. It made it so hard to equalise; some people don't want to equalise. Some people don't even identify the fault of it.

It is why the generalised method of moments estimator of the Gini coefficient in many countries is not even low. We don't want to discuss zero, but it should be low. It's also impossible; the reason for that is the political structure of democracy and non-democracy.

Politicians are who? They are people. How do they get funds to run the nationwide party? They are getting donations. Who is donating to them? Entrepreneurs are philanthropists. So political parties do not have a right to harm them. If they do mean, they won't be funded to spend on politics and advertisements next time. They influence the media to make changes in people's minds. Politicians have responsibility over all people, but due to this power competition between the opposite party and the ruling party, more decisions over welfare stayed on shelves for an extended period. Non-democracy has issues different from democracy. They don't have any power struggle or competition among them. Still, structurally everyone knows it's the King or queen who is superior to everyone. They control everything. The segment of the poor and rich in non-democracy structured in different ways. People are rich in non-democracy for several reasons, some of which are unquestionable only in non-democracy, but non-democracy is a step ahead than democracy in development and equality margin due to minimum factors involved in political matters.

Money is an underlying element in everything. Every political philosophy tries to make people self-sufficient economically. For that, it's trying all sorts of ways. It's implementing policies around that motive. Let's take capitalism as an example; it wants everyone to be invested in the financial market instead of saving it. So, capitalism is securing the lives of people who are investing, knowledgeable people. Capitalism is trying to educate people worldwide to invest. People are moving towards investments worldwide. It is why we have to understand the world will not make more and more people poor when they are bonded with political philosophy, but it will not make people equal and won't force people to become poor.

So, even with inflation, unemployment, and recession, we won't become poor if we stick with the financial market and invest knowledgeably. Capitalism is trying to educate everyone about it. Reducing the segment of the poor is the motive. of the world. So, people also need to understand that even if they happen to be in any political philosophy, it won't guide or lead, or force us to become poor. All it tries to do is make us self-sufficient economically. This structure may take time to convert everybody into being self-sufficient, but I am damn sure that it won't make everyone equal. More people aren't able to work in a field they love.

The world is structured based on money. Investing in the financial market is the only way to safeguard ourselves from becoming poor in capitalism. When we're in other political philosophies, they have their own sticking patterns; only knowledgeable education can make it possible.

Racial, Religion, and Caste

How cool are we now? Because I am going to slam our ancestors to find this differentiation. We should follow a 4-year-old child's mentality because they will tell us the correct answer: what are blacks, whites, greys? It's just colour. They will show us unconditional love. They don't know and don't want to know about religion, caste. How, why did these differences come? Why did these common mentalities come to society? Long ago, no significant issues happened when all people lived in their place until invaders started coming and ruling others' land. At that time, the opposition who lost in the war was treated terribly. All over the world, defeated people are taken to other lands as enslaved persons. Blacks became a symbol of slavery. They were treated equally to animals or even worse at that time, which changed after a long struggle. Even in a few places, we could see injustice happening to people.

100 years before, rulers had the mentality that whites were superior, but blacks were not. It provokes a few current generations of people to act against blacks. We all know that this is wrong. This structure is slowly moving towards equilibrium, which we can see clearly. This difference is a mindset problem. We should practice loving unconditionally; we should accept equal opportunity for all races to cure this mindset problem. For that, we should hire people based on skills, not based on other factors. In my suggestion, I would like to create a wall between the candidate and the employer. They don't know whom they are interviewing. They will only ask questions related to work that create opportunities for people to get the job based only on skills.

People made religion. How many religions are there in the world? Unofficially, there are around 4300 religions in the world. People follow all principles of religions without any sacrifices mostly, this is good, but Adherents of religions are fighting over their religions. It is not correct. Adherents believe their religion is superior, their God is good. They believe other religions are not equal to them. It makes them force others to follow their religion.

People voluntarily moving from one religion to another is fine because it's their right to choose what they want to follow. This fight between people has an unpleasant and harmful impact on human life. Ignorance of the true meaning of religion hurts true devotees. If you ask, what does one never-ending fight mean? Religion's fight. So many lives were sacrificed for it. So many changes happened in the world due to this to calm the majority. Most of the religion's core structure is built upon unconditional love and absolute equality without any difference.

The beauty of religions is the pleasure of sharing wonders with their surroundings; voluntarily, a few people may come while they are impressed by seeing others' pleasure and growth, but forcing them is illegal. It may only increase the count but will never increase their divinity. Bribing people may not help to increase religion's growth. People in religions sometimes hurt people in the name of God, pollute their land and people. Minority religious people are, in most places, ignored by the majority regarding their rights. In a few places, some religious people won't do business with other religious people. A few won't allow their children into other religious people's houses. Most religious people strongly oppose inter-religious marriages. They torture their children if they try to do inter-religious marriage. Those who try to do inter-religious marriage are blackmailed by these religious thugs even though all laws are against it. They fear that other cultures will spoil their beliefs, their cultures, which may change their children's behaviour. Fear of convergence with other religions makes them create a wall against others and used to create a thinking of saving their religion, which will create only pressure in life.

Why does the government need people to be separated? Why are governments not taking any actions against these religions' stupid walls strictly? As I said earlier in previous topics, it's because they separate people through this. They rule them peacefully with malpractices. If governments force laws on them in democracy to converge, then people never choose them to be their leaders, which will end their political careers. So, here people also don't have the proper understanding and knowledge since they are being separated for a very long time. Sudden changes can make them nervous and fearful. What kind of convergence are we speaking about? Accepting other religious people, accepting matrimony without hesitation, respecting each other. Independently approach anyone without any hesitation for help without differences. In a few places, it is happening, but not widely accepted by people in religious countries.

Religious people believe that karma is the reason for the poverty and pain that people face in their life. They try to reason everything with a religious perspective and state that nothing changes fate. They try to dampen others into the same mindset. In this way, they are stealing the hopes of others. Religious people are their own enemy. They believe that these differentiations are there for a reason. They believe that if people try to come out of that differentiation, then the balance of the world will collapse. So, they are standing against curing this differentiation in the name of God. They are ignoring the technological changes that are happening around the world.

A caste is a form of social stratification characterised by endogamy, hereditary transmission of a style of life which often includes an occupation, ritual status in a hierarchy, daily social interaction, exclusion based on cultural notions of purity and pollution as per Google's definition. Why is it difficult to live life within the caste system? Several countries are following it. A few centuries back, we had a deadly caste system worldwide. In religions like Hinduism, people are categorised as Brahmins, Kshatriyas, Vaishyas, Shudras. This worst caste system is still in use in countries of the subcontinent. Overall, approximately 18% of the world's population get affected by this caste system.

Caste-based reservation implemented in India to make people equal and bring social justice. It's good but it's not an absolute solution. It gave a push for socially backward and low people to come up. When India got freedom, it pushed towards the implementation of some kind of social justice in any form to rationalise the civilisation. The administrators thought of an easily accommodatable, long-lasting, and simply implementable way then brought caste-based reservation as a form of social justice. It also provided a much-needed solution but why, even after 75 years, does that plan not bring absolute equality? The reserve system is in place to help low-caste people to grow and get equality in India. Is it the fastest way to bring equality? In my opinion, it is the slowest possible way to bring equality slowly till the world faces another apocalypse. Do you know why? Most educated people are upper caste. A minority of educated people are lower caste. A huge percentage of educated people ruling government-authorised positions are from the upper caste. They will not allow lower-caste people to become equal in society with loopholes in law and order. They need to provide all approvals requested by lower-caste people. Upper-caste people won't provide approvals most of the time or delay the approval or extend the waiting period as much as possible. The government's significant positions are held by upper-caste people. Protection forces use lower-caste people for all illegal activities and charge them for crimes they didn't even commit. Lack of education among lower-caste people gave higher-caste people an upper hand in independent India. Upper-caste people used the knowledge gap and made them again as servants even after independence. I would say the caste-based reserve system is the best to keep discrimination forever.

They should have implemented an income-based reserve system. It's a highly complex solution and needs more work. It needs highly intelligent people to proactively modify the situation according to the plan. It could have been a quick fix in a 30-year time frame, but administrators are not ready for that kind of complexity. They feared that it will upset high-class people. It can't be possible now because India is a highly populated country with 140 crores. If we calculate the working-class, it will come to over 70 crores, but in 1950, it was only 35 crores, and the working-class was only around 13 crores. Continuous support and monitoring could have made everyone equal. If they had used it, they could have erased caste from the dictionary of independent India, but the turn was not taken. The turn that was taken became a wrong turn. It's spoiling millions of people's lives and dreams. A few people may say that income-based reservation would have killed all scheduled castes and tribes. It's not true. This system is created for them. So, we can't eliminate them from the plan. The absolute goal is to bring more income to people who are in the low-income category. If someone is not coming up for long, then analysis will be ruled in and make amendments in the acts to bring them up. It was easy to start from 13 crores.

Politicians have the power to amend the law. They have the power to create a good place. It is a big step with tremendous risk. The political foreground is a caste, colour, and ethnicity, religion system. They fix agendas based on caste. They choose a candidate based on that area's majority caste member primarily. So, they adapt to the irrational system. They fear that if it suddenly changed means, how they would convert people to vote for them. So, they tend to keep the difference forever. The caste system in Indian marriages plays a significant role, the traditional marriage system of Indian culture made matrimony caste-wise primarily. Very few people who are wise to come out of the system. Even though laws are in place to safeguard crimes against it, people do not have the guts to do it in the majority. So, caste-based matrimony sites became a billion-dollar business. Caste-related foul knowledge sharing made younger generations as well blind. It's not allowing to see the accurate picture.

Land, Language and Culture

Communication is crucial to share everything. This world communicates continuously until its existence in any shape. In this world, humans are one of the species only. They created languages for better connection and relationships, but even without them, they can communicate through body language. Body language is the first language created by humans. Later, a long time after, sound then written languages slowly emerged. These languages differ from one land to another land.

Land, language and culture are identities for humans, but humans have shrunk their limits through them. Why did this happen? They don't need to understand or like to see other people in those days.

Other than that, in ancient days, invaders used to spoil the native people's identity. This avoidance has evolved now. It has made people fear other language speakers nowadays. Is it because of fear or ignorance? In the name of globalisation, businesses spread across the world, and products also spread. The business world announced its global language as English because of Western influence or English invaders. Somehow, the business world found a global language to communicate for growth and improvement.

The political world still has a big gap between one language and another. People's trust, acceptance, and opinion of another language, land, and culture are still questionable. So, the truth is we are ready to do business with people of other languages, but we are still undecided whether to share our culture or land on a large scale. In small business dealings, we are ready to accept other people's ethnicity, cross-culture, and political views. The business world has become borderless in the pursuit of earning more money. The business world has realised the value of accepting other lands, languages, and cultures. Therefore, there are only two types of people: business people and political people. Business people have realised the benefits of unity, while political people are aware of the risks of unity. There are genuine reasons and a valid composition behind these risks. Politics is fundamentally structured around one group of people's land, culture, and language because it is their responsibility to safeguard their people's land, rights, and culture. This fear applies to people in terms of their opportunities, growth, and peace. What is behind this fear? The structure of the economy is the reason for this fear. People view land as their source of livelihood. They lead their lives in conjunction with their land. They cannot live peacefully and economically well without their land. We are comfortable in our land even within the current economic structure because we do not depend on the government; we depend on our land. This land provides us with the resources to live independently. Therefore, people do not worry about whoever is ruling as long as these rulers do not act against the people's land. Rulers micromanage people with the help of their lands. When do people become independent? It is when the government creates a situation where land is no longer necessary for people to lead independent lives; it is available for everyone. People have the right to use it but not to conquer it.

If we see the language barrier, the average human can't learn more than 2 to 3 languages. So, the language difference between one another is hard to resolve. We can't interact without grasping the global language. Even with the global language, the true self cannot be brought out. So, there is always a lack of comfort between people with different languages, but people should not consider it a bad aspect. People can't be bad because of the slight difference in the place where they live. Most people refrain from collaborating with other language speakers due to misconceptions and comfort.

Land and culture are sentimental and sensitive parts of people's lives. They are attached to these two from birth itself. Parents groom their kids with a sharing mentality, but parents are always concerned about their land and culture. They don't allow their kids to destroy it and not allow their kids to disobey it as long as they exist. People believe outsiders do not understand the culture. So, acceptance of other people in land and culture only happens on a small scale. From an outsider's point of view, they might see it as bizarre at first. Later, when they realise the reason behind the culture, they understand its value. What can make it easy? We should get to know everyone and then get familiar with them. That is how we can earn their trust and then mingle with them, but we can't be one among them. It is a bridge between two cultures. People join, enjoy, and share respect for each other.

Tourism may work in both ways, bad and good. Currently, tourism is a possible way to understand cross-culture. A country that attracts more visitors is portrayed as a friendly country. It means that most countries are not open to visiting, enjoying, and sharing. This is because of fear of culture and safety. As we all know, World War 1 started because of the prince's murder in the visitors' land.

Land, language, and culture are the borders of people. Politics is designed for people based on these borders. From the beginning, kings and leaders ruled their land based on these borders. We are also no different from them. A person who owns their land, language, and culture knows the value of it. They have the right to rule these things. It is what the common understanding of people developed over the years;

People have evolved, and now these borders are not required to choose a leader in developed countries. In many places, politicians are trying to separate people through these borders. As we all know, the current political philosophies do not give space to cross-cultural unity. Even with unity, we can't get the opportunity on a large scale. Politicians are using this issue as an advantage and keep rocking in the position that they are in now. They can't change unless the economic structure changes, and the structure can't change unless people change their perspective. People can't change unless they understand the politics behind it. What is the politics that stand behind it? When you complete this book, you will get an understanding of what that politics is. Once people understand, then they seek someone who can create a tenet that makes structural change in politics. The person will arise from us at that time. The realisation of this truth has not reached all over the world due to ignorance of social structure. It is a benefit for politicians and businessmen.

Other than politics, land has a complicated issue that is mentally affecting us inside. The devil emerged in the name of the land. Land is an asset for life; buy land and build a house is a lifetime achievement for 70% of humans. It's a lifetime dream. So, for that, people are ready to be in liability for 30 years of their lifetime, too; this means half of our lifetime because the average human age is 65. How people considered this thing in their mind that land is an asset. In ancient days, owning land was a luxury for most civilians. The land belongs to kings or leaders. Civilians had the right to cultivate but not to own it; later on, after a long struggle with stunning sacrifices, civilians began to own lands, and it's our happiness to have a private space to spend some private time. It is what has now developed as addictiveness. After thousands of years of fighting back, there is nothing wrong with owning land.

Reality for most people now is different; the land is a liability. Governments and banks are exploiting society's lack of knowledge. Governments keep people in a lock-in period of 20 to 30 years of debt. Middle-income people either work or sacrifice their assets to pay off debt. Most people choose to work, keeping inflation in mind. Thirty years ago, 100K dollars were worth more than the current 100K dollars. People think it's better to hold debt for 20 to 30 years. People stop trying new things and exploring opportunities because they keep debt in mind. Most of us think it's a better way to avoid risks. Land mainly acts as a stopping point. Few people have the guts to cross it and achieve something; few are affected by it. Few people didn't have the guts to cross and wait for the debt to clear, but the energy, mind, time gone when the debt cleared.

Political philosophy and economic structures operate through them. The bank's number one product is housing loans. It is a faulty system because it operates through debt. People have more opportunities to find new ones.

SEX

Human behaviours are influenced by what we see, want, learn, hear, and problems we suffer. So, this behaviour used to change from time to time based on moods and stuff that we are up to. We can guess one's temporary behaviour with this. Common behaviours are decided by society so do common ideologies as well. Common ideologies sometimes may be stupid and incorrect as well. One who spreads it will not be seen anywhere near, but one buying it spreads it without knowing the whole picture of it. It spreads most of the time and makes a harmful impact on the victim. The victim gets affected without knowing what is happening around them. We can't be able to change or be in a situation to explain everyone once it's spread all over. It's what's happening in gender conflicts. Women and Men both are affected by these ideologies. When someone breaks away from the common ideologies, people around them tend to react harshly. Sometimes it becomes a reason to end the life of a person. The solution is that we should not buy stupid ideologies without knowing what is correct. People once brought ideologies into their mind means it can't be erased if they didn't get a correct vision within a short time; there might be a chance, but if it's crossed generations mean it's irreplaceable. People can't change in real life like they are shown in movies. So, we must wait peacefully until those ideologies vanish forever. It stops people from doing what they love.

Gender-wise and sex-wise, we still face struggles in sections like female, male, tri-gender, lesbian, gay, bisexual, straight, and asexual. So, forcing something we are not is as complex as anything in the world. Standard profiling, like women should cook, men should work, is still an issue in human life. LGBTQ+ is criminalised in many countries. All these indicate that, in the name of protecting culture, people and governments are spoiling the life of humans.

Many countries are unable to equalise opportunities between men and women. The ratio is always off the table.

When an arguable topic is on the table, people do not want to decide because it will cause immense pressure for those in a comfortable situation. A comforting solution in favour of rationalising both sides will disadvantage one side that has already enjoyed more advantage. So as long as it's on the table, they will enjoy the additional comfort.

Pressure in current society on genders is forcing them to do works assigned to them from ancient days like men should take care of outside work. Women should take care inside works of home. Even in ancient cultures both men and women worked. They both prepared food but somewhere in the middle the structure completely left out. In current times in society, we see changes slowly that women can also go to work outside of the home, but part of who should take care of kids, cooking also falls into the hands of women. It's both man and women's responsibility to take care of both. So, balancing both sides is complex and challenging, but it's a responsibility. Indeed, parents can't always give equal importance to work and kids. Still, they have to manage it as a family. Rarely we see men and women switching roles in a relationship, like a man taking care of work in the house, women doing jobs outside and earning for the family. It is slow-growing but a welcoming one because these families break the patterns.

For those who are captivated by pattern, ladies and gentlemen - we are not the same anymore as we were in the past. The situation is changing, culture is changing, even the whole globe's climatic conditions are changing. The only thing that does not change is change. So, we have to prepare to share things in a relationship; the world should also develop an extensive open mind about sexuality. We must stop worrying about old stuff. Everything changes according to situations.

Change should come within all human beings because it's no longer one person's job. Both should equally contribute to work outside and inside the home. It's all about mindset. Once we set our minds to it, it will not be neglected. It's all about sharing and caring. In WBE, cooking is not compulsory. It's an option. If we want, we can do it, or if not, food will be delivered to our home steps.

While practising the current economic structure at that time, we have to share things in relationship with understanding. If one wants to take care of home, it means we shouldn't force them to go to work in the current economy. If someone wants to work, it means we shouldn't force them to maintain the home. It is named as understanding between relationships. Men should get to know all stuff of home. Initiatives should come from everyone. In most places, initiatives are getting stopped by our previous generation. The change we are discussing is not accepted in the previous generation's mind because most of them are not ready for this to happen, yet few people support it. I welcome that wisdom.

How are politics using this difference in their favour? Politics is dominated mostly by males. We can take India for example; they are not interested in thinking about equal gender participation like 50:50 or 60:40 as well in some places. It is male-dominated always. We can see female leaders in many countries, but female participation is not equal to men. Even in politics, equal participation is not possible in the current political philosophy, which is easily achievable, but it still needs to be achieved. It's not because most women are not interested. It's because men are interested in holding the upper hand. They are getting a huge benefit out of it. Politics should be a reflection of society. If we want something, it should give us that. If we don't want something, that means this should not force us; it should take people's opinions then consider them while making decisions. Most of the time, politics is not happening in that way. People are forced to accept the reality even if they don't want to accept.

Gender statistics were taken in the country. It was found that women are the highest number of voters. Political parties announced glamorous plans to impress women; not even a single line is about equal opportunity and sharing of duty. This is a reflection of society. What is this reflection? Politicians will make plans based on how most women see and represent themselves in their society. If anything is raised as an issue in equal rights, it means they know how to deviate people from the protest.

Protestors are always going to keep their goals the same. Politicians' goal is to divert people's attention from it. They have the media in their hands for it.

Psychological differences in the relationship between men and women are more significant. This difference can only be resolved if one speaks about it openly. It's a critical issue that sometimes requires silence. Unless a relationship adviser helps, severe pain stays in life forever. So, this difference needs medical advice.

WORK

Please elaborate on your work; tell me about your profession; take me through your profile; introduce us to your role; walk me through your work experience; work, work, work, work, and work. Wherever we go new, others will identify us by our profession and work. Our work is our identity. We have to choose our identity, not society and family situation. No one can stop anyone who wants to be a Truck driver. If it's their wise. People can advise them about situations and consequences they are supposed to face due to it, but while they are jumping into it with all their knowledge, no one has the right to stop them. The work is the work. They just tell these answers to our questions, 'all works are the same, nothing big, nothing small. No one has the right to judge anyone's profession.'

As a society, we need to create better education about sex. People should not sell their bodies just for the money struggle. We will not have these types of issues when we have a work-based economy.

It is a judgemental difference between societies and works. There are many judgemental workers out there and workers out there suffering due to poor identity of it.

No work is trash; it's just a chain link. If the link fails, that impacts the chain's strength. This impact weakens its structure. Racing is not only dependent upon racers. It includes the track, signals, times, engines, mechanics, even a screw that can change the result of the game, which is why a race is not an individual race. It's a collective effort of the team and the team's skill. The screw also matters a lot.

People are treated worldwide based on their job roles and pay.

So, when an organisation is running successfully, we should appreciate its workers. We should give credit to them. All jobs should get equal credit. A person can be a manager, but it's also one of the roles to play. A person can be a subordinate, which is vital to play in work. If the manager fails, workers will be unsatisfied. If the subordinate fails, then the manager will be unsatisfied. Both will result in loss. So, no roles have lesser importance. It is why all works and roles are treated equally.

No difference in the organisation's role should be followed everywhere because it is all about overall performance. It's not a single person who made the company to the next level. It's a collective effort. So, recognition should be equal.

Most of the underappreciated people in the organisation later showed their talent by creating a whole new organisation against the organisation they worked for and defeated their prior employers. Recognition must be equal. When the company grows, we also grow together with it. It is not possible in the current economic structure. Shareholders and promoters own the organisation. They want to profit from operations with a lower cost of operations through automation and a low workers' volume. The organisation can't give equal importance to freshers and 5-year experienced people based on salary in the current economic structure. It will create mental dissatisfaction for experienced people. Why is it? It's because of the economic structure.

Work overvaluation is a significant drawback in the world. Multiple fields of work and a few top-end roles in all the fields have it. For example, advertisements are one of them, and CEO, COO, CFO, MD are a few roles. Advertisements are essential for selling products. We have a number of advertisements after television was invented. The advertisement world lives in support of products, models, and themes. Corporations need to sell products to mass customers. So, they prefer advertisements. These advertisements need models and famous people like sports stars to reach the mass audience. They impress people to buy products. Therefore, fields like cinema, Sports, Athletics, and television stars become product influencers.

Works evolve in different dimensions because they change the world, which we currently enjoy. Marketing is the main element in the world for growth. Whatever work we do, that does not matter! Does it reach customers? It matters a lot. All our work settles finally through marketing, what we did to customers' attention and satisfaction, development. I also want this book to reach all people in the world. So, marketing needs creative strategy and content if we don't have enough money.

In the 19th century, no enormous respect existed for sports and acting people worldwide. They were treated like sins in a few places. After Cinema and Television were introduced in the 20th century, then, with globalisation and liberalisation, free economy concepts, situations changed. They became famous people because of a whole new entertainment field created around them which entertained and at the same time, helped to advertise their products. It created a new marketplace. It helped people to circulate money. Sports stars and cinema stars, television professions become advertisement models. When concepts and contents get popular alongside actors and performers become famous. Products get advertised through them. Marketing is the most significant industry in the world. Marketing is a survival kit and earning kit for all-entertainment media.

Creators are much more worthy than anything, but what if the most incredible creations are not marketed and do not reach everyone in the world? That's why marketing gets equal importance. Chances of success rates are high for people with creative and marketing skills who work on what they like. They can excel in their life above all others.

All workers are doing their work perfectly. However, people with a close attachment to marketing are always in a higher position because they are performing the role of influencers in society; they tend to balance it with their skills. It's their pressure because if their face value or skills fade, then they get ignored quickly. So, people with close relations with marketing have higher-risk jobs and uncertain incomes than other workers.

All workers close to marketing may enjoy fame and wealth when they are at their peak. They always have a fear of missing out and fear of ignorance when things do not go their way at a colossal level, which they always hate to admit but have lingering in their minds.

The 10% of people are always at the top. The 90% of people are consistently in the middle and low. They struggle, and absolute equality will never happen in the current economic structure. The structure of workers will never change until the work-based economy comes.

We always feel roles like those above the manager level are overvalued. Structurally, it is necessary in the current political philosophy. It's because our net worth increases based on the role we are in. We can't argue about equality in roles in the current political philosophy.

In current political philosophy, local politics in the workplace emerge because of projection issues. A worker who works hard is not recognised, but those who are close to managers get to the next level. Employees of the organisation try to sabotage an equal competitor team with their influence and behaviours for their team's growth. Managers or team leaders like to undertake equal competitors' teams in the corporate world. They sometimes make a mess at work for it. Local politics arises because of personal growth over the organisation's growth.

Coming back to judgemental jobs, some judgemental jobs are illegal too. Governments prohibit these and are very strict around them. Actually, it creates more wealth than regular jobs. So, people don't want to lose any money even if it's illegal.

Work overvaluation; it has to be like that in current political philosophy to maintain the balance in society. Marketers can't use ordinary people's faces for all marketing advertisements and campaigns because viewers can't connect with them as per the corporate mindset; more than that, they are creating branding. Some products need faces.

Finally, Corporations are working hard on automation. It is shortening the labour cost of daily routine work. They don't have a futuristic vision of what the current workforce will do if work gets automated. Governments have laws protecting labourers, but are they accessible to everyone globally? No, 60% of global labourers work in unorganised sectors. Most of them don't have the financial strength to go for any legal proceedings to secure their job and money. Countries like India have 90% of labourers in unorganised sectors. Whose fault is it? They should not be in unorganised sectors if the world is moving towards growth.

More than half of the global population cannot afford the cost of the law and the time it takes for justice within this structure. How are we going to achieve growth? We should think carefully about it.

How can WBE change it? Take Marketing for example, we must understand what makes actors and sports stars more special. Marketing makes their profession more worthy for its good. Marketing created exaggeration in their work and life. Directly and indirectly, marketing creates catchiness in those professions for its motive to reach the audience quickly and hard. How can we change the situation in WBE? If we stopped marketing means, then how come people know about new things? Marketing always exists in any economy because it's immortal and essential, but marketing will no longer focus and revolve around the professions like actors, sports stars, models as in the current economy. The same level of catchiness will be created for all professions in a work-based economy.

Work overvaluation and local politics, what will WBE do with it? In WBE, all roles of work in all fields have equal importance. There is no hierarchy. We will decommission the hierarchy model. WBE will not operate based on money as a transaction tool. The local politics happening in the workplace is because of hierarchy and money. We can eliminate both simply.

Automation: what is the WBE's stance on it? We don't have the pressure of profit, so we can upskill everyone to keep up with the speed of automation. We are structuring a work-based economy, so WBE will not terminate anyone.

Family

Families are the backbone of life. If anyone doesn't have a family in their childhood, they feel for not being in a family. Some people always focus on creating a family for themselves. We can judge a government by how families are doing. The house is the first study room for all people. We can see multiple situations in the family. How elders and youngers make decisions and support each other within four walls.

When people come to a certain age, most of them will marry. Few of them are interested in being alone or a single mother or single father. Where there is a family, there is a child for sure. There are a few exceptional cases, but still, others might conceive or adopt. Parenting will decide a child's future. A family of 2 or more children always has more critical situations because sharing is the first issue that will arise. Only after that will they learn to share things and support each other. After all, growing up, they will have a question again: why should we share things at that time? They will face a challenging phase; a few may cross that phase and support each other. A few will tear apart and go their way.

There are five support systems in the family structure. Those are mental support, physical support, financial support, moral support, and emotional support. Trust, acceptance, sacrifice are the main things to stick in the family. When all these things are bound together, that will be a great family. When there is a break in any single support system, then differences will arise. So, these differences will lead to hatred. So, it will set apart members of the family. Even though they love each other, these differences will never allow them mentally to join and be happy again. So, a few of them get a divorce. A few of them stick together and hurt each other every day. Their children also get hurt because of it. When the marriage is not working, the first thing that is going to get affected are children. Children are mentally struggling in these situations. If parents are not ready to care for their children, they will physically struggle. Differences may happen between family members like husband and wife, son and mother, father and daughter, brothers and sisters, and etc. Differences between husband and wife always hurt more. Domestic violence is the most dangerous level and extreme level. People can't face each other. If they do, violence is the result of that meet.

These differences can't be resolved unless both sides realise and feel them. Unconditional love is pure. It's the highest level of achievement; only very few people can attain it.

Bonding between child and parents is vital. Children having their own space is necessary. Most of the countries which are financially in a vulnerable situation are not able to follow these things because of the situations that they are in. So, some countries are not providing the required independence to their kids. Most of the parents do not allow their kids to mingle with people in the name of cultural safety as well.

Over-controlling will permanently destroy a child's future. It is stored in children's minds as differences. We will have to face severe consequences.

In the current political philosophy, all parents should plan to save some assets because if not saved, it will create a burden and complexity for children in their early career. If they want to switch to other items that they are interested in, it may not be possible if there is no money saved to support such changes. Therefore, they are forced to live life for the sake of the family without inner pleasure. It might be an exaggeration, but there are people working hard on their passions in their free time while being unsatisfied with their jobs and trying to enter fields they desire, although it's not achievable for everyone. It's all about the situation we are in.

Children should be responsible for their parents when they cannot stand at 68 and above because they have crossed the average human lifespan. Only a few people can survive on their own after this age. When a child cannot take responsibility at that stage, differences will arise. Aged parents will be sheltered in nursing homes.

When family members have differences, third parties always find an opportunity to benefit from it. These third parties set the members apart from each other instead of joining.

Family differences took place in this chapter because everyone comes from different families and backgrounds. One is not like another. Whoever got the five supports can achieve anything, but only some have that fortune. It's becoming the reason for who they are and what they do. It's one of the underlying differences which no one speaks of or considers as a factor, but it's one of the critical and undeniable factors.

Parents who read this, please try to give those five supports in any political philosophy.

Finally, these are six differentiation players; we must understand the core motive behind all these differentiations. It is pride. What is pride? Feeling of deep pleasure or satisfaction derived from our own achievements and other people's achievements that we closely associate. While people feel pride at that time, some unknown excitement makes them a new person. After that, all things they deal with will look different. Arrogance automatically comes into their behaviour slowly.

People see their identities like race, land, caste, religion, culture, language, and sex as their pride. People can't compete with other people's identities. So, they fight through it to prove that their identity is greater than others to feel that pride. People want to destroy others' pride, whether it is racial, land, caste, religion, culture, language, or sex.

We can stop being proud of things like race, land, caste, religion, culture, language, and sex. It is something that we receive when we are born. There is nothing we do to feel pride. It's just an identity.

Pride is something that should come from within ourselves once we have achieved something extraordinary. It should not change our character and behaviour.

The work-based economy will give everyone equal opportunity and equal credit. So, there is always equality. We can all be proud.

Six

Kingdom of Fools and Selfish Ministers

The world was once empty with nothing to hold a living, but it changed and is now holding us. Long ago we roamed around without any motive, but we changed ourselves to be civilised. We lived our lives without any tools, but we changed ourselves to using technologies. We were in kingdoms without being able to raise our voices, but we changed ourselves to be democratic in most places. What if one more time? Change ourselves from a monetary economy to a work-based economy for equality.

People are obsessed with the royals. I agree that they protected us. We still need to understand that we provided the sources to fight against the opponent. We educated them to assign complex strategies to win wars. We stood in front and gave our souls for the survival of our relatives. We gave the royal a duty. They have to protect us at any cost. It's their only duty. We did our duties ideally provided the source for our protection based on that only they provided us the protection. We should not be obsessed with them because we did our duties. They did their duties. If we fail to provide, they fail to protect. If they fail to protect, they will die, and we will also die.

Most people want others to treat them like kings and queens. The public glorifies even small gestures when kings and queens do it. People want luxuries like kings and queens. Capitalism gives an opportunity to everyone to become like a king and queen. We need to be talented in some way to become like kings and queens to enjoy the luxuries they enjoy, but being talented is not enough. We need to be in the right place at the right time to be like them. When people float in the dream of becoming king and queen at that time, they forget that, in reality, it is unimaginably complex. It's only achievable for some. They want to be one of them. Few of them want that at any cost. It may be legal or illegal or in the grey area. People work, plan, develop their talents to secure some spots.

Countries came out of the kingdom because people didn't like to be under the kingdom, but everyone wanted to become like the king and queen. People are confused by monetary policies. The monetary policy encourages people to become like the king and queen and enjoy the luxuries, but at the same time, it does not want everyone to become like the king and queen. It's fundamentally encouraging us to fight for our place. We know all political philosophies are not the same. Few have good characteristics, but a large audience does not experience more than one political philosophy.

King, why is a king created? When is a king created? How is a king created? People don't want outsiders to spoil their area and people. So, people selected a person from among them who excelled in strength, command, and fighting as a king to avoid invasion by others. People appointed a few intelligent individuals from among them to advise that person. The king or queen, before making any decisions, seeks estimations and advice from advisers in ancient days. People offered the king or queen some valuable resources for safety, weapons, and support against opponents. They gave the king or queen a bigger and better place than theirs. In case of an emergency, they can also safeguard themselves within the king's place. This is how the kingdom of fools and selfish ministers began.

Approximately 2,50,000 or more people ruled the world as bits and pieces throughout history. It all started with a safety purpose, then the purpose got misread, then the purpose went to the dustbin. Rulers get attracted to be on the throne. It's how the Game of Thrones started. Unwanted insane fights burned down the cities all over the world. Destruction and construction of kingdoms happened over and over and over and over again, but no one monitored when the game changed to conquer money.

When we analyse current situations and search how they started in the first place in the kingdom of fools and selfish ministers. All things happening now started in ancient times in one or more kingdoms that evolved and changed in more ways.

When queens and kings slowly started to behave like they owned everything that they ruled, at that time evil within themselves began to surface, but people ignored to control it then and there. They didn't know this was going to cause lots of trouble for them in the future. We are here as victims of that lack of knowledge.

They have been ruling since humanity started, but they stopped caring about humanity at one point. They started being selfish for some reason. What made them selfish instead of being generous? It's luxuries that they enjoy. Luxuries made them think that they are superior to everything in their city. People were offered sources willingly for protection; somehow, it was forcefully taken from them in the name of tax after kings started behaving like supreme.

The emergence of this cruelty made people fear for their own queen and king. Distance between people and rulers emerged in that place. The distance gave some advantages to rulers. Their ministers kept rulers' activities secret. So, the ministers only communicated to people about the ruler's situation. Giant stories built around them without proper evidence. Ministers became sinister to their people.

When the purpose of safety was within the hands of kings and queens, that time situation slowly turned into economic evolution by ministers. They fooled people by forming a model economy. They stopped bartering and used the evil concept of the coin in the model economy. They framed and publicised this as the country's future by hiding loopholes. People started using it since the transaction tool is easily transportable anywhere, as I said in the early chapters.

The concept of profit slowly showed up as a juicy thing. People getting something extra made everyone happy, but no one noticed malevolence sleeping peacefully inside it. The concept of profit changed the entire picture then and there. Henceforth unity of people in the kingdom started cracking its wall. People started thinking like individual benefits were much more important than anything else—the connection between people set apart. So, the comparison of profits made people feel superior to one another. So, the concept of safety changed. Rulers started collecting more money for safety. One who could not afford it was pushed into dead pits. So, rulers enjoyed more luxuries, but caring for the total population went out of scope.

People selected their 1st king or queen. Rulers gained the people's trust but after they pushed their daughters and sons as successors after them. That is how the 1st son or 1st daughter concept slowly came into the picture. Rulers convinced people that the bloodline of rulers had more power and knowledge than a new ruler. People got convinced over the period. When they had grown big as a kingdom, they used their brothers and sisters to oversee a portion of the kingdom. In that way, rulers resolved the clash between their sisters and brothers. They ought to marry their relatives to avoid a 3rd person coming into ruling authority. They conquered 2/3 of the wealth in all areas. They made more than 90% of people work under them. It is how nepotism developed its wing. It covered all places. When anyone raised their voice against it, they shut them by taking their life, as we all know.

Kings and queens wanted to sustain themselves for a long time in the crown, so what did they do? They started controlling A-to-Z things in the country. Ministers were assigned for all fields. Ministers monitored their designated fields. Kings and queens ensured all decisions and approvals went through them. They created a dependency over the independent system in the name of simplifying complexities. So, when controls increased, people's independence over their livelihood was slowly stolen from them, and over time, they implemented 100% dependency on the government. This dependency made sure that whoever was sitting in the crown had absolute control without fear over the country.

All over the world, we are following this system currently. Rulers achieved what they desired. We are redundantly controlled and suppressed indirectly by governments. They are controlling us in the name of providing welfare, but it's actually for the government's benefit. The government's benefit is the people's benefit, right? Yes, it's for the people, but no, it's not like that; this is for corporate benefits. How come it is for corporate welfare? The government failed in its duty of caring for everyone. They are trying to support poor people by providing welfare, but it's barely enough for living. They can't lead a life how middle-income people are leading. Their standard of living is very low. The political party is ruling the country by using the structured government which is already in place. Political Parties will support corporates for their party's luxuries and welfare. What about government employees appointed to manage the government and support rulers? They always draw a line about how everything should be structured, but ruling parties constantly bend it to their favour. Officials most of the time agree to it. Sometimes come out and expose threats and frauds.

If the ruling party of the government is consistently changing, that's an advantage. Why? The opposition party, which is ruling currently, will try to bring out at least a few malpractices that the previous party did while ruling the government. So, everyone has a small amount of fear to commit the crime. It's not good if the same party is ruling the government for more than 10 years or 15 years unless the public is experiencing the path-breaking changes visibly.

In the kingdom, rulers used their relatives' help when the war was lost. Rulers used their relatives' palaces to hide. They formed troops to reconquer their palaces.

Victorious rulers, what did they do? They invaded the city, enslaved most people, and filled their pockets with wealth. The concept of enslaved people was introduced in that way to the kingdom. They wanted enslaved people to work for their life. They wanted enslaved people for sex. They wanted enslaved people for entertainment. They organised more and more wars. They made more and more people enslaved. These ministers and rulers introduced torture camps for war prisoners to create fear among their neighbours. This cruelty continues till now, with 40 million enslaved people worldwide as of 2018. A puzzling number of secret agents are captivated and tortured somewhere daily to get words out of them. As we all know, nothing has changed significantly in social structures today, but we have to agree the slave system is mainly under control. Governments are trying to find such people and save them.

We can say proudly that it has somewhat improved. But we are still affected by many matters like women being forced into prostitution, plots against other countries, bombing people and torturing people. Somewhat is not enough; it should not happen. It's a slow progression within the next 100 years, almost everything will come under control, they would say.. They would say it will be controlled in the coming generation. Anyways, we are going to witness what is going to happen.

In the kingdom, they introduced the concept of child marriage to ensure bonding between the two kingdoms and make allies. In a way, ministers and kings formed prominent allies. It inspired people; they also started doing it among relatives. Even now, in a few places, we can see child marriages in countries like India, but it's officially illegal and a punishable offence. If it's reported, then the committed parties will go to prison. This is profound pain for children. Their dreams about their adulthood are shattered in front of their eyes, but they are not in a position to do anything but cry for help, which their pitiless relatives and parents also hide. Few people do it because they are poor. They cannot take care of their children. They do not have any idea of Government hostels and child care when they cannot take care of their child. This situation should change.

In the world, God is ultimately in all countries. Gods of countries changed over the period in most countries. There were Greek gods, Israeli gods, Chinese gods, Indian gods, Russian gods, European gods, African gods, but most people changed their gods over time, yet the world still has more gods, as I said in the early chapters. Religion is created based on beliefs. Religion and caste are created to enrich the deeper connection between people, which is one of the reasons for the caste system. The practical purpose of the creation of castes is to identify, divide, and conquer. So, groups are separated in the name of caste. Kings are symbolised as higher than any people. Others are symbolised based on wealth as middle and low. Different religions have different caste systems. Even worse is a few of them feel that it's their pride.

The crown chair is the highest thing that anyone would like to achieve. It represents wholesome power over everything. Even foolish kings may not be so foolish because a minor glitch is eligible to raze their position. They have to be careful about everything. Even a minister can set a trap for the queen and king; they lead an uncertain life. Most kings have spied on their ministers, their movements, meetings. Updates related to their positions are always reaching the king as soon as possible. Those who fail to do it sometimes face brutal reality like Julius Caesar. Politics is a robust business. One who has power can sell anything. So, in the political business, the predominant players are the crown members and ministers more than the opponent party. Betrayal in politics is a so-called old method that has been continuing until now. When it comes to betrayal, no matter what, one must kill either the king, the queen, or a minister to reach the throne.

Current politics is easily definable. It's betrayal politics. Why? Leaders and Ministers are betrayed by their own party people with their fake promises. These culprits somehow try to take over leadership. If it's not possible, they will assassinate their leaders. Dirty politics finds its way to spoil states and countries in all possible ways. Why am I saying this? The birthplace of dirty politics started in the kingdom of fools and selfish ministers.

The most horrible trait among kings and queens is war mania. I want to point out the three nastiest war maniacs in the history of the world. They are the British dynasty, Alexander the Great, and Genghis Khan. They took a vow to conquer the world as much as possible. Where did things go wrong? The upbringing process failed somewhere in childhood. Things they experienced, the society they saw, influencers, enemies, bullies, neighbours all matter. This hysteria pushed them towards violence. Their people and also other people suffered because of it. People paid the price for it.

I just shared three maniacs, but history faced an N number of maniacs. People they slaughtered, constructions they destroyed, lives they spoiled, items they looted we cannot even imagine in our lifetime. Each century faced at least two evil maniacs. For example, the 20th century witnessed Hitler. The 19th century witnessed the British dynasty. They destroyed the lives of millions of people in the worst possible way. They thought when they owned everything, they won't ever need to face another fear or dilemma that they had been obsessed psychologically.

It has become worse nowadays. War maniacs went advance in hand. They influenced political parties. These collective maniacs plotted a perfect breach and invasion in the name of self-protection. They want to control other countries with their power of knowledge and tactics, money. Countries are playing around political chess kind of metaphor. Once checkmate, then no more moves left for the opponent player. This bloody chess costs millions of innocent lives or lives worth of natural resources. Libya, Vietnam, Sri Lanka, Turkey wars are examples of wars that we have witnessed. More wars are not mentioned here. Influencers are none other than foolish kings. They had the bloody wise to own everything at any cost. In the beginning, society was not built as it must be. It's a catastrophic failure. We were evolving as a society from time to time, but we are evolving with the evilest promising quote, "Survival of the fittest." Why? Because for survival, we are killing our own people.

All truths are in front of our eyes. It's about intercepting and connecting the dots. It will provide us with the correct answers. Maniacs are created by society. If one maniac emerges, it means we have also played our part in it. So, as I said in earlier chapters, be responsible and heartfelt human beings.

What gives the greatest bodily pleasure in the world other than sex? Nothing else, right? So, sex gives humans unforgettable pleasure. When rulers had all power to control everything, what stopped them from forcing women and men to have sex with them? Yes, they did that. For their pleasure, they never mind others' wishes and rights. Once they desired, they would get whoever they wanted to their bed. Yeah, history is showcasing how rulers behaved in those days. They built chambers for women and men to have sex with them. They saw others as material to have sex with or without their wish. Whenever they wanted, they had sex with them. It was one form of entertainment for them. These victims were not allowed to marry others. They lived everyday life like others in the ruler's shelter. Only when rulers were not interested in them anymore, that time they would be sent out of the chamber. A few came out of the chambers and started selling their bodies since they didn't know another job. They earned money for their living through this. It became their profession. Some women were sent out along with some wealth to survive for the rest of their life. It destroyed their personal life, but anyhow, they wanted to live because this is the kind of thing that they couldn't raise their voice against. Even when raised, they were murdered like animals. So, they tolerated their pain. They joined hands with victims like them, formed a group. They supported each other. This is how rulers introduced prostitution. For their pleasure, they tortured women without humanity and forced them to be in bed with them. The rulers of the country introduced the bloody term prostitution. Many countries have prostitution in their place. Most countries are announcing it as illegal nowadays. Proper ways out, potential earning resources, and support are not given to victims by governments even now in most places. Situations around them force them to move to this place. Only a few people are coming to this field with desire.

In cities like Pompeii, Rome, Venice, and India everywhere, kings and queens had these chambers. Mostly, women suffered a lot because of this, more than men. It is one of the reasons why we still have men's gaze everywhere. Women's bodies are symbolised as a sexual symbol to impress men. Kings initiated this gaze, and it's continuing. The world needs to learn from its mistakes. It should not be a women's or men's world or any other world. It should be an equal world for everyone.

We can also identify men's dominance over women in today's world. Where did it all start?

We all know it started in the kingdom. Why is this dominance? Dominance is not forced in the model. Women naturally tend to sacrifice. They found themselves making life easy for their loved ones, but men took it as an advantage. They started overprotecting their women. Evolution constantly changes things, as we all know, that changed women's characters in most places. They started finding themselves happy outside. They wanted to share their work equally with the men. During that point, men got used to the comforts that women provided over the period. When they started expressing themselves and wanting to work like men, at that time men's comfort over stuff got spoiled, they were not ready to lose the comfort that they enjoyed. They started controlling them in the name of gods and kings and culture. They showcased stupid books as an example then made women continue what they are doing up to a specific period, but many social reformers raised their voices against it and created awareness slowly. They changed the structure up to a certain point. Most places still allow controlling women in the name of God and family situations. Only a few came out of the box, but most are discriminated by society, but still, progression toward equality has bright hope. A long moral fight finally freed women from their cells in most places. Mutual respect for each gender will bring peace to society. Women ruled a few kingdoms in ancient days, but even though the momentum for change took so long, most places still have not changed their dominance over women. It's a sickness. Mentally we can't grow when we are not leaving space for others. In most places, men are occupied with this mentality: "I can't give up that for others' betterment, but I can have it as waste. This sickness will destroy our society. At the same time, women should not seek freedom from men because it's their right to take it. Women should take that into their hands if they want to be free. All constitutional laws encourage it. Society restricts us only emotionally. Men should come forward to share space which is okay. The issue of women's rights is a hot topic in the kingdom itself, but the solution is not on the table. It's in our hearts. Controlling will not gain anything for us, but liberating can do it. People like Malala cannot even go to her own country independently because she speaks about equal education for all children. Pakistan is not the only country. We have many countries all over the world; so many countries banned so many things for women without reason. It has to change.

Few things never stop following us wherever we go. One among those is religion. It starts from our name itself for most of us. We don't stop believing in God even after millions of scientific inventions and discoveries. Whatever we find beyond outer space does not matter unless we understand where all things started first. Until then, we will not stop believing in God. Obsession over God has made so many people crazy. The average person going crazy is not an issue, but rulers going crazy means what can we do? They were already obsessed with power, crown, sex, and land. Now, God has also joined in. More than anything, like World Wars 1 and 2, all wars put together, nobody killed more than what kings and queens killed in the name of religion and God. The concept of God is the biggest killer of all. The Hindu religion has more than 30 million gods, so think about the consequences. Hinduism is not even a real religion. It is a way of living. Similar religions like Saiva, Vainava, Samana, and a few others combined and recognised as Hindu. See, for one religion itself, we have this many complications and differences. Who knows how many religions in the period of the kingdom? How many obsessed rulers?

When rulers were obsessed with religion, most of them in those days forced their people to convert to what the rulers believed, which was cruel. They did that to all of them, for that, they threatened and killed most of those who disagreed with converting. Most people died in wars related to religion.

Some scientists discovered the physics of the world but had feared to share that with society because religious maniacs established the concept that God is the creator of the world firmly. They killed whoever was speaking against it. Who knows, one of them who feared might end up discovered far beyond outer space or discovered the law of physics that we are still struggling with, and that person ended up without sharing their discovery.

Knowledge is power. Most of the time, people believe that controlling, attacking, and then having a stronger body is the power. It is a skewed knowledge. It showcases that being in the power of commanding and controlling is power, as Cersei said in the Game of Thrones series.

How is it affecting the world currently? We are connected diversely, but minority people cannot survive with their religion. So, they are moving towards other religions to get recognition and support. Political parties are focusing on bigger religions for votes for their party. So, people from other religions have disadvantages. They have to move towards majority religions or protest against them. Governments indirectly converted people through economic and social suppression in the 19th century and the early 20th century. These things are still happening in some places.

The government's political stupidity should be discouraged everywhere. Unity in diversity is beautiful. Unwanted politics make it hard.

Humans missed spoiling a few civilisations. They stay pure without knowing there is another land outside of them. One of them is still in Andaman Nicobar. They are still in the Stone Age era. They have not evolved like we have. They do not care about it much. They do not allow anyone into their territory. Places like those somehow stayed incognito, which has helped them care for all of their people by their king. So, they still follow the ancient motto of caring for everyone within the territory. They are not able to adapt outside of their territory.

There were so many territories like this in the world, but kings who civilised, evolved, and developed captured them then enslaved them and killed them. They saw them as a threat to their land. How can one who only knows how to throw a stone against their opponent be a more significant threat when the opponent has a jigsaw and all-equipped weapon? They destroyed even a trace of them. The best example is "America." Columbus Day holds millions of red Indians' blood in its hand. Intruders betrayed them. Intruders took their lands from them. They enslaved red Indians.

Indians have to thank God because Columbus didn't find India, the golden city of trade in those days. If he had found it, there must not be any Andaman and Nicobar civilisation left; for sure, he might have killed them all.

Why is America showing more interest than any other country in space research? Because maybe they thought that they needed to face a similar situation like the red Indians if aliens attacked them. The whole world fears that. "Karma" as everyone says.

Vultures should be punished by justice for their bitter behaviour, but justice will consider not only the incident of murder but also the nature, cause, and alibi. When it comes to justice, whatever the issue may be, it considers the date, time, cause, nature, alibi, evidence, connections to the surroundings, witnesses, prosecution, and defence.

Nothing has changed regarding providing justice to parties regardless of issues until now.

Justice is structured upon religious books in a few kingdoms and philosophical books in a few kingdoms and is still the same in most places. All punishments and justice are given to people based on those books. Few countries changed their justice system after the 19th century. They wrote their laws and orders. What changed currently? Some minor changes, like previously rulers are provided judgements on their own, but now they appointed someone to provide judgement.

What ideas did rulers had in the kingdom about giving justice? What ideas do countries currently have about giving justice? "Punishments given to criminals for their crimes to make them realise their behaviour and that realization can transform them into better individuals in the end." Has it happened, is it happening, or will it happen? In the kingdom, punishments are more about physical harm, like hitting a person and making them bleed for what they did. They use these people as entertainment property. Rulers made them face wild animals in the stadium. If they survived, then rulers had them locked in cells. Actually, after what rulers did to criminals, how do the criminals feel about what they did? They focus more on how they were treated there, which makes them stubborn both internally and externally. In the current situation, similar things are happening, which is why punishments like these are not changing people in most scenarios. Instead, they make them worse, encouraging them to commit more crimes without hesitation, Criminals get on some intelligence from their prior experiences.

We have to see the hidden picture of the world. Metaphorically, we are all prisoners of the world. We have absolute freedom to roam around anywhere in prison, but we have restrictions in the name of work, life, family, money, responsibility and more. It makes most of us stop roaming altogether. So, not many people experience prison fully. Metaphorically, most humans are in their cells most of the time. We created prisons within the prison and locked people who have the potential to roam around anywhere in prisons. If we let them roam around the world, they will create a mess.

There are grey areas where we can't judge sins committed by people. Most of the time, the rules of society define some behaviours as sins, but the same behaviours in some other country never seem like a sin; people consider them as a sin when society defines them as such. We will get confused about what society is. Isn't it formed by people? Because individuals in society have different perspectives, the concept of sin is shaped by the collective beliefs of the majority. Defining something as a sin is hard. It changes from time to time based on evolution. Women not wearing a hijab is a crime in Iran, but it's not a crime in America. It should be done in better ways. Planning a murder differs from killing someone over triggering emotions or killing someone accidentally. Stabbing someone once to kill differs from stabbing more than 100 times to kill. All crimes, all consequences, situations are different.

Once the prison world opens for anyone, it introduces a new world within it. It becomes the real world for prisoners for the next few years. Most of them are swallowed by that world permanently. While people get a chance to meet and know others like them at that time, developing connections and conversations between them sometimes lead them to terrible things. I didn't mean to say one should not communicate with others in prison, but the surroundings, behaviours of wardens, the way they are treated over there make them stubborn. It led them to a volatile situation. It encourages them to do more when they come back out of prison.

When crime happens under a specific circumstance, controllers implement preventive measures for that particular circumstance only. It hasn't changed till now. They make a note of the reason, but noting it down won't help anywhere if the government doesn't implement plans to address the reasons. Elsewhere, for the same reason, crime will happen under different circumstances anyway. Governments need to concentrate on reasons to reduce crimes. They should not increase precautions for those circumstances or instances. Whatever precautions we take, do not matter; incidents will happen somehow with loopholes for similar reasons. Governments never care about reasons, but they care about crimes because of them. Governments want that to stop, but they fail to understand that without stopping the reason, they can't stop crime. Do they want reasons to exist to make the world entertaining for news channels and social media? Or are they afraid of eliminating the reason due to political pressure and political philosophies? Why does the government think it's hypothetical to eliminate reasons? Structural changes are required to eliminate the reasons. It's not possible with current political philosophies.

Punishments are a crucial part of justice. When something wrong happened, justice would be provided. Punishments are provided based on the severity of the crime. As far as I know, robbing and stealing are not crimes because society pushes individuals into a situation. It's not taken care of them. If we want to provide justice, then punishment should be given to society for pushing them. We have to provide justice for the wrong system of justice first.

The severity of punishment decides whether a person lives or not. If they live, how many years they need to serve in prison. We have to change the structure and atmosphere of punishments because whatever has been followed from the kingdom to till date has not changed people for any good. Punishment should make prisoners realise what they did, what it caused to their surroundings, and prepare them to be good in the future. However, instead of that, we are locking them in empty cells attached to toilets, controlling, treating them like animals by wardens, and releasing them with the horrible experience of prisons. This will not make them change. By the way, it will give prisoners confidence in their abilities. They get a confident mindset; when they do wrong, they become more conscious while doing wrong. They make sure to escape from the situation without anyone's notice; even if the patrol caught them, it means just a prison. This 'just a prison' mindset encourages them to commit more crimes. When people with high power use them as their pawns and accomplish what they want without a trace of them, at that time, they are developing a new level of confidence that we have someone to back them up.

That is why we need structural change in judgements and punishments. A kingdom of fools and selfish ministers started it. We are following it without change.

Mentally rulers developed a mindset that "I am superior to everyone," it evolved, then it conquered the ministers as well. Control is more like a rope. When we loosen it, more irregularities happen, but when we tighten it, it means more trouble. People may die because of it or they will kill rulers who control. People liberate themselves from those rulers. The rope should be in a position to save people from falling. It should neither be tight nor loose.

When rulers had a superior mentality, they behaved over-controlling, disrespectful, and irresponsible towards the constituency. This didn't allow anyone to analyse what was happening. It made them overconfident. Since no one around rulers speaks the truth about the ground reality. If messengers spoke the truth that hurts rulers, then rulers didn't like it, and messengers might get killed because of telling the truth. People are scared of the ruler's mood swings.

These types of rulers went to wars unreasonably due to that wealth of the city reduced. It was affected citizen's economical situation. Many people lost their lives on these instance.

Humans can forget the good that happened to them, but they can't forget the bad that happened to them naturally. The world values bad more than good because good always has positive reinforcement, even if we don't mind, that won't affect anyone badly. There is no harm in good. So good people in those days were not much celebrated and recognised. Most of the good habits are influenced by good people in ancient days, but we don't have a record of who said or started them; Evil is not like that. It's opposite from good. Evil things are always spoken about continuously. People never forget it. All the bad always has a disastrous ending. Why is bad always spoken about a lot? It's because while we are speaking, we are passing information to others, and then others will pass that to somebody else. This is how the news gets spread across lands. People try to fight the bad and close it once and for all. So, when people pass that as much as possible, then only everyone knows the reality of the bad. If people don't share, others can't know what is evil. Ruthless superior mentality rulers continue doing their evil things. They hurt people. That's why bad has more influence on people. Why, even after so many years, we remember it! because our genes subconsciously know its pain. Genetically, everyone doesn't want that sort of situation again. If we forget, a lousy person might get a chance to rise again in the world. So, to speak, people consciously avoid the reincarnation of that bad in the world.

That is why 100 thousand good queens and kings are not registered in history, but almost all bad and worst kings and queens are registered. They are in people's minds till now to avoid the threat.

One **worst** king is equal to a million people's deaths, so there is no wrong in valuing **bad** more.

So currently as well, we have a few evil rulers in the world because every bad always has a new face. It develops itself from previous events. If we do not remember the previous one, it will come in the same form again. It's better not to forget. We have responsibilities to rule out the evil rulers that we have today, but who is terrible? We don't know unless their people and officials expose that with evidence, proof.

What did we do against bad in ancient times? People can't tolerate bad all the time. They also have diminishing marginal utility. Once it's reached means they don't have any control over peace; they want this to stop anyhow and at any cost. Hence, they start a mutiny against rulers and their rules. People express their odium to hit the king hard. They will stop once the king surrenders to them. People will stop after rulers obey the tenets they want. When that does not work, people plot assassination against rulers and their families to get rid of rulers once and for all. They take over the kingdom to start a new beginning. When a mutiny starts, what would kings do? They start to control people worse than ever. Rulers torture critical leaders of that mutiny who are the backbone of the mutiny then kill them. It's like a cat and mouse game. The mouse is the king, and the cat is the people. Why am I saying that the cat is the people? Because it's hungry. The cat wants to get rid of the mouse to calm itself peacefully.

Mutiny has kept its structure the same from the beginning till now. It's in the same form; if a ruler does something that does not have the support of the people, it means mutiny will start. Rulers in the kingdom-controlled people with the force they had; now, presidents, prime ministers and a few dictators are doing the same. They will make the military control people and then make them silent.

As I said earlier, in protective masks, I always wonder, what is the difference between city patrol and the military? The military's duty is to save the country from outside threats, but in times of domestic war, it will control its people who pay for their military force through taxes. At the same time, patrol acts against people's protests. I am not sure when there is a valid protest for a valid reason why the patrol and the military control them. As I said, one thing is sure, patrol should not be under the supervision of rulers. Because they are serving people and safeguarding people from bad situations. So, they are always responsible to people, not to rulers, but they are controlled and directed by the government. The expected structure is far from what we currently have here. If we want to rate our structure, it is 5 out of 10; it never achieves excellence until we structurally change.

Employment is an area that tends to serve its employer. From the kingdom to now, everyone is attached to the employment structure. How did this employment start? The world never employed anyone in the first place. All are independent and found food wherever they go. This is why they never know how to please anyone except their mates. When we introduced the concept of queen and king, we offered them wealth and manpower. That's when humans started working for other humans. Rulers started using them for their luxuries. People never questioned because they wanted their rulers to be free of their daily routines to think and act without day-to-day routine tensions. So slowly it greened the lands with employment. Powerful people employed servants; wealthy people employed servants. People started to find comfort in employment. People collectively registered a wrong perception as employment is an excellent safety. It evolved in many ways. More than 60% of people are employed worldwide by someone. What the employer is taking away from employees is their portion of life, their contribution, their time. They make us beg for promotion and increment primarily, but I am not comparing the world population with 5 to 7% of talented and manipulative workers. Employers offer us pressure, tension, competition, finally little and very little money.

In the kingdom, rulers enjoyed our protection and slavery; currently, rulers enjoy our protection and service. In the history of humanity, what drastic change did we find in the employment field? PF, is it? Gratuity, is it? Insurance, is it? Pension, is it? No, but we actively accepted that it is safe for life. We accepted all advantages taken on us then smiled with ignorance. We accepted that genius people or people who invested only deserve to enjoy profit in the world.

Geniuses will employ people for their inventions then get all credibility and profitability based on employee's work. Employees are structuring the founded items, organising it, marketing it, upgrading it. People worked hard for it and they benefit from salary and maybe a promotion somewhere in the future. It's the structure. There is no "but" here. When initiating a new business or product in the business world, Employees are a significant part of it. Employees are only doing fieldwork for that business. Profit belongs to entrepreneurs, geniuses or people who invested when the business earns profit based on that idea, but do Employees enjoy profit equally as them? Any business or government ready to share their wealth equally with everyone who works for them? The answer is 'No'. The employer always stays as an employer. The worker mostly stays as a worker unless they come out from the structure then try to be an employer. When a business goes downhill, it will affect the employer, the worker who depends on it will also be affected. No one is ready to hire failed company workers. Employees sometimes can't find another job. Not every employee will suffer, but a few will definitely suffer. It's how it is; that's what society will tell. Employees must save from their salary to survive uncertain situations. It's the political structure.

Government or private, whatever it may be, they only want employees, not partners. The government will use the money to structure the country. The private sector will use money to structure companies.

As I said earlier, even if we become an employer from the employee, we won't try to change anything in a significant structure. It remains constant because of the fear of being an odd one out.

WBE never makes anyone an employee, but it will make everyone partners.

I am damn sure in the coming future the population will definitely reduce because most of us are not interested in conceiving more than one baby. I am not being negative here but realistic. Birth only happens when a man and woman want it. A baby comes into the world with its parents' wish. Babies grow up emulating their parents for some time, but when babies grow up and realise the world, that's when they start their journey.

How do they start their journey? They start by knowing things, analysing, and decrypting their purpose. When grown up, they will decide what education they need for analysing and decrypting.

In the kingdom of fools and selfish ministers, children's education was more about knowing and learning what their parents did. Children of queens and kings learned fighting, horsing, managing, strategies of war. In ancient days, parents were the only teachers, but then it started changing. Everyone went to teachers apart from their parents and then started learning new horizons. It was the starting stage of schooling. Few people wanted to know more than daily routines like physics, astrophysics, machines, arts, sports, multiple items they discovered on their own little by little through every single mistake. They discovered much in space and recorded them in history. These evolved slowly. We have structured our education system almost well. Few drawbacks are there, but still, it's not that bad. We made our education system and educators well-versed with their skills in most places. Our education system in the 19th and 20th centuries has given us Tesla, Einstein, Che Guevara, Beethoven, Wilma Rudolph. The education system should develop the thinking capacity of humans toward growth. Everyone is unique in the world. The education system unites everyone and introduces them to society. A healthy society can only be built by a sound education system universally. Good books can be a better teacher and sometimes they're better than teachers.

As per Darwin's theory of evolution, humans evolved from animals. We're learning from each other. Each and everything in the world evolved from millions of groups. Groups give strength to each other. In that group, the best one learns all. They create a mark but without that million in groups, the evolution is nothing but zero.

Learning from each other is happening continuously from when one cell species started its life in the world. We are competing with each other to get improved. Big competitors inspire us. Everyone has a peak point in their life. At that peak point, no one can beat them. Anyways, it's a cycle, when something is at that peak will always come to an end. This peak point will become a target for the next coming competitors. Everyone will try to break that peak point. Eventually, that peak will fade away one day, and multiple peaks will come, but one can't achieve anything without learning how the previous peak happened.

In the kingdom of fools and selfish ministers, they created a block on those competitions. They created a circle for royals. They competed with each other, after that learned and ruled lands. This block of competition made people stay under them and be controlled by rulers. These blockages stopped evolution for some time, but learning again started. People threw kingdoms away in most places, made learning alive, and cleared blockers.

On the topic of selfish ministers, they have been controlled under the oath of rulers. They have to obey orders from their queens and kings. Unless the council of ministers is strong and sound to their queen and king, they won't make the king and queen obey their advice. In most places, ministers had a weak council. They don't have control over the actions of kings and queens, but in a few places, councils led rulers to the destructive path for their wellbeing and wealth. These ministers sometimes avoid advising rulers to make them go down so they can seal the throne.

Few places' Ministers controlled the country over the name of queens and kings. Ministers are responsible for their kings and queens' performance because others can't ask about things directly to rulers, but ministers can do it. They act like a bridge to people, officials, and rulers. Rulers control most of the fields in the land except in a time of war. Ministers hold power to organise during that time. Sometimes they created war and encouraged war by knowing other countries' weaknesses. They are ones who acted in both ways, like a backbone and backstabbers.

The reality is ministers created society's structure long ago. They earned through that for their families, but they have not tried to improvise it after some point in time.

What are Ministers doing currently in the government? They are being the reason for structuring the government in a better place.

Somewhere at some time, they are being the reason for destroying people's lives. There are both good and bad aspects which are unavoidable. Few ministers are approving plan for bribe which are not well-organised. Few ministers are hiding their wealth in benami names. Few ministers are scamming the government for their own wealth. They are trying to overshadow leaders, as I said earlier. They also have a desire to occupy the leader's chair. If they are following the democratic way to achieve their desire, then it's absolutely fine. Sometimes, it's not the case.

Technologies have developed a lot, that's the reason humans are simplifying works continuously and increasing protections. All kings and queens wanted some shield in those days to protect their land for a lifetime, but it never happened. Currently, leaders are also trying. They will never stop until they find one. I am proud of technology from the kingdom of fools to now. We have found many technologies in this world. Finally, technologies are the ones that are going to make the world equal for everyone.

We keep following many bad things, but it's still not wiped out all humanity in the world. We travelled so far and reached here, but we have to be careful going forward. The evolution of the bad may happen through technologies as well. There are both good and bad aspects in evolving. The good is that we can expand our comforts through technologies. We are connected with everyone through technology. The bad is that it's easy to wipe out humans using technologies. Corporates have to stop the fight among them in the name of ultra advanced AI technology advancement, which only advanced supercomputers can handle or control. We should not allow any technological advancement that humans can't absolutely control.

Seven

Failed 6th Sense

Earth is a peaceful place to live happily and equally. All countries are friendly to each other. All humans are friendly with each other, the work-life balance in the world is splendid. Humanity on earth is exquisite. People respect nature; they are doing their best to restore balance. All animals, birds, and sea creatures are protected from harm. Families and children are supporting each other. They live in high spirits globally. Governments and legal systems are ultimately protecting people. All companies in the world are empowering people equally and globally. Humans are in good health. All technologies are serving humans to go to another level. People united over divinity and spirituality. Everyone is doing work that they care about. Everyone has independence over their voice.

We can call this one paragraph of hallucination, phantasm, fantasy, mirage, a figment of imagination, or whatever we want. World people are living under this above paragraph currently. Only 125 plus words of mass communication influenced us to believe we were absolutely fine. Is it entirely true what's in that paragraph? Not a single line over there is true, but for a few people, their circumstances changed their world like that, I am happy for those people. What about others? In India, Mothers feed their babies by showing the moon in ancient times but currently most of them feed their babies by showing the television or YouTube, babies are mesmerised by its beauty and forget what their moms are forcing inside their tiny mouths. Even though we have outgrown that, we are still that baby. Only a few things changed. Our mother is our society, the moon is the first paragraph. All disasters society forces on us by showing the first paragraph are food. Mother knows it's the only way to make the baby eat the crap, but even a baby can't tolerate over some limit if it's too bad.

I am one among that babies who can't tolerate anymore, I wish you to be one among the babies along with me.

More babies did not come out of mesmerised feelings about delusion. What is happening? My mom forcing me; my dad forcing me; my brothers and sisters forcing me; my grandparents forcing me; my wife forcing me; my children forcing me; my friends forcing me; my study forcing me; my teachers forcing me; my work forcing me; my colleagues forcing me; my house forcing me; my car forcing me; my road forcing me; my food forcing me; my foes forcing me; myself is forcing me but for what? All are forced to behave. Behave how? Behave by stopping expressing my true self. What is my true self? Being independent is my true self. What do I mean by independent? I want to be independent in a way, acting like I want, wherever doesn't matter. The only thing that matters is that I'm doing what I like and it doesn't harm or damage anyone. But society changed all the above as forces to stop me from being my true self. It achieved and we practiced ignoring it consciously, being happy along with it wearing masks.

Someone stupidly told me, 'Find happiness even in difficulty.' One nasty statement was created to make people silent, dumb, introverted. Physical or mental, whatever difficulties it may be, most people are practiced to tolerate for some time because whatever pain it may be, it's never going to last 24/7. Our brain and our support systems make it calm over some time. When difficulty lasts intolerably, disasters happen, like killing or taking their own life to escape from it physically and emotionally. People wrongly interpret making it calm, being normal, being away from the pain for some time as happiness. If we see deeply, they don't know that it's wrong. In their situation, it's the only thing they can do, they are not in a position to single-handedly resolve problems. It may be depressing, but it's the truth. Whenever people see difficulties in the system, they immediately visualise the vast structure made that difficulty behind it and judge themselves. Most of them feel that they are not in a position to put an end to it. So, they are left with no choice but to remain silent, that silence moulded them to be in a broken system with unrealistic happiness with real pain. When we think about any difficulties, we see the broken system behind it. Ethically it's not right. People need to be heard by the system. The system should be ready to make changes, that's the only way to be ethical. It's not easy. People should handle difficulty, but at the same time, they should open it up in social forums. The only way to end the difficulty is to face it as a group. It will put an end to being ignorant. I encourage all to open up about their difficulty. It's challenging, I know.

"Find happiness even in challenges" is a correct and accurate statement. Challenges make people happy apart from a win and lose. What is the difference between difficulty and challenge? If we have guts and a risky solution. If we can make it possible with certain risks. If we have the guts to take that risk, then it's a challenge. If we have pain, no solution but we have to come across it anyway means it's difficulty. We consciously ignore the pain and tell ourselves it's not that painful.

People are living their whole life in the world and dealing with real pain. When they want some break from their reality, they seek adventures, thrill experiences, fantasy movies, books. Most people are not encouraging painful close-to-reality movies mostly because they are already facing that for their whole life. They don't want to experience that while relaxing too. People like fantasy, comedy, horror, and adventure movies. They enjoy and experience fantasy and love, and action, thrillers.

People do not like to face real-life pain when they are relaxing. They are enjoying themselves in their own imaginations or in others' imaginations. I never said it was wrong or right. I am not arguing that people enjoy these because they suffer from all life issues, they are creating alternative worlds in their imaginations. In the future, these entertainments will go to the next level, but will pain from the world vanish?

Nothing wrong with enjoying love, music, action, comedy, fantasy movies, books, adventures, and thrills. We should continue doing that for eternity, but we should not practice enjoying that for ignoring the pain in life and ignoring world issues. We can't tolerate real-world issues for eternity. We should find a solution for people's wellbeing.

Most people enjoy it when someone raises their voice against oppression and bullying, but most people do not initiate that in places where it is happening. We are just passing those things regularly. We really have the desire to rise against it, but at the same time, we prefer to avoid catching the attention of others. We don't always have time for that. We hate that oppression, but since everyone agrees to it, we are not likely to create a scene by being against it. It's a typical statement as everyone is disappointed, but most of us do not like to rise against it. Even if someone raises, they will not get proper support. There are many global diversions to turn people's attention from issues. We are good at falling for it.

Everyone in the world knows about sex, but no one talks about it openly in public places in many countries. It's even worse we made that a bad word. Globally we are growing nearly 8 billion because of that one word, but it's symbolised as a bad word in public. It's a great joke in the world. It represents that we all like to do bad things to get supreme pleasure. We portrayed it as a bad thing instead of speaking and understanding, analysing; it may be because people think that "Without understanding and speaking, we grew this fast and do it much often. What if it becomes a talkable topic? Does the world have the capacity to hold that much population?"

Most countries have laws against viewing porn videos. I honestly agree that viewing and making child porn should be a punishable and deadly offence. Sometimes even though the government bans it, people are gonna watch porn anyway by hiding their location online through VPNs. I am not talking about child porn in this. I am strictly against it. Regular porn videos are a multibillion-dollar business worldwide currently. Society has made all acute problems unspeakable and made them more complicated like sex. It's also one of ignorance. It's a societal behaviour that is shiftable when generations change. The same sort of issue we have in all problems.

90s Kids started parenting. In 2030, most of the old habits and cultures that 70s and 80s people followed eventually vanished like old phones. Kids will get knowledge of many things that older adults are unfamiliar with. Constructive parenting methods only make a good human being, not ignoring and hiding or holding back methods. It's not going to help.

People who cannot control their actions, sufferings, or feelings may self-harm themselves in a few places; they derive some satisfaction from that pain. It makes them feel alive. It is a mental issue; there are more problems in the world; many mental issues exist. People living in more difficult surroundings are affected by many mental issues. When they continuously face issues that make them uneasy, they consciously believe in unreal things and arrogantly argue that it's true at that time. Most of them stop socialising due to this. They need to start anew. Some procedures might help them, like changing places, stopping contact with their old contacts, and connecting with new people. They can control this illness with medical treatments.

The reason why I brought this up? Because mental issues are commonly caused by surroundings, for example, family, relatives, friends, coworkers, superiors, teachers, bullies, neighbours, unhealthy places, unclean places. We are surrounded by others. We must be good to each other. We should keep places clean and good. We have to respect others' opinions. So that way, they respect us. We have to discuss our problems with them. If they do not like us, we better leave them alone instead of making their life harder. When we take responsibility, society takes responsibility, these issues will vanish. There are more cases out there, which means we are one of the reasons. It is due to ignorance.

These mental issues in a few places are not only affecting individuals. Affected people become psychopaths. They attack and harm others, as I said earlier.

Trust, believe, and devotion are the most underrated things. People waste most of their time trusting, believing, and devoting to the wrong leaders and things. People are attracted to a few people's talents. People follow them, dedicating themselves. People do anything for them. Even though leaders are wrong, people go to any extent for what they like. They won't accept even when we show all evidence to them and prove they are wrong. All good speakers and talented people can't be good leaders. These people use their followers to earn as much as possible. Leaders use followers for their growth. Leaders manipulate people to do wrong things in their favour. What is the return people get for that? It's "satisfaction", "pleasure," nothing else. This kind of satisfaction and pleasure is not meaningful. It may seem worthy in the early 20s and teenage years, but it will not help us evolve and grow.

Everyone is unique in their way, but wasting our life on some bullshit is wrong. The foremost matter is they are enjoying it, which makes them believe it's not wrong. Hitler had this sort of followers; It's only at a significant level; even in small villages, we could see people following the wrong persons. It's not possible to dislike someone who instantly seems attractive, but once we like them, we have to ensure that we are not falling for wrong. We should not act blindfolded. It's ignorance.

We are slowly recovering from the employment gap between genders. Countries like the United States have made it possible because, in that country, more women are working than men, as of 2020 data. China is close to it, Australia, and the United Kingdom are near less than five percentage gaps. All countries are trying very hard to achieve equilibrium. India is one of the worst countries in the gender gap. People have not realised the importance of gender equality. Arab countries, Iran, and Afghanistan have more gaps. The people and governments of these countries should work on this issue. They should encourage women to do more. More gaps indicate the chauvinistic nature of men in those countries. So, overlooking something like this makes them worse. The world has been out of kingdoms and dictators in most places for the last 60 years. It's slowly changing to equilibrium in gender. People's knowledge about the importance of it matters most. In most places, people ignore such things. It's not going to help.

Countries like this have more barriers, such as caste, religion, gender discrimination, and outdated cultures. It is the reason women are not coming out and working. The lack of independence for women makes it difficult to survive. Women do not have the freedom to choose their life partner in a few places.

Lets compare the best with the worst in the gender gap. USA vs India. India has more cultural barriers than the United States. Indian cultures restrict women from coming out independently in most places. The structure of countries is constructed based on different backgrounds. The independence of these countries matters. The United States gained independence on July 4th, 1776. India gained independence on August 15th, 1947. The United States gained independence 171 years before India. The constitution of the United States started educating their people 171 years before India. Whereas in India, they started just 75 years before.

India was drowning under religious beliefs when it gained independence. These religions forced women to stay at home. National leaders, the father of the nation Gandhi, begged people to send women to schools, work in multiple forums. The situation slowly changed, but the speed was not enough. Most people do not even consider Gandhi's words when it comes to religion and culture. People were so mad about their religions in the early 1940s to 1960s. Parenting methods in these countries played a vital role. American parents in most places groomed their kids independently, whether girls or boys. They allowed them to live outside when they crossed 18. This action made their kids realise independence. It allowed them to work and live without struggle. The Indian parenting method is peculiar; they groomed boys like Americans and showed partiality to women.

Regarding life partner selection, the United States treats boys and girls similarly. The majority of Indians never gave them the independence to do what they wanted. This ignorance continued for a long time due to India having a larger gender gap.

More countries were still out there with kings, dictators, military rulers, and many more reasons unable to solve gender gaps.

---------------------------------cc---------------------------cc---------------------

Climate change in the world slowly started gaining its deserved attention. Scientists have been warning for the last 20 years about it actively. The Nobel Prize for Physics was given to scientists who researched climate conditions in the year 2021. Humans started polluting the earth's atmosphere without their knowledge, but the issue is they're not caring about it even after that came into their knowledge.

Governments concentrate more on profit than on its existence. It's like cigarettes. People know if they smoke, it will kill them, but they do it anyway for happiness and relief. Governments are doing the same in this case—cold-hearted ignorance. The government is also doing it only for money and relief because they didn't find other ways to lead the economy. Governments have just started supporting the climate. A few decades back, the government did not implemented climax control policies and measures it due to trade competitions and insecurities. "Greta Thunberg," remember the name? The 2019 United Nations summit about climatic change, the "HOW DARE YOU?" speech gained the world's attention. We must be more careful and worried about our children's future because it will be more difficult. We have to accept one thing, that we're also responsible for polluting the world. No one is an exception in this matter. We can reduce, but someone, somewhere is polluting it anyway. Few countries are keeping their environment clean but polluting others. As I said earlier, I will explain more about climatic conditions in the coming topics.

Law is constructed to settle only for justice and truth. Humans and animals, what is the difference? We constructed law, but animals don't. I have to confess that, without the law adequately followed, we are also 6-sense animals, even worse than animals. Animals at least have a few basic laws, like saving fellow mates in danger, sharing food, alerting friends in a critical situation.

All we want is the world we deserve. Even if we got everything but not the law, we deserved means, then all we got is just bullshit that will disappear even before we blink our eyes. We agree love is fundamental for constructing a healthy humanity, but without ground rules, we can't make a sensible society with humanity. I am saying this because we can't forgive all rule-breakers out of love in the name of humanity. These laws and ground rules will remind society that there are consequences if we break them, which will make us better humans in the future.

We know the above paragraph is globally well-known; based on this, the world is operating under current political philosophies. We get to know what sort of political philosophies are running around the world after reading all chapters. We must acknowledge that even though laws operate around money, which has many flaws, they are constructed in a way that people should adhere to them. Laws are well-constructed everywhere so that no one can question their honesty because the law is equal for everyone. As per the current economy, manipulators and influencers often bend it to their benefit without a trace. Honesty is not precisely defined by its meaning. People who studied law know its actual sense. The law is constructed in a way that never allows us to question its true colour. If we even try to touch it or its shadow, it means it will go to any extent to symbolise us as terrorists and traitors in most cases or it ignores our voice by diverting people to other stuff.

I am not saying that all terrorists and traitors are questioned the law that constructed because of it they are forced to become terrorists or traitors; I am ready to give the benefit of the doubt. They became one because of little things the world doesn't care about. It may be little thing for the world but its not little for the people who got affected.

The law only favours truth; is it true? Yes, but sometimes even truth lies. Justice depends on how the judge wants to deliver it. All over the world, how many corporates are there? How many lawyers and law firms are there? How many cases are pending? How many people settle only for truth? How many cases settle without trial? According to the most recently available statistics, about 95 percent of pending lawsuits end in a pre-trial settlement. About 97 percent of civil cases are settled or dismissed without a trial. Plea deals are somewhat okay. They accept the guilt they committed, but innocents also take it because they cannot afford the price of the law. The government's budget is not encouraging government lawyers to go to the extent it is needed to prove their innocence.

Corporate firms do anything over the line, they usually settle their misconduct via money, even the death of hundreds of people just like that settled in money. It should not happen that they should be punished without mercy. Few lawyers are doing that and able to keep that going, but most of the time, corporates cover all their dark activities well with loopholes of the law with the help of law firms. They are monetising grey areas of law very well, like avoiding tax,

Depositions happen to discover both sides of the truth. Once the actual material of truth is discovered, they will proceed forward with what sort of punishments to be given. Corporate crimes are not that easy to discover. If it's discovered, they will settle with money and close it well ahead.

Most people fear going to court because of its failed systems, but they are not taking further action. Instead, they are just ignoring it.

Another thing is a biased judgement based on caste, racial, and gender discrimination. We don't know how many people were discriminated. What sort of ignorance are people engaging in? I am not sure. Rumi's famous quote says, "there is a place beyond right and wrong, and I will meet you there," maybe all lawmakers and breakers are already there. They are discussing how to make things even worse.

We are seeking absolute pleasure throughout our entire life. How many of us find and get that entirely throughout our life? Do we know what we like to do? Few know that doing what we like is our most wanted thing. Few of them know that it's their purpose in life; even if situations do not help, they move towards that their entire life. They will get absolute pleasure on their journey, but few do the opposite. They know their purpose, but they don't start their journey for their entire life. They blame situations for those matters; those sorts of people never feel absolute pleasure. If you ask me, "Do people who have already reached their purpose feel absolute pleasure for their entire life?" Yes and No. Why Yes and why No? Most people do not achieve it. Why do they not achieve it? They think of it as a journey, then fixing one unachievable purpose after another and enjoying that absolute pleasure which stays for a short period. Who is declaring whether it's achieved or not? It's the world and sometimes it's the universe within us, that means ourselves. Most people like to do something beyond what they have reached and enjoy short-term absolute pleasure. There are several types of people in the world who have a different perspective about purpose. For a few of them, they fix only one purpose. They work towards that to achieve it all their life. If they achieve it, then they satisfy themselves with it. Their body, mind, soul, heart, guts will stop pushing them, then accept the peace of that achievement. They calm themselves with it. They do not feel like going after another. They stay in the peace of absolute pleasure for their entire life.

Most of us ignore our purpose; we do something to lead a life for our surroundings. So, this mentally makes people feel emptiness even though they have everything; they can't feel soulful happiness if they haven't found their purpose and moved towards it.

The world is continuously battling for survival. People always want to be in a race. In every aspect of life, some unwanted race is going on continuously. When something is limited, naturally there will be competition and fight to get that thing. When we have that something in our hands at that time, we feel like we have achieved. When it's not achieved, we lose in a race, self-doubt will create fear of missing out, which will lead a few people to do anything to get that something. The fear of missing out exists in all fields. When there is one delicious burger, but there are three people, when there is one promotion, there are 12 people. In countries like India, where there are only 1000 government job openings, there are 1000000 people. This lack of supply creates unwanted demand. It makes people feel the fear of missing out. So, to cope with society's standards, they choose to live the way society wants them to live, like doing an unsatisfying job. If we fail in studies, we will have a fear of missing out on a job. If we fail at a job, we will have a fear of missing out on a happy life. Failure will lead people to fear of missing out. It will create unwanted scolding and pressure in life. There will be pressure in all aspects, from A-to-Z; we could identify the fear of missing out in all those aspects. Sometimes this mentality makes people fall for unwanted things they don't want, but since the crowd is rushing to get it in fear of missing out, those who don't understand and don't want it also start to rush for it.

----------------------------------cc--cc-------

This whole book is about keeping up with responsibility. Every chapter in this book touches on responsibility. What is responsibility? Responsible or accountable or in charge of doing something. Our responsibilities change from place to place while living in a society. When we are at work, we will have specific responsibilities. When we are at public places, we will have specific responsibilities. When we are part of the family, we will have certain responsibilities. The list goes on.

Individual responsibility and group responsibility, many types of responsibilities are there. Does everyone in every place take care of this responsibility?

Society is structured to take responsibility in every place, but is it happening? The grey area is something being in shades that's not the right, but at the same time, that's not defined as wrong in any place. So, people are always looking for a grey area in all the fields. They like to escape from the crowd and make life easier. When people start thinking about it, they get to know it.

People always categorise responsibilities' priority. For some people, family is the priority. They will take all family-related responsibilities into their hands and don't give more attention to all other responsibilities. For a few people, it's work. For a few people, it's society; the list goes on. Everyone will not give equal importance to all their responsibilities. If a person takes responsibility for A, then that person will not take the same amount of responsibility for B, C, and D things. It applies to everyone. It makes a big impact globally. The world lost many things due to a lack of responsibilities of people. If two people are in love, it's their responsibility to take protection while making love unless they want a baby. Some people are choosing adventure over responsibility, which sometimes results in unwanted loss to people. They can escape 9 out of 10 times, but one time they have to face reality. When it happens, it's too late to realise. Maybe for some people, luck can favour all ten times, but not many.

You can think about your previous day and count how many responsibilities you neglected. You got affected by how many things due to others neglecting their responsibility. Your affected list is bigger than your neglected list. Sometimes we don't even know our neglected list but others who affected count it on their affected list. It's a boomerang. It always comes back harder than we throw. If we take responsibility for ten out of ten things and inspire others to take their 10 out of 10, it will take the domino effect as simple as that, but it's not as simple as we all know. It takes much more time than we think. If you understand what I am saying, destruction is always faster than construction. If we are frustrated then start taking 0 out of 10 things, the collapse we will cause is immersive for us. It's not always 0. It's not always ten, but it's somewhere between 3 to 4 as of now. Suppose it goes somewhere between 7 to 8 means that is when we can see the real change. We can't blame anyone for not taking any responsibility unless they are our blood relatives. At the same time, we can't praise everyone for taking all the responsibilities. So, think about the importance of keeping up with it. It's the ignorance of responsibility.

We all know moving on from failure or something heartbreaking is as hard as moving the Himalayas from one place to another. Pain that holds time and body, mind forever for a few people. They will not come out of it for a long period. Even if they would like to come out of that pain, it makes them feel impossible to try again. Pain will create unkind and stupid anger towards themselves. It hurts them more than a gunshot whenever that incident comes to mind.

The heartbreaking loss of a loved one makes moving on so hard. Happiness and memories that person shared with us make a permanent hole in the heart. Pain will not allow any other sense to work. It occupies the whole body. Time is the only solution that makes its impact lesser. For some people, it stays still then kills their inner peace forever, but it's inevitable to overcome pain. People who can move on have big chances of success and happiness. If there is a failure, people should not get stuck on the spot and feel sad then hold back themselves, but reasons for failures must be researched. We should never repeat them. Work on other methods to achieve goals instead of fearing an outcome. As everyone says, trust the process. Most people stop trying once they fail. We have to always try on items that we like most. Moving on is vital that we have to remember. People are ignoring moving on sometimes. There is a difference between moving on from loss and moving on from failure. Time heals the loss and attempts with corrective action overcome the failure with success.

All other ignorance directly impacts society, but ignorance of moving on will impact society indirectly. Moving on is a matter of feelings and mind. When a person is not moving on, it will affect that person's work and surroundings. This outcome indirectly impacts society. A healthy society needs healthy-minded people. Without them, we can't lead a happy and peaceful life.

Health is important for spending life on earth happily and peacefully. Healthiness, happiness, and peacefulness are interdependent. One can't live without the others. So, people are always searching for one of these in their life. It's philosophical, but it's true. If anyone gets all these three for a lifelong means, then the earth is a living haven for them. Most of us are not fortunate to get all three together. For a few of them, they were born as differently abled. They are unhealthy in others' vision.

People who are born differently abled don't even know what is normal actually. For them, they are normal, but people look at them in a manner of poor kindness and mercy. It hurts differently abled people. Couples do a scan when they are pregnant. If they get to know about the child's condition not being good and well, they will consider aborting. Some go through a complicated process and care for their child for their entire life. Both are brave decisions. At the end of the day, it's their life to decide to carry on or stop. We should not judge or give advice to go through or stop. We can explain situations and consequences to them. It's what most medical professionals do. The same should be done by relatives and friends as well because parents will be in a confused state of mind to carry on or stop. We should not manipulate them at that time. Why am I bringing this up when it's not even the topic of the failed sixth sense? It's more relevant than anything else when discussing decision-making in hard situations. The human mind and senses will be wandering around multiple thoughts and perceptions. It will not be stable when it's the sudden situation of life or death that is not prepared for. The mind likes to run around on others' opinions, advice, suggestions. Many people fail in making a decision. Their brain grabs others' opinion. It takes that as a decision because of that it suffers a lot. It is argumentative when it comes to manipulation. Whose fault is it? The person who manipulates is doing it for several reasons. They manipulate for selfishness or they manipulate for others' wellness. The person who gets manipulated is used by others.

Once the purpose is over, they get ignored by others. We decisively can't tell that decision-making should be done like this or like that. We have to consider this or consider that. It may be quick or slow. Group decision is better or solo decision is better. It's hypothetical. It depends on situations. We should not be manipulated by others while making decisions. We should not manipulate others for our good. It's a sense-related thing. Everyone faces deadly situations and makes the most critical decisions that sometimes change humanity and sometimes destroy humanity.

As human beings, health is important, but how many of us take it seriously? All medical scientists are working on extending the average lifespan of humans. I like to bring this up now. Most people do not take care of their health. They are just handling their body as if they have taken it for granted, which is why in the first place most diseases are not found in the first stage. Regular body check-ups are not happening due to people not caring about them. Is it because of fear, or is it because of expenses, or is it because of carelessness? Ignorance of self-health leads to the most dangerous diseases.

Why is ignorance worse? One ignorance will lead us to other ignorance. We don't even remember why we are doing it. What generally happens when society collectively starts being ignorant? Collective ignorance can be taken as an advantage by someone who wants to profit from it. For example, humans are structured to work during the day and rest at night. So, most people in the world follow the same. Few people from ancient times worked in the world at night, not permanently but in basic shifts. This, too, is primarily for protection purposes, such as being safe from enemies. When humans started being ignorant of health, corporations also wanted to use it in their favour. In the name of globalisation, multinational corporations started spoiling human health voluntarily for profits. In the name of development, saving the economy from getting spoiled & defaulting, all underdeveloped nations are forced to push their people to work in this health-spoiling environment. Countries like that started chemical factories and drinks factories because parent countries of corporations are not allowed to spoil their people's health. The same corporate wants to save money that costs more labour fees. They want to transfer work to less labour-cost-efficient countries like India and the Philippines. They don't care about employees' health or people's health. They want service to be the same day regarding global clocks because their business is at stake. So, they don't care if employees do the night shift daily for ten years and 15 years. Employees don't mind spoiling their self-health due to personal situations. Corporates compensate with a "night shift allowance." for spoiling health. For example, suppose an IT professional Has five years of experience. In that case, an Indian employee gets 5,25,000 INR yearly, which means that for the same job, an American fresher employee gets 4,50,000 INR monthly as per its currency conversion. If we take purchasing power parity into account, it's still 1 to 3 times more. So, if corporations care about our health that gets spoiled, at least 30% of the amount they provide what Americans are getting, but they are just providing 10% of what Americans are getting. So, corporates don't care if our country says no because 100s of countries out there want that opportunity. They can't say no because chains of ignorance have already spoiled them as much as possible. Someone is always out there ready to say yes if someone says no. The economy is structured in that way. We can't say it's just a tiny ignorance; if we collectively put it together, the picture will stand crashing sky. All countries have to stand their ground for human health as 1st priority over products. What bad will happen if work goes out one day later? Earth will explode, won't it? We need to structure the business. So, people's health won't get spoiled, but we can't because money is 1st motive in the current political philosophy; the reason is ignorance. The same happened with deadly chemicals, cool drinks and many things. When we look deep into this, we can find oceans of things.

I am speaking mainly about ignorance's bad side in the failed sixth sense. If there are bad means, there must always be a good side; we should not generalise anything by only seeing its bad sides. So, the globe needs ignorance, which always helps us lead a happy and healthy life. Humans read all sorts of things. For example, if they read news, they don't remember even 10 news by the end of the day; if we take that to the next day merely, they remember headlines. Humans are structured to keep important things in their mind. So, few things tend to be ignored. I want to share one fun thing, at the same time, the vital fact that, in our faces, our eyes can see our nose all the time, but our brain voluntarily makes us ignore that it's there all the time unless we focus on our nose. Our ignorance is the best way to be away from getting annoyed.

Social media is the best entertainment for all generations currently. People like to be on YouTube, Facebook, Instagram, Snapchat, WeChat, TikTok and Vkontakte. They can manage even without it, that's for sure. Do we know how social media is set up? It will suggest content to us based on our followings. It's up to us what we are following. If we follow entertainment, then we will be entertained by it. If we follow investments, then we will get tips through it. If we follow education, then we will be educated through it. I am sharing this mainly to ensure that our ignorance system keeps us from getting annoyed. If we're using Instagram for 10 minutes, we can see a maximum of 40 to 50 ads. The system is designed so that we will get one ad for every four scrolls. For every 40 scrolls, we get ad-free 30 to 50 scrolls. It's consciously designed to get us focused on the wall or status screens. If we scroll casually, we won't even recognise we scrolled past the ad. Still, when we become conscious and start counting the scrolls, we will know how annoying it is to be on social media walls for a long time.

Ignoring negativity is something everyone agrees on. People try hard to apply it in their life. Whoever achieves that can have a peaceful and focused life. There is a difference between negativity and bad. If someone criticises us badly in a way that hurts us and makes us stop focusing on our goals in life, this someone is our inner self, meaning that's negativity. Many times, it comes from outside as well. We have to concentrate on our primary goals, then find and learn things that strengthen our core belief. It's easy to doubt ourselves. It's hard to stop listening to that and focus on what better can be done to make ourselves the best version of ourselves. When our inner negativity is heard from an outside person as well, that's when we crumble into pieces. It gets us into a mindset of depression. We can't even address our feelings. We feel doubtful due to our negativity, but we can't stop that unless we work positively on our inner self. It makes us continuously worry for nothing. It will make us engage in something that we don't want. Unwanted tears will come, but we can't know why it is happening. Suddenly, we are not interested in anything. We feel something that we want to do but at the same time, we are not in the right mind to do it. It's just a simple formula: stop thinking, wake up, go out, get some air and start doing.

All these ignorances made us live peacefully with misguided or unevolved discipline. I mean peaceful in the sense of the outside, not inside from our soul or heart and mind. This ignorance made us live in the current political philosophies with hapless happiness, which is a hidden source of real pain. Ignorance is the gasoline to run society currently. We are not peaceful and happy, that's for sure. People are landing on God for these two things, but ignorance is the real reason for not getting peacefulness and inner happiness. Every ignorance that we have been doing makes us get one step away from happiness and peacefulness. Even when we pray to God then come home and do the same ignorance, that won't guide or help us reach the happiness and peacefulness we want. It is important to notify them when someone does something wrong. It may be awkward for us to notify them. No one is there except us to notice and notify. We ignore what they are doing to avoid the situation of arguing it's wrong. This ignorance gives that person free flow who did wrong. We are giving a chance to do that same wrong thing again, unless someone notifies them, they are going to continue doing the same. This ignorance stays in our subconscious. It makes us feel worse, spoils our peace and happiness unknowingly. It makes us consider ourselves low.

We may think that society will see us as an awkward person if we start to notify everyone. It showcases us as the most annoying person. Yeah, you're correct, but this responsibility should come to everyone to enjoy real happiness and peacefulness. When we stop being ignorant, we may enjoy real happiness and peacefulness. The task is too hard. If people want to do normal stuff, they can do or try to apply it in life and change themselves first.

Ignorance is a big issue. For ignoring, first, we should have the capacity to think. Yes, we evolved from the Stone Age to the technological age. People in ancient times had the same issue, which is still not resolved. Generationally, people pass it on to one another and keep it alive. I will illustrate how it works with an example; it happened to me; I went in a vehicle to a place. I had to be there by 8:40 pm because my friend was waiting for me. It was already late. While waiting for a signal to turn green in traffic, I saw on the platform a young man lying unconscious near where I was waiting. I didn't know if he was struggling or lying on the street because he had liquor or was sick. I looked all around. All people did not care about it. They were minding their own business. People were moving and walking. I started thinking, do I need to help this man? What if people started staring at me like a stupid or a hero or what if people laughed at me if I checked on him? I was developing doubt within myself. At the same time, I was getting late. There were other situations as well. He may be sleeping on his own, what if I go and check up on him? What if he doesn't like that and hits me? Since he was young, I was not worried. I started staring at him for a minute to find out whether he was breathing. I saw his breath. I decided to ignore the situation and left the place to meet my friend.

In that situation, I felt like my thinking and ignorance were wrong. What would you do in the situation? I leave this question to you. I don't know about you and your thoughts. I should have checked up on him when I realised he was breathing because if he didn't, there was no use, even if I checked up on him. I prejudged him by his looks as an alcoholic without checking up on him and left. So "thinking" is the first thing we need to analyse in ignoring. Oceans of thoughts will come across your mind when you're facing a situation, but more bad circumstances make the mind think bad and leave the situation. When in a peaceful place, you sit and rethink; you will realise it's wrong.

If we are ignoring means, we weren't found any material benefit in that thing that's the matter. It might be right in some cases but not in all the cases. So, sometimes we are thinking from the wrong perspective. It's psychological. We must go deep into situations and analyse our process. We don't have to worry about ignorance because everyone is ignoring something daily, unimportant or immense.

People point out others and say, 'they are ignoring but they are not facing any trouble. He was ignoring them. He was not facing any trouble. She was ignoring them. She was not facing any trouble.' It's always hypothetical. We don't know until we face a situation. The result of ignorance is always hypothetical. We don't know when it will affect, where, or how it will aggregate. Individual ignorance becomes collective. Collective ignorance will cause destructive impact.

In the example, I only said my side of ignorance. If we take that example and analyse it, we could find multiple instances of ignorance. When ignorance reached me, it was at the 20th or 25th level. This meant that in all the 19 levels, there was a chance, but they ignored him, left without checking up on him.

----------------------00-----------------------00--------------------------------

Sometimes people have a grudge against other people without reason. The grudge will become permanent over time. When that happens, people start finding reasons to hate them. People hate them for small political actions or setbacks. So, people ignore the importance of reasoning. In some places, it hurts the growth of that person. What do I mean by growth? For example, in sports, if Rock hates someone, Rock will be developing an unreasonable block within him. It makes Rock stop thinking about the purpose of competition but entirely focuses on defeating the particular opponent. It will make Rock divert from the competition. When Rock focuses on the person he wants to defeat, that focus and aim can't give him a chance to reach his full potential. Rock may win that person, but Rock can't win in a competition with his full potential. The same things apply to every situation.

"Thinking" is important in life. Sometimes getting good feelings, positive reinforcements is tough. Still, we can stay away and avoid the bad as much as possible because it's nowadays more than good. The goal is to analyse the bad then take out lessons and keep only the lessons that are taught, but don't fall into the fear and pain of those bad things. We should not stay in touch with people dumbing us with bad words, damaging, shaming, badly hurting or undermining our efforts. "Thinking" will make us understand everything clearly. When we start thinking about ignorance, we will understand how badly most things went out of the zone then affected us. If we want to avoid ignorance, we must think, realise, share, act against it. When people are not even thinking about it, how can I expect them to realise it, where can I ask them to share and act? They will laugh at me. So at least enlarge our limits to our family and friends.

How impactful has ignorance changed our society? Just look out and think.

Time to Switch on the SENSE.

Eight

Subconscious World's Conscious Survival Battle

Survival is ultimate for every living being. If we take any issue, we could capture a certain part of survival being hidden or an established agenda. We could see it in society, status, money, fame, border, language, religion, food, animals, political parties, MNCs, entertainment, health, protection, sports, everything, including things I missed out on here, always in the competition of survival.

Homo sapiens first appeared in history 3,00,000 years ago approximately. If we take the graph of our development, we can see survival has only taken us this far. What prepared us, trained us, tested us, killed us, educated us for this survival? Nature. Nature prepared, trained, tested, killed, educated us in sound, vision, smell, communication, alliance like this. It altered our organs based on our geography.

If we look at the graph, we can see an overall hike from the last 30,000 years in history. The graph shows another hike from the last 3,000 years. The graph depicts an additional hike in the last 300 years. In each hike, many things have been the driving force for survival, taking the survival mode to the next level. We can't conclusively say that any particular thing is driven by force just by noticing something. The evolution of survival has made the life of humans more stable. We have evolved from food only required for survival to needing food, shelter, clothes, and the internet for survival. We have included many things over time for luxury. We will include even more things in the future. There is a chance that what is important for survival today may disappear in the future. Over the last 3,00,000 years, we have seen more items being added for survival. We can't stop adding up. At the same time, we can't stop following what we are doing; it's a prolonged movement that has happened over centuries. It's the movement of collective subconsciousness which is irresistible and irreplaceable.

Answer the below questions truthfully from your heart and consciousness.

1. If society is constructed as if everything is equal for everyone, whatever work we do does not matter. We get equal treatment, like food, shelter, and luxury.

   Which type of work do you like to do?

   - Knowledge-based hard work
   - Administrative and support work
   - Both

   Everyone is independent in choosing their options. They finally choose what they like without hesitation because nothing changes in treatment. Whatever work they do, they receive equal treatment.

2. In the current societal structure, it treats people based on what our work is

   Which type of work do you like to do? (Read the paragraph below before choosing)

   - Knowledge-based hard work
   - Administrative and manual regular work
   - both

   The treatment is top class for knowledge-based hard work and average for the rest of the work. Now also, everyone has independence in choosing options. Finally, we can see hesitation in some of them because of their choices; they will be treated differently because of their choice.

Common question between capitalism, socialism, communism and many follow-up questions we get over the period. What is the value of talent?

What is the value of growth? What if everyone wants to do simple work? No one gets to evolve?

All these questions! It's such a joke. The modern survivors tried to convince people that money is energy that drives technologies, unites people, and brings peace to people and lands. They got everyone with or without their conviction because people have to take a side. The opposite side of money is not a well-written or structured path. There is no path there at all in old times or the path not explored globally in many places which is successful in rare places. So, the marketing openly established and convinced 8 billion people. It made them follow the money as hard-core followers. It's threatening people currently who try to think about structures beyond money to run the society. What do the subconsciousness and consciousness do in it?

We must understand the capacity of the subconscious and consciousness, how it affects us, how it's saving us, how it's being helpful throughout our life. Many people want to improve the world into a better place in all ways, but when they try to introduce alternatives for money, society will stand against it because it's a change of unimaginable scale and risk. So, there is always a flaming fight between consciousness and subconsciousness.

Consciousness analyses facts, methods, and possibilities. Subconsciousness is filled with the collective data of minds of generations and intuitions. Both stick with their analysis and data. The solutions of these two combined make societies force to go one step ahead, but the fight is about the larger picture of survival directly. So, the aggression of it is vast. Therefore, decisive solutions are on hold indefinitely. Consciousness works hard to stabilise the existing structure. Still, leakage is unstoppable; if we close one place, it comes out from another. As I said in earlier chapters, people in their comfort zone don't want risks.

The dilemma is people judge solutions based on a percentage of success. Most of the time, subconsciously driven ideas result in failure. It makes people fear subconscious forces.

Consciously sketched ideas often achieve success, but subconsciousness is the movement that won't get its way in one step. It's a movement that takes time. Push has to be injected into people over generations, and the solution will be achieved collectively.

So collective minds of support globally are required for this. Someone has to succeed. They should promote like-minded people at any point in time.

So, we can't keep it aside. Subconsciousness gets its way one way or another. The world is structured to learn from the push and pull of consciousness, subconsciousness. So, at some stage, we can get the solutions. It may get delayed. We won't be there to address that, but the truth is we are also the reason for society's all upcoming changes in the future far away. We also made a move for that change, due to that it's changed. We could see many things changed in the current time, so why not in the future? Let's hope for good.

What is the value of talent? What is the value of growth? What if everyone wants to do simple work? No one gets to evolve? Capitalists and individualists threaten everyone with these questions without knowing the real truth behind them. "What is the value of being talented?" If we stop the capitalistic structure, we will not recognise talented people. We treat stupid and talented people similarly. It is what capitalists feared most or used those questions to threaten others. First, we should break down the brutal face of capitalists, so if we are taking this to argue the above question. How many talented persons are recognised correctly, if one vacant position and two equally talented persons there means, who would we rather choose? We will test them even if they are equally talented. Only one will crack the test, another will lose. So, these tests will select the more capable one, but the rest of the equally talented people won't be taken into account. They have to choose other firms to get that position or wait until they get it. Suppose we don't agree to their agreements. In that case, they will choose a million others who agree to the same because they created small demand with their stable capitalistic structure with vast supply. They argue that choosing one and dumbing all others in graveyard works is value for talent. So, they should not raise the questions like these.

The next question is growth; what is growth? Improving, evolving, finding, discovering things. The growth that we have achieved today is significant. From the perspective of growth, the world has achieved the next level, we have computers, smart televisions, cell phones, internet, food supply, motors, medicine, cameras, an enormous amount of computer applications, mobile applications. We are at an early stage of artificial intelligence. The last 300 years of modern era world history made us an intelligent civilisation. This growth is what made possible the work-based economy even more reliable and effective. This growth, if you ask me, I will value at 35 out of 100 because even more technologies had bright chances to turn the world even more effective and show growth, but it's not possibly made it into the market; the reason is business people don't want those big changes because they want to mobilise the technology they invested in first. If it comes up, it will spoil the items they invested in. We can say the structure of money traps them. They can't risk it. It will collapse. For example, free electricity is still ineffective in all places but was invented more than half a century ago.

So, we can also take this as an example of how the subconscious gets its way. We can delay it, but it will find its way one way or another. Capitalists only decide what growth they want for society, but it's very slow. So, they could not implement it quickly; it is bad.

What if everyone wants to do simple work, and no one gets to evolve? It's the thoughtless thing to say about humanity. If we asked anyone who made the world move one step ahead in society-wise, technology-wise, humanity-wise, literacy-wise, did you do it for money? Or did you do it for fame? They will immediately respond with one nasty look that tells us they didn't do that for money or fame. If we ask Albert Einstein, Nikola Tesla, Mahatma Gandhi, Vint Cerf, Steve Wozniak, and anyone directly that you did what you did only for money and fame? I definitely say most of them will say "NO." It's the passion that drives human life, not money. When we open all kinds of doors, they will do what they like to do. We don't need to worry about all will select simple work. Most importantly, people will do work based on their characters. Due to that, we don't have to worry. All people don't have the same characteristics. All great achievers don't do what they like to do for money.

We are in a world that motivates us to work subconsciously. When we start something new, we will get conscious. Once we learn how to do it, we won't be worried; it will happen subconsciously in the proper manner almost 99%. Research works can't be included in it because it always requires analytical thinking.

Transactions in the world are always in its consciousness because it's always in people's attention. It's structured in a way that it's most vulnerable to ordinary people. So, the transaction is always conscious; what the collective subconsciousness wants in the world is to make the transactions work subconsciously.

I will explain it more straightforwardly; please listen and follow as I said, go to some place, anywhere, even your room, stay alone. Try to switch off your gadgets for some time. Turn off your conscious thinking, listen to the inner self, think about what you really want. The subconscious will always be deep inside you. It urges you to live happily by doing what you like and loving something unconditionally. Do anything to make you feel better, live without pressure. Our subconsciousness always wants us to be independent. The journey is the only thing the conscious mind always worries about. It mostly steps on the wrong thing.

For example, subconsciousness wants independence, but consciousness doesn't know how and from what, or consciousness is feared after realising how, from what, ignoring it, as I said in earlier chapters, making people focus on unreliable small things. Students are the future of our society. When students don't know how and from what items, it will create unwanted and waste skirmishes. In 2022, Indian students from Karnataka state started a big battle against the government of Karnataka state, which was about allowing students to wear hijabs on educational campuses. As we all know, India is a secular country, but the majority of the population is Hindu religion people. I like to reference previous topics in this issue. For the political party's wellbeing, they motivated Hindu students to wear saffron shawls and stand against Muslim students without thinking about politics behind the curtain. We understand religious politics and student rights issues when we see the battle from up top. When we deep dive into an issue, we can see the real picture.

India introduced a uniform culture for a few purposes. The first one is to make everyone feel equal. In the beginning days, wealthy students wore great suits to come to school, making others feel like well-suited students were above them. This domination and advantage favoured rich kids. So, governments wanted to stop inequality, and they introduced uniform culture. The second reason is that India wants to stop the religious advantages for the same reason of inequality, which is also an add-on reason to wear a uniform. Still, when some Hindu students, almost everywhere, always wear religious symbols on their hands and neck, for some seasons, they wear saffron shawls, red, black shawls then come to institutions. In most places, this negligence is ignored, but the same negligence done by Muslims at that time gets questioned, making Muslim students protest for their rights. So, the real problem here is inequality, a lack of understanding. We can't be able to stop religious influence because the truth is, it starts from our name itself. We can't recognise people without a name. In that case, how can we stop religious inequality? We can't spread equality only by dress. After independence, India should have educated people about equality over the period to bring equality economically and socially to make people understand others' independence over religion and practices, but it failed. Instead, it developed restrictions and tried to implement equality by law forcefully. So, breaking the uniform code stayed in law as illegal but not practiced by a vast set of people due to a lack of education. Most people have unity in their hearts, but this restriction makes them stand against it. So, a forceful restriction does not work consistently.

Most of us want to express our religions independently, but restrictions in the name of equality make people stop expressing themselves.

People face difficulties and discrimination based on inequality between the rich and the poor. The uniform is a temporary solution. Truth is never realised. Students have to realise it and then change the direction of the battle against the core problem. The subconsciousness knows the core problem permanently, but consciousness never has the guts to acknowledge it because of factors, complexities, and fear.

When people discuss the rich and inequality, they subconsciously jump into the topic of being selfish. Is it good or bad? Is it a subconscious thing or a conscious thing? Being selfish is not a bad thing unless it hurts others. All creatures in the world are selfish. We provide for others only after we are satisfied with our needs. When someone is not providing means, they are unsatisfied with their needs. So, we don't need to force others to be selfless. Society is structured to be selfish. Everyone knows how many trillions of currencies are circling? How many millions of people are starving? The percentage of starving may be reduced comparatively, but suffering is not gone yet. We don't need to blame others for being selfish. Everyone knows a maximum of 3BHK is enough to stay comfortable, but look at billionaires; they could have helped people instead of building palaces. Actually, they are helping people by building palaces. What if they didn't build one? Then how come construction workers and mortgage-based economy live? So, there is no use in objectifying elite people.

When a wealthy person has an exceptional educational background with a welfare mindset, we can see tremendous changes in industry and society that completely change the path. It transports people to a new level. I haven't said that others couldn't make that sort of change. People have made that sort of change, but it's more challenging for them compared to wealthy people.

How the British monarchy changed the structure of the world through its rulers. It may have wounded and killed millions of people, but somehow it made most of England's people wealthy. It's hurtful, but it somehow changed the structure of many places and people. We can use wealth and education together for construction or destruction. The above two are used for different purposes, but the consequences have changed the world. Take India for example; rich people only had an excellent education in a time of independence. Few good-hearted people sponsored knowledgeable students. If they might have thought, why should we waste our knowledge in India? then flown to America and Britain means India can't be in a position that it is now. Education makes people self-sustaining. Dr. Ambedkar is a self-sustained man who was poor before his education. Once he became a lawyer, he stood against India's societal problems. He later created and wrote the laws for India and structured the constituency. Rich people like Tata, Homi Bhabha, Vikram Sarabhai, Nehru constructed India's Future around the birth of independence. So, it's evident that it's easy if the rich take a stand for it; that's whatever it is. We can't expect more from selfish people. If they think for society, then boom, they will make it. It's their piece of cake, but they need to think that matters. Two persons and their team structured the monetary policy in the Bretton Woods agreement. They convinced 44 nations with it. Yes, that's what knowledgeable rich people are capable of.

There are at least thousands of economic experts worldwide writing millions of books and theses on developing and expanding the economy through the existing monetary system. They are trying to fit into the mould that two people and their team created for the whole world with an American perspective and prioritised Americans first. In 1971, the Bretton Woods agreement ended but the core motive of that agreement remains the same. Why didn't thousands of economists find alternative or more capable structures and experiments? The only experts there who lived in the world were Maynard Keynes and Harry Dexter White, who structured the monetary policy in the Bretton Woods agreement, is it?

See below Figure 3. It's only American data. The same thing is happening worldwide, maybe except in a few countries. Now comes a subconscious and conscious battle; almost 50% of people subconsciously want better economic and monetary policy, but all we do is try to force them into the mould. It's a battle between consciousness and subconsciousness; consciousness has the upper hand till now.

Figure 3

All countries have intelligence agencies to know what other countries are doing. If we research further, we can realise that the structure is protected by people who don't care about their life. Their only motive is to get orders from higher officials that need to happen. If the government wants someone to die for some cause, they will execute things in their ways, as we see in movies. They must obey and do anything at any cost. Millions of operations are happening worldwide. Intelligence agencies like the CIA, MI6, DGSE, Mossad, KGB have executed many. I mentioned only a few agencies. The point is that we don't know if agencies only protect people against terrorism, safeguard the nation from threats, protect countries' secrets, or if they are protecting the monetary structure from threats as well. We don't know how many hidden agendas every country's intelligence agency is handling. Is monetary policy one of them?

Life or death competition between consciousness and subconsciousness in this segment. Conscious people want to continue the monetary policy. Whenever it gets faulty, they do some magic and make it stand and run again. Experts do magic, which is nothing but infusing money, cutting interest rates or raising interest rates, giving haircuts to borrowers, writing off loans and much more. Magic has not changed over the century. The same magic has been working perfectly for over a century. We should appreciate ourselves and the world because we are still hoping and waiting peacefully, encouraging our children to hope the same. We are making them fit into a mould. My father did the same to me. I am waiting for the same magic that he waited for but still have not seen. I lost my hope.

I realised that waiting could do nothing but postpone time. I started to work on the change. This book is my work.

When we talk about the subconscious and conscious things, one question arises: does everyone like to be equal consciously or subconsciously? When we think from an individual perspective, it differs from person to person. We can't make everyone equal. It's not our motive to change individuals forcefully. We want the system to operate equally.

Even if all basic things are equal, someone who does more for society is naturally treated more than equally. It's impossible to stop it. It's impossible to stop those who hate the way others have been treated more than equally because it's natural that good and bad are indivisible sides. What is good and bad here? Or who is good and who is bad here? We can't define good and bad in some circumstances. One evolves from the other. One gets better than the other. The competition between both is life. Bad need not be purposely wrong all the time; some good might look bad in others' vision. Vice versa, some bad looks good too. It's subjective to matters and situations. We can't live in a world where everything is good. That's the law of nature. Bad can't survive without good. Good can't survive without bad. Our subconscious may poke us; they are treated more than what they deserve when someone is treated more than equal. Sometimes, others get disappointed then become jealous if we are getting the treatment of more than equal.

If others get treated more than equally at that time, we try to become greater than them. We try to replicate or hate their things on that urge. We lose our purpose and our motive then drowns in such things in that process. For example, I like Michael Jackson; I haven't understood most of his lyrics while he was singing, but I like his voice and emotion. I like to treat him as more than equal, but for someone different from me, who doesn't like him treated that way more than equal. They have adverse opinions of him in that process. They start to hate him more and forget their purpose then drown in useless things that do not belong to them.

So even if they are treated more than equally, remember that it's not our place to judge.

I always say to people, I like Michael Jackson, but I don't want to become like or be like Michael Jackson. Because everyone has their travel, we're not able to bring anyone with us. We're not able to stop anyone from their travel. Live in the space that is ours. If we did well, the treatment that we hated, which people gave to Michael Jackson, will be given to us as well, but even if we're not received means, that's not an issue until we did what we like to do. We provided our whole heart for that process; we achieved our self-satisfaction for that. It made us happy. We got our inner peace. It's all that matters. If we're not getting what we want in our journey, we have to create something to get what we want. We have to start focusing on that creation. Once we have created, then we will get the journey we wanted. Even people who tried different ways other than those I mentioned above in detail may have been successful. If it's a good way to reach that fame means they will get that inner peace. Few people seek others' validation and follow shortcuts, but I am sure they can't enjoy inner peace. They may not want that and don't consider it a big thing. We can't define something as wrong or right equally from everybody's perspective because it's impossible.

Most people do not realise that, but it's the truth.

We subconsciously want to be united even though lands, languages, religion, caste, culture, heritage separate us. The core of land, language, religion, caste, culture, heritage is unity, celebration, peace, and sharing. We must understand that all these separation factors formed to simplify the lives of human beings. All have their ways and style of achieving it. All people like certain ways, certain styles. They follow them. Few learn it and unite with it. All these separation factors are conscious things. Even though we get it naturally, and all prologues come spontaneously, it's a conscious thing. These separation factors are labels. Our labels always identify us. I know 9 out of 10 books spoke about it. You consider this as a 10th one, but it's the unavoidable truth. Sometimes our label makes us proud. The same label also makes us guilty. Most problems arise because of labels because we can't live without labels unless we are monks, but even monks have labels. How to solve this problem? The problem once it arises, we can't solve it without hurting each other, but we can stop the problem from happening. For that, we have to understand that we don't have ownership of our label. We should not force it on others.

When do we realise purpose? When we analyse it? Then we all come to know that the subconscious is right. So, that's why we all want to follow our collective subconsciousness. As I said in earlier topics, there are always people around us that can't live without making problems with labels. We have to find them and stay away from them.

People are so different from one another. Their paths are different from each other. Mainly if we take a family to check on its members, the father does some work, the mother does some work, their sons/daughters do something, their wife or husband does something, all these are different. Mostly, no one travels on the same path. They all travel with different people outside their family, but they all join hands at dinner and share things. Even though they all do different things, they like to stick with their family. Even in the family business, the family members are carried away with different tasks. So even though they are from the same family, there is all sort of differences we can notice, like each of them has a different ideology and belief, follow different leaders in politics, different styles, different habits and different hobbies, like different tastes. Few may be very particular on what they want to eat. Few may eat anything. Few have restrictions, everyone likes different stories, a different hero, few are more spiritual, few are neutral, few won't have belief. Even though they don't like someone among them, they stick together for others in the family and support, so what binds them? A little movement of joy, love, the feeling of being around all the time. If they are conscious all the time, they can't live with people around them for a minute because they are different from others. Consciousness is always put in front. When we started thinking about it once, we started feeling we wouldn't be able to be with them close and normal. We will alienate ourselves because of it. Few left from their family for some reason of trust and oppression, but people mostly stick with family. Most people have exponential tolerance levels. It's the main reason for being together. Consciousness always makes us look for something and make our brain active all the time, which, over time, will create pressure and stress. We can't always be conscious of people in general. Most of the world is operating subconsciously. The trusting comes from subconsciousness but not from consciousness. That's why we are currently able to live and operate in society. We trust that society won't harm us all of a sudden without reason. Over some stage, we started believing that society will always do good for humans. There must be valid and rational reasons behind everything that is happening. The whole world is living and operating in that collective subconscious faith in society and people, but people in power politics misuse this faith. People in politics betray that good faith sometimes. They use that unconditional faith to make people as dolls. Politicians make people fight for politicians' benefit. People want to live together subconsciously without borders. They want to visit and explore new things. So, whenever power politics hits people's collective subconscious desires with rocks, people get fearful and disappointed by pain.

Many wars happened in 2022. The war between Russia and Ukraine made both sides' people frightened and fearful. People never liked war throughout history because it will always create a loss for both sides. It created massive tension in the world because Russia is assertive. If any other countries were involved as well, that might have become a world war. Since no one was willing to intervene to make peace between both.

It created scariness among people in small countries that if the same situation happened to us then at that time also no other countries would help other than watching it simply like a school and college fight. They shout, enjoy, who knows, even bet on it to earn money as well. When we search for the reason for the war, we will realise how fear is the only reason leading to war. Russia's fear of European countries and America. Ukraine's fear of Russia triggered the war. Is America a sleeper cell behind it? Why? People think because of that, America encouraged Ukraine then asked them to sign a NATO agreement for protection. Russia is against NATO; it's not okay that Ukraine is joining NATO. Russia started the war because of that, but America is not supporting Ukraine directly in the field but supplying weapons to Ukraine to protect themselves. America is aware of the nature and impact of wars. The American dollar is the world's reserve currency. If America spoils itself through this war, they won't be able to stand as the world's reserve currency. All other countries believe in the United States dollar value standing still but they will take a step back if it goes to war directly against Russia to support Ukraine. The world will find a new reserve currency other than the Dollar and Euro in that case. It's the reason America is only threatening Russia verbally. As I said in the previous chapter, "Masks of Countries", we must understand the importance of collective subconscious behaviour and stand by it.

When discussing politicians' betrayal, we have to look into the predestination forced on normal people by politics. Our fate is fixed even before we were born based on where we were born, to whom we were born, maybe 1 in a thousand overcoming that, that's what figure 3 explains to us. We may quote Jeff Bezos, Bill Gates, Mark Zuckerberg, Dhirubhai Ambani, Jack Ma as 1 in 1000. When we lose ourselves in the politics of the system, then we can't change our predestination fixed by political people. To overcome predestination, we need our family's complete support. They have to support our dreams and believe in our dreams. Politicians don't even know us, but everything they decide will affect us one way or another.

One thing immortal in this world is materials and their complexities. It will live on until the end of civilisation. We can't achieve 100% formulation with rationalisation because people are different from each other. They always seek different things at different times. People always behave as if a sprinkling amount of something is missing even after we have finished reading all the philosophical and economic books in the world that have ever been written and researched to come up with the perfect solution for material equalisation.

People, in general, always like a 'keep it simple' oriented solution. They want what they want without restrictions. It's not possible for everyone at any time. In today's world, only billionaires have the luxury of it. Monetary tools ensure that it's not available for everyone. The billionaires take it as an advantage and enjoy their life, quoting their hard work as the reason for that. They invest billions that are sleeping in their wallet to create wealth. Employees as well are working hard for those billionaires to create wealth.

So, as ordinary middle-class or poor people, we can get whatever we want with our money. We can't spend more than the limited amount of money that we have in hand; as middle-class people, we can take loans based on our creditworthiness. Still, one way or another, we have to repay that with our work. Billionaires have the luxury of unlimited credit facilities because of their intelligence. Still, they also need to repay that, but for that, they have to manage their employees smartly, create strategies, business models to repay that vast sum. In a few cases, they also fail to repay it. When a middle-class individual person fails, that won't affect the country's economy much, but when billionaires fail, that will collapse a small portion of the economy. Billionaires have great potential, so their risk is greater, their luxury as well looks greater to normal people. Normal people forget about potential and risks when speaking about luxury. Billionaires are not ready to be philanthropists at a bigger level because billionaires know if they do that at the biggest level, they will drastically affect the economic situation. So, even if they are wise, they can't do it considering the balance of the monetary economy. So, money is a restriction that avoids a material deficit from people's over-usage. Some restrictions are needed in any economic model, but they should be rational. What we currently have is money, that's irrational. Why is it related to consciousness and subconsciousness?

It's such a complex explanation; materials attract people. Desires are the reason for such attractions. Desires come from what we listen to, watch, experience, enjoy. It's consciously connected with our inner self. This inner self is our soul. It's hard to separate the soul from its desire. These desires trigger our consciousness then pump us to get it. Subconsciousness doesn't have any role in these materialistic desires because these materialistic desires are connected scientifically with body chemicals. It makes us only focus on what we want for quite some time, but that will go away within 1 sec or minute or hour or days sometimes. The world has more than enough supplies for people's needs instead of desires. People always desire more in the materialistic world than they need. Most of the items already secured their place on shelves without being touched for months and years. We have to encourage children towards achieving something to get the materialistic benefits rather than buying every product they are requesting. If we groom kids this way, after they grow up, they won't line up behind materials. We need to educate them on the importance of acquiring materials and their essentials and their availability.

Stories are essential for people's lives. We construct ourselves with stories that we hear, read, and see. Those stories enrich our subconscious connections in the mind with the world. They help us understand the world clearly, which will help us find our purpose. Famous people in the world always encourage everyone to read. The truth is that new doors will open within our minds to inspire and create something new. Stories of great authors in books like Moby Dick, War and Peace, Crime and Punishment, and many others have given the world some examples of living, showing how hard life is and what the greatest thing in the world is, other than love. More than a trillion stories exist in the world, so reading and listening enriches people.

How is subconsciousness getting new connections from books and new stories exploring? Why is it essential in the world we deserve? According to scientific research, people are gaining more empathy by reading storybooks. Empathy is the only way to become a better person. The matter is that the conscious world believes that only the outside world's chaos is the reason for all incidents that we are suffering. The truth is that people's inner state of emotions is the expressions of the outside world. People can't control the outside world because it's a mess of a billion people's consciousness. People can only control the inner self. People have to understand that to make an excellent inner self, we have to develop empathy. When we have that level of empathy, it's easy for the subconsciousness to explore good ways to live peacefully.

Scientists have identified 27 distinct types of emotions, challenging a long-held assumption that our feelings fall within the universal categories of happiness, sadness, anger, surprise, fear, and disgust.

There are 27 emotions: admiration, adoration, aesthetic appreciation, amusement, anger, anxiety, awe, awkwardness, boredom, calmness, confusion, craving, disgust, empathic pain, entrancement, excitement, fear, horror, interest, joy, nostalgia, relief, romance, sadness, satisfaction, sexual desire, and surprise.

All these emotions are expressed in action in the world. We haven't realised those connections and impact. We know that emotions are reactions to others' actions or our state of mind.

People are working on channelising their emotions with the help of doctors, monks, spiritual leaders, and philosophies, but they consciously believe that if they channelise all their emotions, then they can achieve divinity. However, we can't be divine all of a sudden once we channelise our emotions. We may achieve a state of happiness and peace, but when we can't maintain that position permanently, we are not divine beings. Given that there are too many ashrams, gurus, churches, and mosques, it's encouraging all people that they can achieve a divine state of mind. But the truth is we can't collectively make people follow and fall for the magic of the divine in a short period because that can't be accepted by the world. Divinity is something that arises from within ourselves. Every being has different characteristics of divinity. Our subconscious will not agree with the standard protocols in the field of divinity; it always sticks with its characteristics. The world has a population of seven and a half billion, but less than one in a million can rarely achieve the actual state of divinity. We can't follow their ways. If we do so, it will be a failure. This is what the excellent philosopher Gurgeesh said throughout his life.

Most people consciously believe that philosophies are not interesting to participate in. Those People are not aware that philosophies are constructed the society. Everyone should explore multiple philosophical paths; then they will get to experience what is truly important. What we avoid is worth consuming for the good of society. The subconsciousness of individuals is attracted to different types of philosophies, which is good because collections of multidimensional convergence will give a new colour and bring unity among the people. Subconsciousness always pushes us towards the right path, but the path is not well established. It needs to be constructed in most places. People didn't try due to fear and discomfort. People are not likely to waste time to implement the new society because of the lack of people involvement in philosophy. Involvement in philosophy is much lesser than in other scientific departments, which is why the scientific world is constantly improving rather than the social structure. That's why we have been stuck in a failure structure for a long time. This structure was successful once, but that's a long time ago. When the use of equal distribution becomes a question mark, we started facing ultimate discomfort, which is happening now. Our collective consciousness categorised a few items that are all important components for the good of humanity, but that improper categorisation made people believe that creating wealth and enjoying that is happiness. It's why we have to be in the world. This sickness ignores the voice of subconsciousness. What is that voice communicating? The construction of a good society. It makes people mature towards free will. Every human likes to live with free will, but maturity is important, guidance and pathways are missing because the collective consciousness didn't allow us to explore. People have to explore it with the help of modern philosophies.

When did people start doing work without liking it? That's when they started working for profits. I already shared many things in the previous chapters about profit, but when I tried to think about evil beyond profit in every chapter, I didn't find any. This one word traps all topics. It gives different reasons to sledge it. Profit made people work a lot for more profit and mental illusional competition. What is this mental illusional competition? One person wants to gain more profit than the other person. It's happening all over the world. These profits introduced the concepts of inflation and deflation. People were produced for the demands. It's the situation before profit was introduced. After that, it completely changed. They started producing for luxury.

Subconsciously, people found some inner peace in work that they did before the profit concept was introduced, which made them keep away from personal life thinking. It made them concentrate on work. Now, after it was introduced, the majority of people are not finding peace at home and work as well. They are continuously listening to something else like radio, music, video, which is making them forget the problems and stop focusing on both the failures or overthinking and going into mental stress about it. Subconsciousness is missing the life it enjoyed before the arrival of profit.

This thing made people restless; it's joined hands with science. All new inventions made people advance in comfort. People started believing that they were progressing too fast in science. Actually, we want students to pass all the subjects that they selected. When a person gets a 90 in some subject out of 100 but fails in other subjects continuously, then we do not consider that person a successful graduate because we want them to pass all subjects. If we take the world as a student, it has distinction in science and maths but just passes in Money management, then it fails in social, which means it needs more effort to get a passing mark. The world thinks science is a major and can only grow with it. It's not going to work that way. The growth that world think is a failure. It's conscious thinking. The subconscious wants at least a pass in that subject.

People want a peaceful and joyful life that is not happening equally for everyone. We saw how consciousness and subconsciousness play their role in it. Once these issues are identified by people, they will mature and realise the chance of success in a work-based economy.

Nine

A New Element – Misused

All things have their purpose. When a thing doesn't have any purpose, at that time it will go to the waste bin, as we all know. People may have a sentimental connection to things, but when it reaches its end, then its life is over; we should somehow find a better replacement for the things we lost because we have to move forward, no matter what, for the good of ourselves and the society. We can't have tea in a broken pot because that will ruin us. The metaphor here is none other than money. What else can it be?

So, people who like the taste of money and who have the luxury to taste more and more don't have any issue with pot. Normally, people always have a floating mindset; when they don't have any ways to earn money like others do, they hate money so much at that time. When they know ways to make money, they will enjoy it. They don't see mistakes in it at the same time. People usually connect money with talent. They symbolise it as a talented person who can earn more.

Why should we divide that as talented and the rest of the others then give the talented more money than others?

First, we have to understand what talent is. Doing something that we are doing more efficiently and effectively is called talent. Everyone does something. Every particular category has a number of persons doing the same. They are forced to compete with or without their knowledge because of the same category. What makes them more efficient and effective? It's the time they dedicate to that something because they love it; they have their heart in it to dedicate that time, which does not feel like pressure, but instead, it feels like pleasure. Since they love it, they update themselves continuously in that something. They want to improve it, innovate, combine new things, invent and discover new things. When they are finally able to excel in it, that time they are identified as talented persons.

The luxury of doing something that we love is not possible for everyone. Few don't even get a chance to study. Few will not get a job in that something. Few have other personal issues. There are 'n' number of social and structural issues that are being barricaded to move towards what we love. So being talented looks like an impossible thing in the current structural society. Everyone recognises them when someone does that. People who are lost in the barricades were not identified as talented. The barricades are the issue for not being talented, but society registering it as people without these social issues can't construct a balanced society. The balance they suggest is that a few people should be at the top and a large number of people must be at the low. If everyone goes to the top, then the system will collapse. The competition to achieve a place at the top of society by crossing all the barricades will make society survive in the world with continuous updates. If we make everything equal for everyone, then the momentum will stop. It's the stand that society has taken and operating on it currently. Monetary policy perfectly keeps the imbalanced balance.

We have discussed all the barricades in the previous chapters. People being talented is also in the hands of time and situation. Even when we are ahead of our time, the people in common won't understand.

Everyone assumes that changing the system is nearly impossible due to these problems, but people have a misconception. They can be able to make the change constructively. We have to think about one step at a time. People have to agree that we are stuck in a dysfunctional system.

People have to analyse the faults in the system on their own and write that down. This book is my analysis of all items that went wrong when everyone analyses the system on their own. At that time, we have the chance to get different perspectives and different solutions. When more and more analyses come out, then we can identify common themes. We can work towards improving it. No one is obliged to accept one's analysis, but they can at least read the allegations they are expressing on the failed society. Continuous reading can make sense. Motivate everyone to take action proactively.

In the Hindu religion, people do one common thing when they go to the temple. They pray to God. They make an agreement with God in their mind. If the prayers they wished for really happened, they would do the thing to a god that they agreed. Another one is they sacrifice something to God for things they wish to happen ahead of it. In many different cultures, we have the same thing all over the world; we started it before the Stone Age era; what is it implying indirectly in its hidden layers? We have to remove cultural procedures and gods to see a clear picture. Whatever we wish to happen for the good of us and our society, we must sacrifice something, which is a universal thing. We can't earn something without sacrifice. If we don't wish to sacrifice for what we want, then we will reach the stage where we can't move ahead without sacrifice; we can leave that behind to continue what we previously did and say goodbye to the desire we wish to happen. As I said earlier, we are enjoying what we are enjoying because of people previously sacrificed for that in any way.

The materiality of sacrifice is based on the impact it creates against the strength of the opposition, who is wise to stop it. Turn back history to check what sacrifices were made for wars that happened, what sacrifices were made for independence, what sacrifices were made for the name change of places, what sacrifices were made for women to wear dresses, and what sacrifices were made for the saving of language and heritage. These sacrifices were made against power, control, superiority, lust, ownership, pride, and selfishness. How many sacrifices were made by black people to achieve at least the current level of somewhat equality? These sacrifices create a forceful dilemma in structure; when force gets aggressive, the opposition has no options to stop and open the gates of change. As I said in previous topics, the opposition created 'n' number of divergences to stop people from joining hands altogether.

People in ancient days conceived as many children as possible because they didn't initially know why it was happening. When they came to know why, they intentionally conceived more and more, possibly because of the situation and global condition. When one child was unable to survive, they had another, but later it improved. They started controlling the process in the 20th century; the process of childbirth was a do-or-die process. More and more people died in the process of labour. The pain of losing a loved one is unimaginable. When you plan to spend all your life with that person, but she died in conceiving a child. Nothing is more painful than it. This happened frequently. Most people didn't even want to conceive naturally at one stage; they started going through caesarean. Scientists are working on giving birth without the help of a woman's womb. The future will be like if we want a child, they use technologies to create a baby without a female body as a womb in the near future, as we see in many movies. In the process of perfecting humans, we are in the near future of creating superhumans.

The world has evolved in many ways; we are the latest upgraded version and ruling the world. We will not be there till the end, but the data we provide will last a long time. Now, data is stored on servers. Previously, they had it in stones and leaves. Evolving is a continuous process. The future will have only our data; superhumans or AI will be there. Physics is something that we haven't even discovered five percent of. While we master it, we will become superhuman. Perfecting the AI is in progress. If we provide automated access, AI can also occupy our place with our data. So, an important element is focusing on and realising the limits of anything.

The Kardashev scale defines the types of civilisations. These civilisation types start from 1 and continue indefinitely. Kardashev originally defined only three types. Later, scientists added all the remaining types. These types will show people what we can do and where we stand now.

All these types are scintillating for people. Every type will show people what the next big thing after what we have done previously. Type 1 civilisations will be capable of using all the energy on earth, manipulating all the elements like air, water, fire, climate, land. We have not yet become a type 1. Scientists fixed a 100 to 200-year time frame to become a type 1. We are just on the edge of becoming a type 1. There is a huge possibility that in the process of achieving type 1, humans may become extinct before becoming a type 1. What are all the problems that we are facing in the process of achieving type 1? We are facing all the problems that we discussed in this book. People are the real enemies of humanity when we don't find a rational solution for all these problems. We will kill our species in fights like Hiroshima and Nagasaki. It will take only 15 minutes maximum or maybe less than that if I am sure. All countries launched their nuclear missiles. One good thing is that it will be a painless death. Once the bomb reaches the land, or maybe seconds before that, we will be in heaven and looking into the destruction of humanity of the home planet. So, scientists said we are waiting to see how it will turn out. People once crossed type 1 means it's easy as pie to reach 2.5 maximum, but after that? Who cares about after? That's the problem for another millennium.

This book aims to perfect people in the process of reaching type 1. Did you ever think about it? I believe you will; the world has evolved in nature. We are just nothing in this world. We are one of evolving beings in nature. What if a new creature, nothing like a human, started to evolve in this world? Will humans go to kill that new creature that is going to come? That creature may be in a new sex. The only option at that time is to unite without any difference; at that time, people will unite to kill it because they wanted some problem as a reason to unite without the border. We are creatures that never accept something evolving above us. In fear of survival, we somehow try to end its legacy without a trace of its branch. It's just hypothetical because evolving takes time. We didn't find any trace of a new species or anything that can think like humans till now. It's not going to happen in the near future of 100 to 200 years. That's what the time limit is to become a type 1 civilisation but don't be happy about that soon because we are endangering humans with artificial intelligence, as I said in early chapters. We have to handle the technology segment more carefully since this issue. It will be catastrophic if we miss stopping before it goes overboard. Too easy can lead us to too much danger. It is why people need to know their limits.

I always feel sorry for people who buy books on a few topics. Millions of authors have written books on the topics of How to make money? How to become a millionaire? etc. These books are sold in millions, but only authors and publishers benefit from this. The fact is they can only advise us on the path to earn, but even on that path, the unexplained topics or skipped chapter difficulties will burn us, which we have to face on our own. Learn to lose then realise nuances. Finally, we can start earning from it, but the way that they showed to become a millionaire in the book always comes with risk. Most of the time, those risks will make people lose hard-earned money. It's not wrong to show people the way, but naturally, it's not possible for everyone who understands a book to make millions. It's always limited in that sense. If we take a survey of people who ever read a book after five years to check if they became millionaires or earned from that book, then only less than 2 to 3%, we can find the success rate. It is because the system is structured so that it will not allow more and more people to earn much money from middle- and low-class segments. If they started to do so, it would increase people's purchasing power parity to equalise order balance. Middle- and low-class people balance this world. They must achieve all things slowly and steadily. They can't fast-forward things to grow as a group. It's because the system will collapse. There isn't enough supply for that growth. So, society should always guide people to move towards equilibrium. All authors need to shift their focus from money to the reality of the world. They can advise more on equality.

Nothing will change whoever comes to power. It is a statement that most people make when talking about politics and changes. All arguments will end with this statement about politics and power, but did we ever think about why we are saying these statements? We are saying it because we are not seeing any structural or systemic changes in society for over 1000 years. Technology is upgrading itself, but as I said in the earlier topics, our society structurally and systematically has mostly stayed the same. Governments worldwide are upgrading their military, technology, power. They are not ready to bring changes in structure and operations on a systematic basis in society. So, people can see the changes when it's visible around society.

What is more visible than changes in structure, cadre, operating system? The system we are operating on was introduced several thousand years ago, stage by stage, it increased its cruelty little by little. We haven't seen the real problematic phase, that stage will be catastrophic. It showed its glimpse into all wars, recessions, economic meltdowns. What is this structural change and systemic change? This book is all about it, or maybe not all, but it showed a glimpse of it. We can develop it effectively and efficiently together.

We must consider people of all religions, languages, and lands if we want to bring systematic and structural change because we can't change anything with a single perspective. It's entirely unethical. When we put together everything, it will give us the whole meaning of something that we wish to change. We need to be aware of everything to get the complete picture. We must see things with an open mind to know their nuances before prejudging anything.

We are better at one thing, which means keeping up with rules that governments created. It is why more than 90% of people live peacefully. If more than 10% of the world's population likes not following the rules, the world will fall apart. We can't control that mass. So where is this mass accumulated altogether? The middle class. Therefore, the government's concentration is focused on the mission to keep up with the middle-class level. For the obedience that people show to their governments, the government should consider new technologies to make people equal without borders.

When more and more is added to the population, when average life expectancy increases from 65 to 75, at that time governments can't handle this sort of growth as far as I know. Countries are fighting for the reason my people should get more while humans are struggling to survive as a society collectively. This mindset will tear us apart. The supply and demand should be rational. We are taking out twice the lifetime worth of resources from the earth because we need to meet the profit curve from those resources, which is irrational. We are using technologies to do it. The sole purpose of this chapter is to stop misusing technology like this. Is technology the new element? Of course, it is a new element. What else can it be? We're making progress more and more in all fields using technologies that we previously invented. We are creating new technologies using old ones. We keep upgrading and innovating them for better efficiency. We have improved in all areas essential for life, but the power of money circles all these technologies. Transaction tools are controlling technologies instead of putting them to better use.

We entered the world of technology 300 years ago. All fields are currently filled with technology. A-to-Z departments are working hand in hand with technology. We have to move to the next level. All these technologies have fast-forwarded growth, but society is moving towards being more materialistic. They buy things only because they are available and affordable. Most of us are not thinking about one thing, 'is it required? or needed or essential?' This question is missed in society. More resources are already being exploited which are there for future needs. We have depleted resources equivalent to 200 years in advance. People want it because companies and governments don't care about future generations. Companies and governments allow what people want. All couples love to have a baby, but they are not saving anything for them, but spending all things that belong to them in the name of living in the present and enjoying as much as possible. If we want a healthy, happy grandson or great-granddaughter or both, consider the steps we're taking currently. We must make sure we're using things up to their capacity. We should not overproduce. We should not overconsume. People can argue about recycling. It can be a saviour, but how much and how long can it be possible? All over the world, experts and social workers are advising people to stop being materialistic, but since companies have targets to sell no matter what, the motive for their survival and profit. Working on consumers' psychology and pushing them hard to be materialistic. We can't blame corporates and at the same time people. The structure that we are operating on is pushing everyone. The transaction tool and society structure make the situation harder to save. It is where we have to think about what can be the thing that uses technologies wisely. If we genuinely want to love our own kid, we first have to start loving the world. We provide something for that by stopping being materialistic.

How many people know this story? "What I am suggesting is worthy of trying": - Muhammad Nabi, the Islamic prophet, went to a town for a visit. All the people waited for him in the street from rags to riches, praying to God to receive a blessing from Muhammad Nabi. As he walked down the street, people from both sides showed their respect to him. At the same time, everyone waited to see to whom he would give a blessing. They were ready to provide anything to him to receive his blessing because it is very divine and powerful. He walked near a rich person. The rich person thought that he was going to receive the prophet's blessings, but Muhammad crossed him and went straight to an older man who was a poor daily wage earner. He took the poor man's hand, placed it on his head, and then asked for his blessing instead of giving him a blessing. The people around him were shocked and shaken by his behaviour. Later, people asked him why he did that. Muhammad responded with a smile; the man is working hard for what he has. He eats food from his actual work. So, I received his blessing. He tried to make people understand that being rich or poor doesn't matter, but what matters is working for the things you deserve.

I am saying this because it's not wrong to be rich. People think that they are rich because of their intelligence, but that's not the matter. People have to work continuously for things they deserve instead of making money work for them, which is impossible in a world where money is the transaction tool.

There are only seven essential things in the world. All other things are created to elevate the quality of these essentials. Those essentials are food, shelter, clothing, communication, entertainment, medicine, and transport. All the other things are there to support, elevate, or protect these essential things. We are leading our life only for these seven essential things, but what is problematic in getting those things? It is where rationality, equality, quality, quantity, greed, inferiority, superiority fight with each other. Tag team wrestling takes place to get these seven essentials. We are separated by land, language, culture, religion, nationality, caste, colour, and many more things. We can list down for 100 pages all the things that separate people, but we are all united by all these seven essentials. We are all classified by these seven essentials as very poor, poor, below average, average, above average, rich, or very rich.

Finance and power are separate controls that can support others' motives but never contradict each other's core purpose. All these seven essentials are protected by power. All seven are produced by finance. These are the core purpose of these two controls. So, now we can see that all these separation factors are divided into two categories: protection and production. What is problematic in getting those seven essentials? Oversimplified into two; protect and produce. Finance crossed borders for its reliability. It expanded its scalability. Power doesn't have the option to cross borders because it's restricted to people, culture, land, all separation factors. So, power uses finance as a tool to control other borders.

Why are essentials needed to be protected and produced? In the beginning days of civilisation, people lacked communication. There was a high insufficiency of essentials. People had a lack of knowledge about it. So, people went across borders and stole from others. They attacked others to conquer essentials to overcome the fear of survival. When they started evolving, they needed an effective tool to exchange. They used the barter system. Then, after some time, gold and the gold standard came. The rest of the events took place, as I mentioned in the previous topics.

In the current situation, do we need to be protected and produced? Most people say yes, arguing that if we didn't have protection and financial means, then who saves us from terrorists, thieves, and exploiters of finance? It is where I differ; when we observe the world, we can spot where we are struggling and getting annoyed. Power and finance are those places. So, people who cannot get the essentials are becoming poor then dying or becoming terrorists then killing. Those people say power and finance are reasons and it is the destruction tool. Terrorists' motives always, no matter what, make tenets come true, whether peaceful way or blood path. If not possible, then kill who is innocent to create pain in society. They make governments feel for their activities. Have you ever thought about it? How many terrorists possibly killed people to make the governments feel for their activities against terrorists? It's very low. Governments never feel for such things, but they will give baseless warnings. How much is low, very low? It's not even 10 percent of World War 1 and 2 combined. As per the book's definition, so-called good people sadly are the reason for more deaths than bad people like terrorists due to the political system's fault.

Globally, people have a better understanding, education, and technology. No one in the world wants war unless they are obsessed with power or finance. So, it indicates that protection is over-exaggerated. Protection was once vital and uncompromisable due to people's lack of understanding, knowledge, education, and technology. However, currently, we can confidently say we are at ease with all things, but still, we are lacking in something, that we haven't believed we can lead a happy borderless life. We lack belief.

Borderless life is good, but how come we sleep peacefully without the fear of thieves if we remove the patrol from society? We are going to become equal. The concept of a thief will not exist because everyone will have everything that's required. No one will become a thief in the first place, but anyway we will be protected by patrols because there are other kinds of life threats there. Advanced security systems will be there to protect us from everyone.

All essentials are produced by finance, aka money. We have to take a look at the forex of the country. It is where finance plays its part. The same question here as well, in the current situation: - do we need the finance? After reading the above paragraph, you probably have been confused or in a steady state of mind of "no." If so, I somewhat tried to make you understand well, but if you said "yes" again, my answer is "definitely not." Finance is something connected directly with money. As I said in previous topics, it should not be an independent tool. Due to its incapacity, we are facing the worst financial meltdown, inflation, deflation, economic crisis, and gambling. The world has resources reserved for almost 200 years, even when we use them as we use them now. No country necessarily goes into an economic crisis, but we witnessed many economic crises over the years. Why is it? It's because of the transaction tool. The crisis may have happened because of poor governance, even though in a real challenging situation, other countries can give their hands to the affected countries, but monetary policies that are constructed around forex, demand and supply links will never allow such humanity-based things over an extended period because it's the system that we are operating and constructed to keep materialism, money alive forever. It is one way of controlling others' borders through money combined with power. Market Crisis is a frequently used term in the financial world.

Share markets have caused more significant losses to people compared to frauds and thieves all over the world throughout history combined. Share market wipes out what frauds and thieves have done throughout history in just one day of a market crash. The market will rise again from a clean slate anyway. Families that invested, especially in derivatives, can't stand a chance if they wrongly invested or bet. Yes, derivatives are pure gambling. We have to enter there with an acceptance of our risk. If we stupidly put our entire savings in derivatives and want to risk, We're putting ourselves in deadly situation. Nobody will stop us. There is always a chance of a win. If we do so, we are a billionaire; if not, we have to sleep on the street the next day. These are all extremes, but calculated risks can be acceptable if we are knowledgeable about it to play with it. Acceptance is the key we have to develop in ourselves. Even in 2008, nobody expected the bonds to crash and make a huge chunk of money wash out, but Americans didn't worry. They just printed money to solve the issue of corporates going to zero, but what about people invested in it or small businesses that survived with petty cash? Unbearable loss. It's the structure. We can't raise our voices against it. It is how it's structured. We have to enter with an acceptance of market risks. We have to invest only after research. We have to be up to date about it. Even after all things, there will always be a spot of a grey area. When regulators find it, they will try to close it, but until then, it's the spot where people who spot it earn without risk. It may be structured, regulated, but people with the luxury of robot trade and coding skills can grab more money than others. So, there is a question mark in rationality always.

All financial crises make people fall deep. People sometimes die, but we can't keep it aside and say finance is structured, regulated, entirely rational. We can see a massive gap between the wealthy and middle-class ratio. Some people nowadays teach their kids that this is the structure. We have to achieve tremendously to get into that 2% somehow. If not, we can't lead a financially independent life. Some people don't even share anything related to finance, letting their kids face the reality on their own. These parents are all philosophically wrong; misguiding younger generations; Either they advise that inequality is incurable or they are not sharing anything about inequality. They expect us to adjust to it to achieve the top or stay in the middle.

Few people educate their kids rationally by explaining the situations of finance and advising them on how to escape or change reality based on what their kids want. Most places' education does not explain the realities properly. Few people aren't even aware of it, so how can they advise their kids?

We are all born into any one of the religions in the world. Once we become adults or teenagers, our perspective on God might change or stay the same. Most people believe in God unconditionally, but how can most of us be in a sacred place like a mosque, temple, or church and have these thoughts? Because those places always tell everyone that everyone is equal in everything. There should not be any difference in the standards of treatment. So, in all places, our knowledge is not fully utilised. It means most of us hear what people say and simply agree on things before leaving, without implementing it in our lives. It means most of us are not examining, analysing, or thinking about what they are saying. As a society, collectively we are fundamentally collapsed. Most of us are not completely following anything. Most of us are upgrading ourselves in bits and pieces, but with that small piece of the upgrade, most of us behave like we know everything and tell people that everything is perfectly alright.

Most of us failed to grasp knowledge and understanding in finance. So, famous people with bits and pieces of incomplete knowledge advise us not to start falling into philosophies before becoming rich. They are encouraging people to be rich, but they aren't aware of the truth. The truth is that only 2% of the place is there. It's also very hard to go. Stop manipulating kids and others wrongly without complete knowledge because situations are not the same for everyone. Opportunities are not the same for everyone.

We have better technologies. We can lead an equal and happy life with that in the future without money as a transaction tool. Valuables are the reasons for protection. We need to have that understanding. It is related to finance; it is protected by power in the current economy. So, when we remove only power from the current economy and then continue with money as a transaction tool, then it's suicide. When protection is not there, it's easy for frauds and thieves to steal comfortably.

If we remove the money from the current economy and keep the powers borderless, as I said, then power over-focuses on things that it's already protected and makes it even smoother to enjoy. We can create something new to replace the money. Finally, make life easy.

Why do we need to protect people? I simply say that we are protecting people because they will fight baselessly to prove that they are stronger. It's a valid reason. It might happen because we are, after all, humans. We can't stop feeling those matters. How can we stop getting those feelings? As all divine scriptures say, love them like our own blood and create a better understanding of humanity within ourselves. Yep! No other way. We can stop protecting borders because we are structured in a way to hate having borders, but we are still evolving. So, we can't remove other protections altogether. We have to ensure that people are getting a better understanding. Until then, we can't completely go ultra-advanced. What is ultra-advanced? It's the topic for another time. I can give you a gif. Power can be replaced in the ultra-advanced stage. WBE - Power can't be replaced, but it can be used effectively.

It's very easy to provide people with essentials equally. We can easily avoid small countries going into an economic crisis since we are moving into a borderless world. We must understand one principle: not all countries are blessed with genius and knowledgeable people. Due to a lack of expertise, most small countries are struggling to survive currently. These are overruled by overpowered nations. When we move into a borderless world, the committee can analyse to provide the subject matter expert from anywhere to the requiring nation to resolve the issue. More productive and progressive research can be done independently without any interference from threats and attacks. We can effectively use resources globally to create and manipulate new sources more quickly than we expected.

You may ask me that, currently, we are using all the technologies. What changes does WBE bring that we are not having now with those technologies? Technologies are not working to their 100% potential. They are used as money-making tools. Economical experts' intention is not to kill money, but they intend to kill the reasons that use money's weakness as a moving point to earn something which is not ethically correct. It spoils the globe for its happiness, which is fundamentally wrong. It is where the whole equality is being questioned because of these reasons. We cannot move to equilibrium along with money; in the world, being equal becomes a laughingstock. Social workers want equality in religions, equality in caste, equality in colour, but the range of people who raise their voices for all these is subtle on equality in money. Why? It's because of the gap in understanding of finance.

How can we use technology effectively to achieve what I said? Please read the short glimpse below.

Here is a short glimpse of the efficient use of technologies. All Essentials are effectively managed and maintained by technologies.

Food

Food is the 1st thing in essentials, as we all know, but the availability of food is still not there for a few million people, lets leave numbers and accept the fact that there is a shortage. It may be small or big. We must understand that there is someone out there who still does not have food when we have it. A wasteful quantity of food per day can be fed to thousands of people. So, what is the solution to this? How can technologies be improved in the food sector? We have to mobilise a large quantity of land that is unused all over the world that has the potential to cultivate organically. We can elevate cross-cultural research facilities to maximise the talents of brilliant minds.

Toxic fertiliser that kills the nature of land should be examined under surveillance. Observe the potentiality of growth factors in it. Try to analyse the molecular structure then segregate toxic factors that can spoil the land. In that process, we all know that people are working hard in the current political philosophies as well but even if they find results to that good thing, they try to mobilise it to gain more profits then again it will circle back to profit curve. Countries that have money can use it, benefit from it, but those countries without money that can't make it, borrow that from others. Over a period, that can lead them to a vicious circle of debt. Countries have to be obligated to the lender for that debt. It will be dangerous.

The solution rests with the unity and cooperation of the globe. The work-based economy binds countries together without borders. The solution found anywhere can be used everywhere to make the world a better place. The food distribution system will be introduced into the work-based economy with the help of technology. How is it different from the existing one? We are using monetary policies to get food and ingredients, but some options will be introduced in WBE that can give us options to select food that we want for the day or ingredients required for the day. We can make it possible with the help of food apps. We can cook or have food, and it's our wise, but we always have options. The system can minimise wastage. It gives efficient time for those who don't want to cook. It allows us to make a healthy diet and problem-free food habit. As I said earlier, technology can revolutionise all essentials in WBE. It's a points-based system that treats everyone equally. We don't need to terrify of sudden changes. Systems will be introduced only after multiple years of examinations, crisis handling, shortage management test. Healthy, quality checks are made and ensure after a 100% success rate.

Shelter

Indians have a saying, "it's harder to get married, but it's even harder to build a home." Worldwide, people have their dream home in their minds with at least four bedrooms and a lift inside, expensive restrooms, expansive dining areas, comfortable viewing areas, and good scenery. These dreams must be in our minds. If not, we are just robots or we just scared to dream because of cost. Most people have the desire. What does a work-based economy say about it? How are technologies going to handle this? As I said earlier, we are not going to own anything other than essentials. WBE will ensure that everyone has their own home, but what will technologies do in it? A home we own is shiftable. People of all kinds only have the right to own one property. Technology will ensure that it will be up to our mark and desire, or I could put it in the way of minimum desire. Once a person shifts from being a student to working in the WBE, they are eligible to own a home. Our work is our eligibility. We can design our home with our luxury points as we wish, but everyone will get their minimum desired home once they enter the job, which is shiftable. What do I mean by saying it's shiftable? When we get a job in another place, we don't need to worry about our property in our current place. A place where we get a job will have a home for us. Our luxuries will be shifted from the old to a new place. So, our old place will be allotted to someone else. It gives us easy mobility, comfort, and a stress-free environment. What is the minimum desired? People may not be able to get a big bungalow, but they will get a minimum of 3 to 6 bedrooms based on their family size.

WBE will feel sorry for those who like to have a home like Ambani or Bezos. It is not possible to build a palace for everyone. It's not under an equality scale. We are trying to make people equal. The current economy builds its empire over real estate, which is the primary source of income for most countries and investment firms. It's safe and secure. It provides a maximum guarantee to run an economy. Countries build infrastructures with money. So, countries can grow more when people are willing to spend more. People are praying to God that the real estate rate should go down. It's fundamentally wrong in the current political philosophies because if that goes very low, then our country is nearing a financial debt crisis that is going to kill the life of millions, the source of millions, and which is horrible. So, it's like a loop in the economic structure. WBE Governments can utilise technologies to advance our experience and comfort in the home. The economy can act independently without the support of real estate. Technologies can ensure our protection, privacy, our belongings will be easily handled without any negligence. WBE will never hold us in a loop of an unsatisfied job and the pressure of money or a points-based system.

Land is the most complicated essential of all essentials. WBE has to handle it very carefully. It's because 100% politics are happening surrounding it in current political philosophies. People have to sacrifice their land and house. We will get a spacious big house from 3bhks to 6bhks. Billionaires are having million times worth of lands and houses but the pain is the same for everyone. Why are people afraid of sacrificing the land and house that they own? It's because of the struggles that they faced throughout their lifetime to hold one piece of land. Our ancestors struggled to own it and passed it to our generation. People have the fear. What if authorities plan to capture our land and house like they did previously? WBE will reserve all the rights and ownership to the public equally. No family politics will be there. We will have equal ownership of the lands of our nationality. It will be documented after it's authorised in our name. Everyone will have every right to go anywhere to relax.

Cloth

Gorgeous looks are most important for humans, but not all the time. People like to dress as they wish based on the places they visit and the people they meet. What are technologies going to do with clothes? Clothes are essentials, but they have to be bought with luxury points because not all essentials can be distributed unlimitedly and equally due to insufficiency. It's not only clothes that require luxury points but also ornaments. We have to reduce the holdings of ornaments to a certain level. It will make the world a better place. An ornaments account will be created for people worldwide. All the core metals will be credited to the accounts equally for everyone; it can't be taken by anyone, but they can use it when required and return it after its time limit. People have to use their luxury points to use the ornaments. Technologies can smooth the experience of buying clothes, using ornaments; technologies will ensure nobody neglects rules. We have taken resources from the earth more than required, which caused the deficit. We already have more than enough rare raw materials sleeping in the lockers, which are fundamentally not required in WBE; they will be put to better use by society. So, we don't have to worry about the ornaments' availability.

Communication

Globally, one day's worth is more than we can imagine. 21k crore years' worth of data is transferred daily by humans alone. As far as I know, only 1% of data can be possibly registered or stored; maybe I am wrong. It might be even more significant, but I am sure 100% of the data can't be stored. So, the power of communication is bigger than all controls. So, the same question, how will WBE manage it using technologies? WBE will not restrict the freedom of speech in any manner. People can speak about revolutionary things that can improve the economy. They make the society a better place. Communication helps us enjoy life. We analyse matters about all information that we receive then pass on to others about hidden layers in them. We enjoy engaging in them. All social media that help people communicate will have an autonomous body that no government officials own or control. This way, we will only receive news as it is without manipulations. Rational views can be portrayed without deviations. Communication in WBE will engage the general public in all decisions, opinion polls. WBE will decide to sanction the agenda based on reactions of people to further proceeding even current political philosophies following it to some extent. So, leaders can't get a chance to make destructive decisions autonomously. Communication language converter apps will support 1000+ languages with the help of technologies to stop hindrances to communicating with each other. We know it's already existed with minimum language assistance, but technologies will take it to the next level in the work-based economy. The app will be on everyone's mobile. Communication is not just a tool to convey messages; it's a core part of a transaction. Layers and the importance of communication will be taught to people daily. It can reduce cruelty.

Entertainment

Fun is the primary source that makes all problems bearable. It gives breathing space to think through a tough time. What makes people relax? Things that keep people away from stress. Most of them choose entertainment. A relaxed person has a clear mind to think. People are working hard in the current political philosophy. They need relaxation. Besides sleeping, they should refresh their mind and body in some other way. So, they focus on entertainment. People have a different set of entertainment based on mood, place, time, situation oriented to their attitude and behaviours. All entertainment makes people engage in activities. It makes people feel lively. There are 'N' number of entertainments in the world with the cost of zero to millions. The same question arises, how are technologies going to change this segment? When we look deep into society apart from essentials, entertainment is driving society forward continuously because people, stories, music around us continuously entertain us. Whatever work we do, we automatically connect with one or multiple essentials and with entertainment. We are connected to the earth with time which is constant. We are supposed to pass the time somehow because even after all that we wish for is completed, we are still left with endless time which can only be filled with entertainment. So, the demand for entertainers is always at its peak. The odd one out used to excel in it. They can easily catch the attention of children to elders. Entertainments are subject to the luxury points in a work-based economy. They can spend as long as they wish to spend. These luxury points help people spend it wisely on things they wish and like.

The workers in the entertainment field will not have the pressure of existence in WBE. People have security over their job in the entertainment field in WBE. It will not follow the lame policies of the current political philosophies. It won't give a hard time to artists, sports persons, entertainers. So, what technology's contribution to it? Technologies don't have much of a part in it but technologies will ensure that we get our luxury points, which are equal to everyone. It expires monthly. It's not salvageable. It's a method that does not force us to use all luxury points but will give us independence whether we want to use them or not. It will stop us from thinking about saving for the future. It makes us live in the movement. Technologies of WBE will enrich the entertainment experience. In WBE, entertainments never be the ignorance tool for us that stops thinking about pain. Real painful things will be addressed properly.

Medicine

No words are needed to explain the importance of medicine. It has improved in many ways in the current political philosophies. The progressiveness of this field is tremendous. This is the main reason for our population growth. We are going well with it but still facilities are not available for a few million people. Even though progressiveness is noteworthy, crimes around that never stopped like illegal testing of drugs on people, creating diseases to attack enemy countries. Even though it's related to the chemical industry, it's based on medicine. Compared to the global medicine-related GDP, these crimes are insignificant, but the impact on people is enormous. Covid-19 is the best example of it. It isn't a man-made disease but killed 6 million people as of April 2022 worldwide. How are technologies going to improve that in a work-based economy? Technologies will ensure that everyone gets proper treatment for their sickness. It keeps the doctor-to-patient ratio on track. All sorts of treatments will be provided to everyone equally without any difference. Technologies will ensure that if any differences are monitored and raised by patients, then that issue will be rectified within a day. Technologies will ensure that all sorts of medicines required for patients will be delivered to doorsteps based on their sickness and severity. Production of medicine, raw materials, supply, availability, alternatives will be tracked continuously by technologies. The creation of raw materials and alternatives will always be on track. It ensures there is no rise of deficiency in supplies. Technologies will help people to maintain a healthy diet to have a good body, consciousness, peace. So, technologies in the medical field of WBE play a big part. We have all the technologies in hand currently but the potential usage of it is not achieved because of the structural restriction, but WBE will not have any such restriction to the medical field since it's essential.

Transport

Technologies are the reason for all growth in transport. We can travel through sea, air, underwater, out of the earth and land with any speed. Currently, all options that we are enjoying are because of technology. We are manufacturing the vehicles unlimitedly every year. Everyone will agree that manufacturing of vehicles needs massive raw materials like water, metal, rubber, plastic, aluminium, and electric components. There is a myth that EVs are environmentally friendly. People must know the mining process of rare earth materials before arriving at any such ideas. Pollution is high in that process. We commonly agree that vehicles are exposing more pollution to the environment. Continuous extraction of raw materials from the earth is poisonous to the earth. Scientists and technologists are working on saving the environment by discovering practical solutions to the problem in the current economy due to transportation. How are technologies going to change that in WBE? The current political philosophy is utterly dependent upon export and import. Exchange is the primary source for a wealthy society; transport is the main source of exchange. WBE will have strict public transport rules; its availability will be well organised. All people will have a proper transport facility in WBE with the help of technology. WBE never restricts people's rights to use personal vehicles, but for regular transports, like going to work, we will be adopting entirely public transport unless it's an emergency. People can enjoy their travel with their vehicles, but usage of it will get reduced due to this. It can save us from pollution but not only this going to save us from that pollution. Technologies will analyse transport-related pollution emissions which will be controlled in more effective ways. Technologies will ensure to safeguard raw materials of the earth. It will prevent us from overproduction, unwanted recycling of it. Recycling will be unavoidable that will be there, but unused, overused items that go into recycling will be mitigated by technologies. Technologies will ensure that anywhere local can be possible within 30 minutes in WBE.

Ten

Where is the World Going?

Why current political philosophies have to change? Those who still believe that current political philosophies are better and need to last forever are still madly in love with current political philosophies. They have seen some potential in current political philosophies. I would like to see that too. Please mail support@economicstealers.com. I will try to discover what they have seen but has gone unnoticed by us.

One sentence is more than enough to close this chapter. Google "Earth History". For those who don't know, you have to check then get to know how the world has changed in the last 30 years, which has stayed still for a million years. If we had a time machine, we could pause time then move the entire timeline of the world that we structured into millions of years in the past to check, "Is 100 years enough to spoil the earth?" really, whenever, wherever in the timeline we move, it gives more or less the same outcome. This noxiousness is led by the current political philosophical structure's interconnected strings and knots. It's a whole web of dust. Removing one string or knot will never help anyway because the money spider will rebuild it how it's like to build.

Earth's temperature is scaring scientists because of its vulnerability. No wonder in it because just small climatic temperature changes capable of raising sea levels. This change will be enough to sink New York into the water. Anyways, that is slowly happening. The sea water level is rising. Scientists predict that around 2100, some areas, I mean essential areas, will sink into the sea. How hard will it be? Can't governments stop it? They can change the situation to be as good as they did for the ozone layer. Fixing it is an effortless task, but governments should decide it. What makes that climate change? Is it pollution or rotation of the solar system, or any secret agenda going on within governments to increase the sea level? Solar systems can't be the reason because a slight change in the earth's axis can cause an ice age in some places. The sun provides the source ideally without any significant change. The next is the secret agenda, sorry guys, we have to wait and see after the target is achieved then the investigative reporters leak the files. So far, all are accusing pollution. Net zero is the world leaders' goal in 2035 commonly. We have to wait. Is it going to net zero or net XXX numbers?

Do we all know what is polluting the world? All vehicles, all-electric goods, all chemical factories, all dye plants, all experimental laboratories, radiation, gas, plastics. I need another 100 sheets to fill the other list. We can't lead society without these. We can't expect people to stop using it all of a sudden. Even if they try, it's not possible. We can't stop what we started, but we can control one thing: overproduction, over-usage, wastage, alternate, productive shredding. Corporations and governments will not do anything until they see some tremendous loss of things because they are not ready to consider small indications; everyone always takes action when it's out of hand. If we want precautious changes to happen as planned, the system's flow needs to change; adoption can't come that quickly. So, fear of change will not encourage the profit curve. Losses will be huge that can't be manageable by governments and companies that value their currency against the United States dollar. It will affect the exports and imports of the countries that rely on the United States dollar. It will be considered as a chance for mega-powered countries that try to use that situation then occupy and dominate the country that tries to take precautionary action against climate change. So, if something needs to change, it must happen together. One country can't change anything alone. Biggies need to decide. When will they decide? When they see the potential loss that affects them, as I said earlier. It's not the people's place to decide because we are all controlled by the governments that we choose. Whoever we choose, they will be doing all decision-making. It is a structural problem. Countries can't do anything that affects people in bad ways. So, they postpone these small issues for another time.

What harm can scientists do to society if their products are not adequately researched in every way possible? The transport industry was looking for a new type of gasoline. Thomas Midgley Jr and his team researched and then found something useful that can be used in cars as fuel, but they didn't correctly research their findings' side effects. What is that going to mean for humans; they created something to smooth the car ride. The industry's lack of research skills and profit rush stood as factors for the new fuel to come to market fast. The scientist Claire Patterson found that the new fuel is causing a disastrous effect on the human body since it contains lead. It is mixed with air then pollutes humans on a massive scale. He had to try hard to prove that it was causing millions of deaths just to smooth something for the luxury of something. Industries created this new fuel. Industries are not ready to stop what they constructed using billions of dollars. Finally, when he proved that it was causing deaths worldwide, they decided to find some alternative. Again, Thomas Midgley Jr stood as a villain for humans with another invention of smoothing refrigerators, which spoiled the ozone layer. Finally, that too was discovered too late, which made a hole in the ozone layer. Countries are trying to reconstruct it. The work is in progress for decades. It will take more decades. The profit motive is the main villain that makes people push towards these things without proper funding, research of side effects, testing. One person and his team funded by industries. They spoiled the earth's atmosphere without proper research. They spoiled human health just for a profit Curve. He is just an sample but world is still holding many people like him.

We have to know what Nash equilibrium is. More specifically, the Nash equilibrium is a concept of game theory where the optimal outcome of a game is one where no player has the incentive to deviate from their chosen strategy after considering an opponent's choice. When we follow some structured rules in anything, that time our opponent and us both take the same strategy to end the game, which means that a particular item won't end because both are stuck at the same point. If there is no change in strategy, then we have to tie that thing. In the power game, countries' leaders have that in mind then started building nuclear missiles. They thought if we have one, then others won't threaten us—currently, there are nine nuclear states worldwide. Nine leaders only have access to it. These nine countries can't compete with each other since they are in the same league, but when all the countries in the world have access to it like these nine countries means that time almost 200+ countries have access to it, which means 200+ leaders. Precisely 200+ mental mind games. They can't keep quiet for much longer; somehow, they will rise on their instability; they come to a revenge mindset that I don't care about my death or my people's death or a million households; I want you to suffer like me, I will launch it without regret. So, this mind game of Nash equilibrium will only work out for a while. People must know that it's not like World War 1 or 2. In the last paragraph, we discussed what could possibly be done by one team of scientists. I know that it's already been discussed worldwide that no one should use nuclear or more dangerous weapons on anyone, but secretly, every country in the world is trying to build one, like India, Pakistan, and North Korea. It's just a matter of formula how long that is going to take. Even creating and storing it in place will cause harm if a millimetre of a thing goes out of hand. People can't be conscious 24/7, as we all know.

How hard will it be? Nine countries are creating this much mess worldwide currently, then think about 200+ countries; I know more countries are the territory of super-powered countries, but still, the counts are more. The expected level of mess is 1000 times bigger. Russian war, American war, all border threats, economic meltdown, we have few reasons only today, but what does the future hold in it? There may be more reasons. Unexpected countries will become super-powered nations then start creating new threats. Fall of existing countries from that status. Mind games do not always end in favour of someone we think. The systemic structure of the economy forces us to hold on to this. Loosen up from the structure is the only way out.

Password, lock, firewall, secure ID, VPN – we use these to protect the items we use; we are liable for them. So, they can prevent us from data loss and theft, robbery. They are used to safeguard materials in general that we love and own. Let's look at it from a different perspective. From childhood, if we look back on ourselves, we can identify children wanting the same thing that another kid has. We never taught a child that we should have the exact item as another child. Then where does this attitude come from? Just think about it. It's simple that children create equality within themselves without anyone's influence. They expect that whatever things other children have, the same thing that they want to have too, to keep equality alive within themselves. When it's not happening, at that time children express their pain by crying, then registering this in their mind. As parents, we can't buy everything that children ask for because of so many reasons. Some parents are educating their children with that situation as an example, then implementing that "everything is not equal for everyone". "You will not get everything that you ask for". There is no equality in the world that we are in. We have to keep that in mind, then start to accept it and afterwards behave like accepting it. This suppression is almost registered in every child born in the world. Some parents are educating their children that parents are not in the position to buy those items and as children, it's not a good habit to ask parents to buy everything others have for them too.

Children don't know the concept that people created something unequal. When that child becomes a man or woman, at that time, those who accept it don't do anything against it and don't spoil anything, but those who are not accepting it always create all messing up things. Few people want to change that constructively by coming to power for change the system that is not rational. They make the system legally and peacefully rational. Few others stole things that they didn't have. Almost all these thefts are hidden symbols for the representation of wanting an equal world. Now go and check criminal records of the world every year regarding thefts; all are the unheard voices of wanting an equal world. Sometimes it goes one step ahead by making people think that the world is not giving us equality; we want to give the same to the world. They will get bigger and bigger than everyone in any way possible without regret. These types of people become harmful to society eventually. Every wrong person has some reason why they want to create a mess in the world because everybody is not the same and wants to change something constructively. They don't even know the depth of it, but they will do it without knowing it. All these securities that we have are to showcase that this world is not equal, there are valuable things here that are more valuable than our life, and for that, we have these securities. If anything happens to these valuable things, people are never afraid to stop thinking about killing anyone to protect them. It's because they have ownership of it, that ownership came from hours and hours of hard work. When it goes out of hand, they can't stand on it and watch. Due to that, they are acting on their rage to protect it with their life.

It's the generalised consumption of inequality, but there are an N number of layers in it. When we read the newspaper, we do not realise why it is happening worldwide in society. The structure is not just connected only with money; it's just a tool; it's interconnecting all major differences then helping its survival. As I said in earlier topics, it keeps the society in a permanently discriminating way. We have a law that we should not do discrimination, even if it's a mild and tiny discriminating thing, but if an affected person went to complain based on that created law, at that time society will tell them that it's just a tiny thing. They ask them to resolve it within them. People who have luxury and time bring even tiny problems to court. It's not convenient for everyone. We have bigger problems to deal with. The range of these small struggles keeps increasing in society, leading to big issues. The system structure is built that way; if we want to change, we must avoid these irrational political philosophies.

When we generally talk without detailing; at that time, everyone wants to be equal in everything, but when we explain details of difficulties, hardships, challenges, and sacrifices, 90% of the people who agreed to be equal in general conversation will not step forward after hearing the details. It's because they want it, but they are not ready to push themselves to struggle for it. They start to argue by supporting the idea that old philosophies are the best. 'It has to be like that to maintain balance in the world.' They argue that 'it's okay to make 1 billion people suffer for the good of 7 billion'.

People always hope that something will change for good in the current political philosophy because people can't systematically completely change from what they have followed for these many years just like that. They are naturally looking for better things in what they currently follow. Is it even possible? Can we make things better in the current political philosophy? Governments and banks in most countries operate as separate entities, but both are equally involved in maintaining the balance that we are arguing. We can't bring change to current political philosophies because they have to move with strict rules, which should be undeniable. The major complaint is about the profit curve; can we cut the profit curves which are the backbone of political philosophies? People who studied economics and mastered it know the real challenges in it. The profit curve that we created leads an economy. The profit curve keeps it running, but at the same time, because of the profit curve, people are struggling to keep up with it. We can't cut the profit curve in the current political philosophical structure.

We can't make a better system because we have to struggle with other components of its structure that are connected with the profit curve. Consumer cost is always greater than manufacturing cost. Manufacturing cost should include costs of raw material, production equipment, electricity, labour, place, transport, and marketing. Companies can't give the product at the manufacturing cost because they can't move their organisation to the next level. They have to add the profit cost, and that's when they can move to the next level. If they don't include the profit cost, then they can't produce more if demand increases, or they can't even produce without a profit curve if the manufacturing unit operates with the help of a loan. They will supply only for the demand that previously existed if they run the unit with their own capital. They have to take a loan to meet the new demand because they don't have cash in their hand as surplus since they gave their product in manufacturing cost. Financiers are eligible to provide a loan because they have the power of holding money as a source. There are 2 types of major financiers: NBFC (Non-Banking Financial Corporation) and BFC (Banking Financial Corporation). BFC can print money then provide a loan through the credit creation process, and for that, they will charge interest. They can't provide loans free of interest because this interest is their income. The bank needs money to maintain itself. The interest that they get from customers helps banks for that purpose. Banks have to pay for their protection, workers, services, land, and transport. NBFC can't print money like BFC, but they are a big institution. They hold money lump sum as capital for their business. They will have the same expenses as BFC. They will get those expenses covered from the interest they charge to customers. This interest as well holds the profit cost. So, BFC and NBFC can move ahead in their business to the next level. If they are not added profit cost, then it's the same as the companies' scenario for NBFC; they only have supply for existing demand. They can't supply for new demand. BFC differs from that because they are not providing a loan based on their cash in hand, but they are creating the money through credit creation under the central bank's norms when someone is applying for a loan. So, the BFC sector never runs out of money unless there is a worst recession or investments devalued.

Now, come back to companies that reached NBFC or BFC for a loan to meet the new demand. They will get a loan to meet the new demand. They pay interest for that loan. This interest is also added to the manufacturing cost. Take for example, Demand is not stable in the market. Sometimes it goes up and sometimes it goes down. Most of the time, nobody knows when it goes down. It's depending on market conditions. If demand goes down but supply is not adjusted to it, then the manufacturer has to reduce the consumer cost to make the consumer buy more, but when that doesn't work out, at that time, they have to face the loss. Companies will have expenses that never change but if they can't produce income, they can't provide interest. If NBFC provided the loans but it doesn't get its interest, it means a loss for them. It's the same for BFC too, but what is the difference in loss between NBFC and BFC? BFC is mostly backed by the government or central bank, but NBFC is on their own. So, NBFC needs to maintain its business. NBFC will take a loan from BFC to cover its loss. NBFC and Companies are making a loss if the profit curve is not there. So, BFC as well can't get their interest. Their loss can't be recovered if the profit curve is not available. They are forced to write off the loss cost from their books of accounting, which can't be recovered because we eliminated the profit curve. We have to completely change the accounting principles that we are following now. The golden rules of accounting are void if the profit curve is not available. If the profit curve is there, once demand becomes normal, companies can raise the manufacturing cost by including the loss cost and profit cost to come up with the consumer cost for the consumer. This will recover their loss.

Even if a profit curve is present, they can manage up to a certain level because they have the money earned from the profit cost they charged to customers. They can't manage beyond a certain limit. So, BFC will also not get interest because others are at a loss. BFC usually invests 90% of our money in financial markets. When everyone is facing a loss, people will seek their money saved in BFC. At this time, banks can't provide deposits back to customers because they invested 90% of the money in the financial market. If the investment is profitable, then BFC won't have any issues, but if it's a loss, then they have to bear the loss. This loss will also affect governments. Even with the profit curve, we have to face losses. It will increase the consumer price of goods. So, to acquire products, consumers need more money than they previously required. They demand employers to raise their income. This increase in income will be added to manufacturing costs as well. Now the price of goods has increased. It's one of the models of inflation. It's a cycle that will continue to rotate. That's why the prices of goods continuously increase over decades. This is why the profit curve is inevitable in current political philosophies.

It will collapse the structure if we cut the profit curve from the economy, which will be a catastrophic failure. We can't cut the profit curve in only one country because the whole system is structured in a line. A separate line can't leap out of the existing one. The world won't support it. If the world likes to withdraw the profit curve, it changes the entire system as we imagined, but the world can't do it if it's not seeing anything catastrophic in the current system. Indigenousness and individuality can't be motivated if we cut the profit curve. A product's success is accessed based on its profit and loss. When we cut profit from it, we have also been forced to cut loss in it. Then, we can't be able to operate or access something in the material world without PandL in the current economy. We can't re-engineer things in the current political philosophy because of this.

We could see the 1940s' 1 dollar value was more than 2022's 1 dollar value. One of the many reasons for inflation is speculation in the stock market by big players. The speculators of the financial market are one of the reasons for inflation. The hedge funds and similar other instruments are the reason. The government is injecting money into the economy without narrowing down on which aspects need to be improved with that infused money. So, the injected money spreads across all fields, then the fields that didn't need any injection of money also get benefited from it. These unwanted field players use that money to bet and speculate with it, hiking the prices of necessary goods.

This devaluing of money happened because of the profit curve. When profits rise, at the same time, we have the risk of loss, and to compensate for loss quickly, the price of the product will increase. That time profit will get generated. The price increase will create an impact on people's purse so that we have to pay more for the same thing that we bought for less money in the last quarter end. This cycle slowly devalues the worth of 1 dollar. When we get hit by inflation, the government will increase interest rates on repos. The government will decrease interest rates when countries are together in an economic struggle. So, people get some more money in circulation. It's fine when people are moving towards growth slowly and steadily. It's not fine when the collective movement of growth is unexpected and unprepared by governments. Resources for that growth are not available in the material world. So, governments have to hold people in their current position. The government is not ready for further growth which required more resources that time the government hikes prices of essential goods then they increase interest rates on loans. They try 100% hard to hold people in the current position until the resources that get ready. Growth is measured by money in the current economy. When people have more money that time, what will naturally happen? They try to spend more on things, sometimes they are wise to spend on stuff that has very minimum availability. Sometimes since a huge volume of people is acquiring something in particular that time the availability of that stuff becomes very minimum. In that case, the price of that item will be increased. It's not structured to reach more people. When people get more money. Everyone tries to spend on that very minimum item, that time the resource will go out of hand on the government side. The balance of the economy will get spoiled. So, this imbalance unavoidably falls heavily on people irrespective of their work. We can't blame governments for it. They tend to maintain balance at any cost. So, they increase the cost based on demand and availability.

Laissez-faire is an economic philosophy of free market capitalism that opposes government intervention. It believes that economic success is more likely when there is less government interference involved in business. Globally, people have an idea that if there is no intervention of the government, then it's easier to grow more. Developed countries are identifying themselves as laissez-faire countries. They are proud of it. Banks are managing and keeping the balance in countries that have the position of laissez-faire. We can take any model in the current economy and then do research. The final results will show up as the "keeping the balance at any cost" motto. What is this balance that we are talking about? Balancing is nothing but controlling resources that are minimal and making sure that they are available for everyone who can bear the cost of it no matter what. This cycle can't be improved. We have to follow this if we want this current political philosophy.

The financial world has been moved towards digital transactions. As I said earlier, currency changes its face. It transfers itself to adopt technologies. Its true nature will always stay constant. Whether cryptocurrency or simple digitally manipulated currency, governments always try to show people that nothing has changed but society has evolved technically. They convince people simply with rules and coordination of all players of differentiation. Suppose people got the disclosed economy method after arguments and protests then. In that case, governments openly do their manipulative things. They showcase the side effects of what would happen if they didn't follow it. These effects will automatically convince people to stay in the current political philosophies.

People want complete independence in the economy. They don't want any involvement of corporates, banks and governments. It is only possible when everyone in the world has a complete understanding of the economy. People must know the importance of using things to their 100% potential and understanding the minimum usage of resources. Even then, people need a centralised entity to assess, report availability, productivity. It's a topic for another time. It's not possible in the near future. First, people should realise the value of equality about WBE. Only after it is possible.

Take the history of civilisation then check how it has systematically changed. I never argue about the knowledge of the people, technologies that systematically changed work and entertainment. It's a tremendous systematic change, but I am questioning whether society has evolved mentally towards equality with the help of current political philosophy. If that happened, I wouldn't have been writing this book in the first place. Differences modernised its face, but the root of all these, deep inside, completely lifting all historical causalities. People always think it's okay to make 1 billion people suffer for the good of the 7 billion population. Anyways, one day or another, within this 1 billion people, most of them will move to the 7 billion population. Few in the 7 billion population will move to the 1 billion population. It's just a cycle. This rotation only makes human life interesting.

It is how people consumed philosophy throughout history that it's just the cycle. I am not one to advertise it as a wrong conception of philosophy because if society has not changed as I imagined, then I also have to be in that poor old philosophy. Why do I say it as poor old philosophy? It's because it's encouraging the ancient things that need betterment. It's encouraging that some people should be at the top and others should be at the bottom. We must depend on people higher than us. We have to accept the inequality. We might as well move to the top sometime; we should behave like how the top behaved these many centuries, or else the balance can't be maintained. Poor resource maintenance is also part of it.

We as humanity started from scratch. We initially followed equality naturally, but we slipped from that somewhere in the middle. We lost track of it. We don't have a grip on it currently. We are trying to become equal like we started in the beginning. It seems like a cyclical effort. We made ourselves worse, but again, we are trying to become good. We made mistakes collectively as a society. We structurally enlarged an unequal system. It's a movement. We lived as a group, then we transitioned ourselves to tribes. We moved from tribes to kingdoms slowly. Now, in most places, we have replaced kingdoms with democracy. We are still in that process because we have not completely figured out everything in societal structure globally. We will move from here too soon.

We can categorise workers in three ways: good, poor, and illegal. What are these good, poor, and illegal means? Good means workers who do the work excellently. They improve it to the next level. Poor workers are those who do not perform well. They make more mistakes. As we see in previous topics, mistakes are the reason for all the improvements. If we didn't make any mistakes, then we can't be able to grow anyway. Poor workers are not always poor; they will move to good workers at any time and vice versa. Good workers can't be good workers always. They will also become bad workers at any point in time. It's just a cycle. As we all know, it's a never-ending one. Illegal workers are those who do work illegally for survival. What are all illegal works? The works that harm people in any way are categorised in this. We have illegal workers in society, but this is unavoidable in the current political philosophy. They sometimes survive in grey areas of the law and sometimes get caught by law.

There is a difference between illegal immigrants and illegal workers—a topic that is unexplored in any of the above topics. Illegal immigrants are emerging because their countries cannot care for them or their wellness. So, those who don't have money are moving illegally to other countries for a better chance of survival. Illegal immigrants are emerging because of the financial crisis and wars mainly. They may be illegal immigrants, but most of them are not illegal workers. They do small work. They live mostly hiding from the sight of governments. Illegal immigrants sometimes get the citizenship of the country where they immigrated illegally and start enjoying subsidies that countries provide for their citizens based on their tax income and government's public debts. This is where the problem arises because they might have immigrated 10 to 20 years before and started a family and running successfully but the government only has the supplies for the existing citizens. So, when these immigrants put their hands on these subsidised supplies that's when the shortage problems arise. So, governments start searching for the reasons. They will find out the immigrants' issue. So, the government, naturally abiding the law, will decide to send them back to their own nation. This process will not only affect immigrants but also their kids. Their kids don't even know that they are illegal immigrants settling in a foreign land illegally. So, the future of the kids as well spoil. The survey taken from most countries agreed that illegal immigrants are helping the development of countries. They are not a burden to the country. They become a burden when they enjoy the subsidies that they are not eligible for. India is one of the examples suffering from illegal immigrants. Countries that suffer financially, like Greece, have a different opinion. Illegal immigrants always focus on financially strong countries. Financially sound countries are not in a position to accept illegal immigrants in large volume because if they start doing that, the country's balance will get spoiled.

How can we judge the economy based on its performance? There is a saying that goes, 'One serious goof can spoil what we build throughout these many years, but our current economy doesn't worry about that at all because even after millions of allegations, stupid decisions, even after a heavy fall, our current political philosophies never lose their track. It will firmly stand without changing anything of its pace. What is the reason? The government is a structure. This structure is managed by people. The people who are managing it have made all mistakes. All falls and allegations are happening because of them. Economists showcase all collected data then argue that current political philosophies have a balance of demand and supply. It has a proactive monetary system. All these are the only ways possible to run the world.

The economy should not be vulnerable. It can't be manipulated by the people who manage it. The economy should not be affected by natural calamities. When any natural disaster happens, it spoils millions of people's wealth. Losing their position and earning back what they lost takes decades. The economy cannot recreate what they lost within two years. Because of that, people in a good position yesterday can lose everything the next day. Stability is missing in current political philosophies in the disaster situation.

If we ask people one question, "Do you like your work more or the money that you're earning from that more?" most of them will say the money they are earning. Few may say both. Few may say work. So, people are attracted to money more than anything because it helps them survive. It entertains them as a tool. We are naturally attracted to things that make us happy. So, humans are attracted to money. This attraction moves slowly toward addiction. When these types of questions arise, people quickly respond to them. This shows that their psychology is very weak towards money. People also know deep inside that nothing can be earned without work. These psychological questions help us understand people better. People idealise riches. People want everything that rich people consume. It drives people towards attraction then addiction. They feel insecure and out of fashion when they don't have something rich people have. They just consume the idea that rich people live up to the trend. Companies are using it to create unwanted demand for products. These products create a projection in people's minds that buying and enjoying it is happiness. It is where short-term artificial happiness is manipulated by products. This core concept is the same, but it has different roles in urban and rural areas. This addiction is more on prestige rather than money in rural areas. What are all the prestigious things for them? All the items in players of differentiation.

It is happening because of a lack of understanding of society and the economy. Common people tend to lead their life in a short circle. When this force drives society in the same way, the usage of unwanted overrated goods circulation increases worldwide, costing more raw materials from the earth that potentially need to be used for the growth perspective but are wasted into unwanted goods. This waste will make the environment poor. People will lose their grip on what is essential. This psychological analytical capacity will fade away over the consumption of unwanted goods. People will act violently. When we bring up this topic, they feel like someone is pulling their legs. It will get worse as time goes on.

Artificial intelligence is sabotaged from the first topic itself. Companies depend highly on it because of its profitability, quality, speed, and accuracy. The world population is growing higher and higher, but the actual problem will be the data we are generating in the world. Humans can't manage that without the help of technology. Companies want to smooth the process of managing it. They work hard to create artificial intelligence, particularly for some categories that can manage data efficiently. For custom calculation purposes, categorising, simultaneous research of data, analytics, better production, protection, marketing promotions, analysing customer behaviours, collectively correlating and verifying topics, arriving at solutions, intelligence, investigations, monitoring, wiretapping, grammar correcting, spying, and many more. All these major areas require AI intervention. Most AI is created only based on object-oriented purposes. It gives a better analysis promptly.

As long as the AI is created for object-oriented tasks, it's fine, but if AI is created for a complicated task that requires object-oriented research purposes, then AI will create its consciousness and self-awareness through trial and error, which will endanger humans. When we create something to save milliseconds, that destroys our 50,000 years of heritage and legacy, it means there is no sense in creating it. It's worse than nuclear missiles. Companies have already created AI that can think independently but then stopped it from operating after realising its criticalities. So, we should not try something we cannot control. It can result in severe loss.

The inner emotions won't leave us when we have the knowledge and all the resources to create something like that. It urges us always until we get severe hits and pain that we can feel. We continuously argue against people who talk against AI, then judge them that they don't know how to create one due to that they are interested in stopping someone who knows how to create one. People with knowledge and resources always hear a voice within them encouraging them to do or create something like researching AI, but when we presume that voice then act on it without analysing risk factors, we have to face the consequences. If we leave the world like this, we can witness the movie Terminator in real-time.

We have to understand the circumstance. Since we know about the inner voice, it's essential to know what's causing it. Humans are triggered by different types of circumstances. Our circumstances are created by the social circles around us. These circumstances are classified into two types: good and bad.

Nowadays, people have the power to be atheists, but in ancient days, many centuries back, everyone had to believe in God. It created two types of circumstances. People who lived around those centuries saw one circumstance as good and the other one as bad. They believed that believing in God held them towards divinity without harming others in their circle. They saw it as a good circumstance. What they saw as a bad circumstance now looks like a good circumstance. What is that other circumstance? People lived in a society with conflicts of believing in God. They called themselves atheists. They tried finding the laws of physics but mostly didn't express themselves as atheists in front of society because of the threat to their lives. Theists believed that atheists were their bad circumstance.

Here is an interesting fact: our circumstances provoke our emotions. Our emotions provoke our inner voice. It prompts us to act when we are restricted, as I mentioned earlier. So, when we are limited in some way, we not only attempt it but also aim to safeguard what we have gained to show to our circle. It's the main reason how we obtained most of the valuable scientific research papers from ancient times. When there is no restriction, there is no need to safeguard it because it's freely available to everyone. Whoever has an interest can read or acquire it. In this case, sometimes previous generations failed to pass it on to the next generations. It vanished over time as time passed. We don't know how many countries had restrictions on atheists or how many precious documents disappeared. It's not necessary for scientists to be non-believers in God because many people who believed in God discovered many mind-bending laws of mathematics and physics in the 19th century, 20th century, and even before that.

Centuries back, people believed that non-believers of God are bad for society. When people faced a hard time, they prayed to God, symbolised God as the saviour of the soul. People who faced cruelty in the name of God were held in bad circumstances, but the balance was not equal because good circumstances dominated. Places where bad circumstances dominated were hidden by history mainly to avoid diversion. The bad circumstance does not always need to be linked to bad things because people's perspective towards seeing something will change when time changes. People always need the option. When that is not available or the path that other people don't want to explore, which is even followed by most atheists. Atheists choose against something which most people are not agreeing. This bad circumstance triggers to prove something which the world has not seen ever before. Most scientists are triggered by bad circumstances. They tried to prove everything needs to be identified with science. Followers of God feared it. Why did they fear it? The chances of these discoveries spoiling the unity of people within their circle. If bad circumstances triggered people to prove that everything is science and God has no part in anything, then people's inner demons started taking revenge on their own instead of praying meaninglessly to God. It will spoil humanity completely. This is why people in good circumstances avoided and argued against bad circumstances. Currently, naturally, most people have developed their knowledge.

As per science, the concept of God is not accepted, but it's taken as a uniting source. In the later days of the modern era, many things changed. The core of uniting sources is still stable as a god. More than 65% of people have belief in God, 7 to 10% don't have belief in God. The rest have something in that place that replaces God in any form. Good circumstance is directly related to happiness.

Our Expressions are reflections of our government's activities and our ecological incidents. People will be in a bad circumstance when something unlikely happens. So, humans are subject to circumstances. When people feel something collectively going out of hand, which can affect society, this is considered a bad circumstance and people collectively join effortlessly to act against. So, this circumstance automatically covers a mass audience. Mass is nothing but the volume of people. The force acts as a speed in an incident. This speed will lead to consequences. It may be anything. Sometimes decisions at that speed will take the ruling parties down. In the ancient days, it was hard to manipulate circumstances because of the networking issue; word of mouth was time-consuming. Most of the time, governments' ruling parties will control word of mouth smoothly before it gets spread to a broad audience. The crucial issues only get a broad audience. People in bad circumstances are suppressed even more, mainly in ancient days. This is why the French Revolution, American Revolution, and Russian Revolution took place. When the time changed, networks got broad improvements. Social media became a platform for propaganda; manipulating mass audiences became simple. Governments are trying hard to keep the audience as good listeners because when people are manipulated by social media about governments' inefficiencies towards problems that affect society, it will create considerable domestic violence in all places. The governments can't control it. The governments have to stop bad circumstances. Governments use internet bans, tight restrictions. This news spoils the government ruling party's positions. They can't keep their place secured under challenging circumstances. If the governments can't stop networking. It will end up with huge domestic violence. Governments can't stop this. Other political parties will use situations then take over the governments.

When something is created that cannot be destroyed forever, it stays forever in any form, one way or another. The world is changing daily. The speed of changes can't be analysed, but that can be felt inside us. Where is the world going? We started by asking the question. Now we have come to the near end of it. The daily changes can't be monitored. The decadal changes can't be unmonitored or ignored. The world is upgrading; it automatically erases things that have been untouched for years. It's eliminating living beings that can't change themselves even after multiple lifetimes. Stubbornness towards staying without upgrading can't help to evolve. All these years, the world has been teaching us only one thing: changes are keeping us alive. It's pushing us towards crossing the space-time dilemma. The decisions we make help us. We have to own the consequences of decisions. Sometimes it ends with gain. Other times it ends with loss. All these years, we felt sad for things that vanished from this earth. We lost many languages, species, specimens, historical buildings, scriptures, legends, technologies, and scientific research. We lost in the speed of changes. Many went undiscovered and destroyed. All things that were created gave some input. It helped the world to change.

What is driving us towards changes and decisions? The most complicated question ever in the world. We are well aware that everything has a reason. So, discovering it became essential. Take a piece of paper and a sharp pencil, now put a dot on that paper. Metaphorically, this is what we created in the world over millions of years together as living species. Imagine that we draw a circle that is the most prominent ever possible. It can be even more significant than universes altogether. It is what stays collectively in all living species' minds that is uncreated but has been there for a long time as a model, prototype, or idea. The created things never equalise the uncreated things because when something is created at that time, the uncreated circle becomes big. So, it's impossible to equalise. It is because when something is created, that forming and inspiring new uncreated ideas. So, naturally, one created thing led to millions of uncreated ideas. So, whatsoever created will come from this uncreated idea circle. We can imagine the nano-particle level in the dot that we draw. It's the level of mass hitting the circle in sense of inspiration, evolution, releasing, unleashing converting the uncreated things into a created thing in the material world. So, people are running towards materialising their uncreated ideas daily. It is what encourages them and leads their life. Some people are running for themselves. Some people are running for others. So, money is just a tool to make it into the material world.

So, when people realise the value of an uncreated circle and then try to make the dot bigger, the human race will evolve to the next level. They will eventually realise the weight of money in the process of evolving and later create alternatives for that money. They equalise themselves and then unleash the universe within them. It is where we are going.

We have alternative methods for everything. If we take medicine, we have allopathy, Homeopathy, Ayurveda, many other methods. If we take coding, we have many coding languages. For communication, we have 1000 languages. For cooking, we have alternative methods. We have many modes and methods of entertainment. If we make buildings, we have alternative methods to build them. For clothes, we have various fabrics and many various methods to loom them. So, the world has options of choice for almost everything but money. If we look for an alternative to the monetary system, we don't find any. People have choices and alternatives for everything but don't find anything as an alternative to money. We are surrounded by legendary technologies, but alternatives for money are found nowhere. We found $E = mc^2$. We found how to compute numbers fast. We found many things. Still, the economy always relies on money. When people understand what is the fastest way to make a dot bigger, at that time, they will find the alternative for money to run the economy. Why do we need it faster? Because the universe is moving faster than the speed of light. The scientists confirmed that the moon is getting away from Earth day by day. We may have lakhs of years. We can't achieve anything groundbreaking without moving from money and equalising humans faster in the speed of 100 years to 1000 years. Else, we have to start from scratch again, you know why. Why? Because humans don't have patience, tolerance in the power war.

When there is an apocalypse, 2% of the top table people may think or may not, but if they think that they will escape from the earth, leaving 98% of people to die on earth. They think that they can survive with 2% or maybe less than 2%, but they will just be leaving a source archive on the earth. They can't collect more than 2% of data overall to survive without earth. So, they can't survive if they are not protecting and equalising people. If people are leaving with 2% from earth, then people are making their dot even smaller and making their circle even smaller. So, survival will be much harder than expected for those 2%. There are high chances of a fight among them, then people will be moving backwards to the Stone Age. This is why the world will be going to find a prototype and model or demo economy without money as a transaction tool to survive with all luxury.

What will be the next hard thing if we all equalised in the future? Putting the roof on top of our head, feeding our tummy, or educating us will not be hard, but serving our luxury will be really hard. People will go crazy about their luxury. People will get ready to die for the luxury. People don't care about the side efforts of their craving towards luxury even after people studied all about how the world is structured. They can't control their desires because of fewer social problems encourage them mentally to riot against something that the world has less that can't distribute to everyone more than what they are currently acquiring. I brought this up because nothing is a permanent solution. Moving towards the next level is the only solution. What is the next level? Once the world is equalised, it will run smoothly. The next level will be decided based on daily movements, news, chain of incidents occurring over centuries, leaders' behaviours, the world's structure. Political situations change based on all these. We can't predict over some generations because this is not predestination. Nobody predicted that we would be growing this well at this time. The same will apply to the future.

In the previous topics, I discussed the players of differentiations that separate people. Our ancestors created most of these differences to keep balance in the world. Actually, in the future, these differentiations will disappear when they provide no material benefits to any kind of people. Currently, people are getting all kinds of material benefits. So, differentiation keeps itself alive with the help of monetary policies. Most people in the previous generation have not forgotten how society used these differentiations. Due to that deep inside, they have not changed, but time will give the answer. All these castes and racially based differences will disappear when the money system changes and if a work-based economy comes.

People's search for finding divinity in the current period is more complicated. Few people use it to earn money through others' beliefs, but in the future, understanding God and searching for divinity will be travelling on an entirely new path. These searches may take us all into a different dimension. I mean in the sense of metaphysics.

Woke culture is followed by many people for many different reasons, one of them being independence about sexual identity. In some places, children are forced to identify themselves at very early stages, which is not a good sign because children are always in a confused state when it comes to sexuality. As a society, we should explain and educate them about everything around it, but we should not influence them towards any side. We have to give them an independent chance to figure it out on their own. If this is missing, then more people will be spoiled for someone else's business and happiness.

So, that's it. I am quitting my assessments of where the world is going. You can continue to write your predictions of where the world is going and post it on any social media, tagging economic stealers. Let's see how many possibilities we are getting, how far and where the world is going from your point of view.

Conclusion

Money is constantly disgraced in this book. Why? It's because of its substandard. The majority of people can't understand it. People in finance, industrialists, politicians, business people use money's grey area, which is not accessible to ordinary people. Even though they influence money, the world does not collapse. Why? These influencers manipulate a tiny portion. The volume of money circulating in the world is more. So, it won't collapse; still, it's dangerous. Why? The law keeps the monetary policies safe. The world will collapse if the vast majority of ordinary people over a period get influenced by people in finance, industrialists, politicians, business people, manipulate money through grey areas, then start enjoying the taste of money. It's not structured to be available for everyone. It will be considered illegal by law. So, this time laws need to seal that grey area then punish people in finance, industrialists, politicians, business people who manipulated it. It can't let them leave this time like previously because this act will collapse the current structure. Why? The world operates based on political philosophies. It can accept then let go of small levels of breaches, whoever it is, but when something wrong happens that affects the fundamentals of that political philosophy; it won't consider whoever it is because it can't keep its standard if it leaves them. So, people, even at the top, have to accept and cooperate with it even if it's a significant loss for them. So that others can survive in that system. Due to that, laws need to be there to keep the system alive. Everyone is liable to the law. Even people at the top create new political philosophies that should be structured with laws. People can't construct something that only favours the top of society all the time by laws. So, laws should be made equal. The problem here is that the top of society escapes most of the time. They will be captured if there is a tremendous problem. It is called substandard in finance and law.

Politicians made people believe that equality, social reform, and peace are the core of politics. Worldwide, all politicians take it into their hands to collect people's votes. People have to understand that financial management is the core of politics. What are politicians doing for the majority during their tenure? They are managing the country with the funds in the house. They are creating assets for survival. They are trying to increase the balance of foreign exchange. If politicians fail, it means countries become bankrupt.

As I shared in this book, we can't wait for leaders to bring equality and social reform while managing the country's finances. They can change one after another in current times slowly. At the same time, they have to make sure the changes won't impact the finances of the country. Politicians prioritise finance over equality and social reform because they can change these whenever possible. But if they lose their position in finance, they can't manage to stay at the place at the global level. Isn't it supposed to grow together? Politicians reduced the gap in equality in some categories. They haven't achieved what they achieved finance-wise. It won't provide absolute equality in the near future. We categorised all the reasons into different chapters.

We have to split finance and equality, social reform, and peace. We should select different leaders for both segments so globally we can achieve what we desire, even though absolute equality is impossible.

All tech giants are in the process of introducing AI. It won't be an issue if we keep it object-oriented. ChatGPT is the talk of the town. Even more object-oriented AI we have now. If AI occupied the object-oriented jobs, then we have to find an alternative for those who survived via object-oriented jobs. If leaders fail to do it, we must face the world's worst recession.

People have to get some perspective on the recession. Why is it coming? How is it coming? Consider the economy travels in a straight line. People will keep themselves updated on the current technologies and stuff, then educate themselves to travel along with it. Suddenly, the economy takes a spike in travels towards the upper curve slowly due to new technological adoption. Companies will convert themselves to adopt them in that travel along with the economy. They can't be able to back the employees in large volume since the technology simplified its requirements. So, a certain volume of the labour force in the adoption has to look for a change of employer or work because that field of work all over the marketplace vanished. They backed only certain employees who performed well. Companies are tightening the rope that fits for their growth. Overall, due to this adoption, a large population is moving out from the workforce who seeks the next job. The market is empty with no jobs to offer them because of it. The small business as well gets affected by it. There are several types of recession. It's a change in technologies related recession.

We have to face recession in several situations - like natural disasters, public health crises, global destabilisation such as wars, disruptive changes in technology, and a sudden rise in oil prices. We discussed recessions in earlier topics, but that is different. Those are caused by the inefficiency of financial institutions. These above recessions are because of the global situation. Most of the recessions are man-made. Recessions lead to unemployment and poverty in most places.

Recessions are painful only in present political philosophies because no government has plans for them. We can avoid most of the recessions in WBE. The recession is the place where people lose their positions in current times. The other issue is inflation. WBE can lead the world without these.

One person, entity, or government is not responsible for people's current struggles because everyone coordinated and created everything. People need unity and coordination to create something new that works for everyone.

www.ingramcontent.com/pod-product-compliance
Lightning Source LLC
LaVergne TN
LVHW091302150826
845673LV00006B/1509

* 9 7 9 8 8 9 6 1 0 3 0 4 2 *